Finance for Executives

A Practical Guide for Managers

Nuno Fernandes

British Library Cataloguing in Publication Data

A catalogue record for this book is available from the British Library

Library of Congress Cataloguing in Publication Data
Fernandes, Nuno
　　Finance for Executives: A Practical Guide for Managers
　　　　p. cm.
　　Includes bibliographical references and index
　　ISBN-13: 978-9899885400
　　ISBN-10: 9899885401
　　1. Corporations—Finance.　2. International business enterprises—Finance.　3. Corporate Finance

To Isabel, Francisco, and Luísa

About the Author

Nuno Fernandes is Professor of Finance and Director of Strategic Finance at IMD, a top-ranked business school. IMD is ranked No. 1 in open enrollment programs worldwide (2012 and 2013) and No. 1 in executive education outside the United States (2008–2013) by the *Financial Times*. At IMD, Professor Fernandes directs the Strategic Finance program, as well as many partnership programs for leading international companies.

Professor Fernandes works with senior leaders and executive committees to help them with investment selection, financial strategies, mergers and acquisitions (M&As), international investments, risk analysis, and general governance issues. Professor Fernandes is a specialist in corporate finance, international financial markets, and emerging market risks. He has published in the leading international academic journals, including the *Journal of Financial Economics, Review of Financial Studies, Journal of International Business Studies*, and the *Journal of Portfolio Management*. He speaks at business conferences in Asia, Europe, and North America, and is a regular contributor to the business press worldwide, including *The Financial Times* and *The Wall Street Journal*.

Professor Fernandes advises companies and financial institutions in Asia, Europe, Latin America, and the Middle East in formulating winning financial strategies, global portfolio investments, international valuations, M&As, risk management, and emerging market investments.

Professor Fernandes is Portuguese and holds a PhD from IESE Business School (Spain). Prior to joining IMD, he was Director of the Master in Finance (CFA Program Partner) at Católica Lisbon School of Business & Economics (Portugal) and a Visiting Scholar at Columbia Business School (New York). His work has earned him some distinguished awards, including the AEFIN prize and a grant from the FDIC (the US regulator for financial institutions). In 2008 he received the Lamfalussy Fellowship from the European Central Bank. This fellowship is conferred on the top researchers in finance worldwide.

What Is This Book About?

Finance is an exciting and key area for executives to master. Over the course of my career, I have developed a significant number of educational programs for executives that cover many fields in finance and their links with business. But I always faced a challenge. One question was frequently asked after these sessions: "This was great, and I'd like to know more about it. Can you recommend a book for me to read that covers these topics?" Most finance textbooks are too complex and long, and the practical relevance for executives is obscured by more theoretical and technical topics. Some other books are too basic and limited in scope, covering only a very limited set of topics, such as accounting ratios. When faced with this question, eventually I would recommend a couple of chapters from one book, some readings from another, or the kind of 1000-page handbook that people love to carry on the plane back home. After several years, I realized that too many people were asking for the same thing, but "that thing" did not exist in the market. That is why I decided to write this book.

I have noticed when working with general managers that many of them fear finance, the culprits often being jargon, complicated math, and non-standard concepts that do not make intuitive sense. In this book, I try to avoid all these pitfalls by using sound academic research and theories (many of them Nobel Prize winning), and focusing only on the important "nuggets" that are relevant for practitioners, without delving into all the complicated technical details underlying the conclusions. In addition, the book presents several practical applications of key finance tools, how they link with strategy, and how to implement them with Microsoft Excel.

This book has been designed to meet the needs of executives, both finance as well as non-finance managers. Any executive who wants to probe further and grasp the fundamentals of strategic finance issues will benefit from this book.

OBJECTIVES

Finance should be fun, and practical as well. With this book at hand as a reference, executives will have access to a set of tools that will help them develop their intuition for solving key financial problems, analyze alternatives in decision making, and formulate strategies.

Finance is simple. It is about connecting money with ideas. There are several investors with money available, and there are several ideas looking for financing. Finance is just the engine that connects these two forces: money and ideas. And, of course, the overall goal is successful companies that create value for both the suppliers of money and the suppliers of ideas!

These core personal premises regarding finance led me to build in the following features into my book to maximize its utility:

- Simplicity — The core concepts in finance are simple, and they should also become intuitively transparent after using this book.

- Conciseness — The chapters are short and self-contained to appeal to busy executives who are keen on value-added activities.

- Practical focus — The core concepts are explained, but the reader will also learn to identify the problems and pitfalls of different real-world choices.

- Application of theory to practice — It is important for top executives to become familiar with important academic research that impacts their companies. This book is grounded in world-class research, and only presents the salient highlights of academic research on each topic. It is therefore not a literature review of all that has been written on each topic.

- Real-world focus — The book features examples from actual companies and empirical data on many companies and industries around the world.

From my experience, working with real-world problems and real-world data is more fruitful than theoretical discussions on formulas. Because practice with real-world data is crucial to learning finance, each chapter of this book presents empirical examples of the concepts, uses real-world data to illustrate the key ideas, and allows global executives to "think finance" and have fun with finance!

TARGET AUDIENCE

Most executives need to understand and drive the strategy of their company on the basis of sound financial principles, but with the overarching goal of value creation. This book targets them.

Finance for Executives is a book for business executives, from all backgrounds, seeking

- To focus on the links between finance and the strategy of their company, be it a private or publicly traded company

- To discover how to create value for their company and boost its financial performance

- To understand the key ingredients of long-term value creation

- To create a cost-of-capital culture within a company
- To refresh and broaden their understanding of the latest financial concepts and tools
- To learn not just about accounting numbers, but also about sound financial decision making in areas such as financing and payout policies, mergers and acquisitions (M&As), project valuation, or risk management and derivatives
- To ultimately make better decisions

This book can also be used in executive training programs in finance, as well as in MBA, master's, and executive MBA programs. Indeed, the book is based on many years of executive education and consulting with world-class corporations from all continents of the world. I have been teaching corporate valuation, capital structure and other financial policies, M&As, and risk management for different audiences. I have learned a lot from my regular interactions with practitioners, including CEOs, CFOs, and other senior executives who are interested in the broad world of strategic finance. I have therefore been able to identify what key topics are relevant to different companies, private or public, and what difficulties exist (often language related) in addressing them in practice. Each chapter in this book has benefited from this rich experience.

EXCEL TEMPLATES

In most of the chapters, concrete examples are explained step by step. Further, an Excel spreadsheet containing all the models used in the different chapters is available for download from the book's website:

www.FinanceforExecutives.net

Practitioners will find the file easy to use and to customize to their own requirements. It is useful in a variety of situations: value creation and its decomposition into managerial drivers or key performance indicators (KPIs), cost of capital estimation, project evaluation, mergers and acquisitions, company valuation, options valuation, etc.

ACKNOWLEDGMENTS

The ideas in this book have been developed and reinforced by many people. I have greatly benefited from my regular interactions with hundreds of executives from all backgrounds, including CEOs and CFOs of many companies around the world, teaching sessions, developing company-specific programs, consulting, and even informal conversations. I am grateful to them for sharing their wisdom with me and inspiring many of the ideas in the book.

I owe a big thank you to the following academic reviewers and colleagues for their constructive advice and insightful reviews of this book through its many drafts: Yiorgos Allayannis (Darden), Bo Becker (Stockholm School of Economics), Geert Bekaert (Columbia Business School), Arnoud Boot (University of Amsterdam), Guilherme Brito (Católica Lisbon), José Manuel Campa (IESE), Andrey Golubov (Cass Business School), José Guedes (Católica Lisbon), Campbell Harvey (Duke University), Pedro Matos (Darden), Igor Osobov (University of Connecticut), and Daniel Rogers (Portland State University).

I am also extremely grateful to my colleagues at IMD, professors Arturo Bris, Salvatore Cantale, Kamran Kashani, Stuart Read, and Leif Sjoblom, for their comments on this book. At IMD, I must specifically thank people who have generously read, edited, and provided comments on drafts of this book, namely, Susan Broomfield, Marianne Foerster, Beverley Lennox, Lindsay McTeague, Michelle Perrinjaquet, and Susan Stehli. I am also indebted to Raphaël Thiébaud, my assistant at IMD, for his diligent help and support along this journey. Among many other things, he expertly oversaw the production of all the exhibits in this book, an amazing task given the multitude of databases and formats employed. He has been instrumental in getting this book from its early stages to its final form. I also appreciate the support received from a very good and capable friend, Kyryl Lakishyk, who managed the entire cover design process.

I could not have created this work without my students, who read and used virtually the entire book in their finance classes at IMD, in MBA, and executive education courses. Over the years, they endured reading earlier drafts of the book, corrected mistakes, commented on the content, and provided additional thoughts and insights that helped shape *Finance for Executives* into the book that you now hold in your hands.

Many business professionals were kind enough to read various chapters and share their observations with me. Among this group, a special word of thanks goes to Marc Chauvet, Viktor Dobrikov, Natalia Filchakova, Jacques Guillemot, Luís Henzler, Hammad Hussain, Tracey Keys, Paulo Marcos, Pedro Marques, Alexandre Mesquita, Urs Rohner, Severin Schwan, Isaak Tsalicoglou, Stephan Wullschleger, and Yingjie Yang.

This book could not have been written without the love and support of my family. My wife, Isabel, gave unsparingly of her time and effort to support my writing. She has read and commented on different drafts of this book, and has always been a sounding board and source of ideas for my work. Finally, my two children helped me with their patience and uncomplainingly sacrificed time with their dad on account of his work on this book. Francisco had to put up with his dad typing away for long hours instead of helping him assemble and disassemble his Legos, and Luísa had to count her teddy bears and PLAYMOBIL toys on her own.

Introduction

HOW TO USE THIS BOOK

This is a book to be used, not a book to be read from beginning to end.

Each chapter is highly readable and practical, yet rigorous. The self-contained chapters include fundamental concepts, analytical tools, and demonstrations of applications of those tools. Executives can then tailor their reading to the specific circumstances applicable to their company.

This book contains empirical evidence, based on real company cases, of the value of financial techniques/tools. In essence, each short chapter is written in a way that allows executives to put the concepts immediately into practice.

Outline

Chapter	Title
1	The Main Accounting Metrics and Ratios
2	What Is the Cost of Capital for My Company?
3	A Managerial Framework for Value Creation
4	Selecting the Right Investment Projects — Capital Budgeting Tools
5	Deciding between Different Sources of Capital — The Capital Structure Decision
6	Borrowing from Banks and Capital Markets
7	Raising Equity — IPOs and SEOs
8	Returning Money to Shareholders — Dividends, Buybacks and the Payout Policy
9	Key Principles for Company Valuation
10	Value Creation through Mergers and Acquisitions
11	Derivatives and Risk Management
12	Management of Corporate Risks with Futures, Forwards, and Swaps
13	Management of Corporate Risks with Options

This book starts with a chapter on the main financial ratios and key accounting terms. **Chapter 1** reviews the key accounting statements, focusing on the main points executives should look at when analyzing financial statements.

Chapter 2 covers questions such as the following: What is the cost of capital, and how does it change over time? How does the cost of equity vary across different companies? How do I compute my company's weighted average cost of capital? What is the relation between risk and cost of capital?

Chapter 3 focuses on what value creation is and how it should link to the company strategy. Indeed, value creation is the responsibility of every executive, yet not all executives have access to the latest strategies and tools of value creation. This chapter outlines a best-practice foundation in value creation for different companies and organizations.

Chapter 4 focuses on questions such as the following: Which of two apparently profitable investment projects should my company choose? How can I ensure that my company allocates capital to projects that add value? What criteria should we use to decide between different capital expenditures? How do I decide between different cost reduction projects? How do I evaluate brands? What should we pay attention to when we evaluate projects outside the company's core business?

Chapter 5 addresses practical issues associated with the financing policy: Why do some companies have sustainably very high amounts of debt? How much debt should we have in our company? How does the optimal financing mix vary across industries? What is the impact of debt on operations (customers, suppliers, employees, etc.)?

Chapter 6 covers capital-raising activities in debt markets, addressing questions such as the following: Should we issue fixed-rate debt or floating-rate debt? My company has traditionally used only bank loans. Are corporate bonds an alternative? How do rating agencies look at different companies? What is the risk of investing in bonds? What are credit default swaps (CDSs)? Should we have long-term or short-term debt?

Chapter 7 addresses questions such as: Should my company go public? How do equity-raising processes work? What are the stages in an initial public offering? What are the costs and fees of public equity issues? What happens when a company issues rights? Why do companies have stock splits? Is there value in being listed in different exchanges around the world?

Chapter 8 answers questions such as the following: My company has been trading on the stock exchange for 8 years, and is profitable. Is it time to start paying dividends? What is the best way of returning money to shareholders? When should a company repurchase shares? Why don't we keep all the cash in the company? How do I design an optimal strategy to remunerate shareholders?

Chapter 9 describes the main methods used to value companies, addressing questions such as the following: Our company is considering spinning off a division that is no longer core to our business. What is its fair value? How many years should we use when valuing companies? What are the different methods used to value companies? How do different multiples work?

Chapter 10 covers mergers and acquisitions (M&As), their objectives, and the techniques used in the valuation of a target company. We address questions such as the following: When do mergers create value? What are the appropriate methodologies to value potential acquisition candidates? How can we ensure that our acquisitions create value? How do I choose between different payment methods? What happens after the M&A deal is concluded?

Chapters 11 to 13 cover key concepts related to derivatives markets. Effective usage of derivatives can create significant value and allows for effective risk management strategies. The functioning of the markets is described, and several pitfalls of using derivatives are illustrated. The chapters address questions such as the following: Why and when should we use derivatives for risk management? What are the differences between futures and forwards? How are stock options valued? How do derivatives markets work, and how can companies use them effectively? How are futures, swaps, and options priced in the market?

Overall, this book moves beyond spreadsheets and accounting, and takes a broader perspective on finance. The main objective of the book is for executives in any part of the organization to understand and internalize the links between company strategy and finance. The unifying thread running across the different chapters is the emphasis on the managerial implications of financial analysis.

Contents

The Main Accounting Metrics and Ratios

This section presents an overview of the key items in the

- Income statement
- Balance sheet

The main difference between these two statements is the timescale: The income statement is a report of a company's financial performance over a certain period (a year or a quarter), whereas the balance sheet is like a static photo; it represents a snapshot of the different items on a company's financials at the end of a certain period.

INCOME STATEMENT
Financial performance **over a certain period**

BALANCE SHEET
Static snapshot **at the end of a certain period**

1.1 INCOME STATEMENT — MAIN ITEMS

The income statement presents the operating and financial transactions that affect a company's equity during the period of interest.

The key output of the income statement is the profit (or net income), which is the difference between the revenues and costs during the period.

Revenues

| Net sales generated by a company during the period.
| "Net" means *inclusive* of any price discounts.

COGS (cost of goods sold)

| Direct costs attributable to the production of the goods sold by a company
| All material costs as well as the direct labor costs used to produce the goods

Gross profit

| **Gross Profit** = Revenues – COGS
| The difference between revenues and the cost of making a product (or providing a service) before the deduction of overheads, charges for assets, taxes, and interest payments

SGA (selling, general, and administrative expenses)

| Overhead expenses, that is, costs incurred by a company that relate to its products and operations
| All general and administrative expenses (for example, electricity, rent, salaries)

Depreciation and Amortization

| Used to spread the historical cost of an asset over several years.
| Can be interpreted as the loss in the value of the asset due to the passage of time, usage, wear and tear, technological obsolescence, or other such factors.
| Has no relation to the market value of the asset.
| Tangible assets (also called *fixed assets*) such as cars, machinery, and buildings are *depreciated*.
| Intangible assets (assets that are not physical in nature) such as patents, trademarks, copyrights, and goodwill are *amortized*.

EBITDA (earnings before interest, taxes, depreciation, and amortization)

| There are two equivalent ways of computing the EBITDA:
   ○ **EBITDA** = Net Income + Interest + Taxes + Depreciation and Amortization
   ○ **EBITDA** = Sales – COGS – SGA
| An indicator of a company's operational performance
| A useful comparison indicator as it eliminates the effects of financing, taxation, and accounting decisions
| Used as an indicator of the ability of a company to service debt

| Does not represent the cash earnings or cash flow because it
  ○ Does not account for the cash required to fund working capital
  ○ Does not account for the replacement of old equipment
| A good proxy for the cash flow generated by a company's operations if there is no major change in the net working capital

EBIT (earnings before interest and tax)

| There are three different ways of computing the EBIT:
  ○ **EBIT** = EBITDA – Depreciation
  ○ **EBIT** = Net Income + Interest + Taxes
  ○ **EBIT** = Sales – COGS – SGA – Depreciation
| Sometimes referred to as the operating income
| A measure of a company's profitability that excludes interest and income tax expenses

Interest expenses

| Also known as *financing costs*
| The annual amount of interest paid on the debt held by a company
| The cost of borrowing money
| The price a company pays for the use of the lender's money
| Does not include repayment of the debt amount; only the interest part is included
| Often presented as the net interest income received from a company's financial investments

EBT (earnings before taxes)

| **EBT** = EBIT – Interest
| The amount of earnings after accounting for all expenses related to operations, assets, and financing
| The measure of a company's profitability without considering taxes

Minority interest

| Minority interest exists whenever a company consolidates a subsidiary's results but does not have 100% ownership. The minority interest item in the income statement represents the portion of a subsidiary's profits that is due to the minority, non-controlling shareholders.

Equity income

| Equity income exists when a company owns part of another company, but not enough to justify considering it as a subsidiary. The holding company will report a separate line — equity in income of affiliates — that represents its proportionate share of the invested company's profits. In this case, the revenue, costs, assets, and/or liabilities of the invested company will not appear on the holding company's financial statements (not consolidated).

| Equity income commonly appears when a corporate investor (typically) owns less than 20% of the voting stock in another company.

Net income

| There are three different ways of computing the Net Income:
  - O **Net income** = EBT – Taxes
  - O **Net income** = EBIT – Interest – Taxes
  - O **Net income** = EBITDA – Depreciation – Interest – Taxes
| Profit generated in the period.
| Often called "the bottom line."
| A measure of the net change in owners' equity resulting from transactions during the period.
| Can be paid out or be reinvested in the company (see chapter 8). If it is reinvested, it will appear as retained earnings in future accounting statements.

1.2   BALANCE SHEET — MAIN ITEMS

The balance sheet is a snapshot that shows the health of the business as measured in terms of its accounting assets and liabilities at the end of a certain period.

Balance Sheet

Assets	Liabilities
	Equity

1.2.1   Assets

The left-hand side of the balance sheet includes the assets. We now describe the main categories of assets.

Cash and cash equivalents

| The most liquid assets on a company's balance sheet
| Assets that are readily convertible into cash
| Include physical cash, bank accounts, money market holdings, short-term government bonds or treasury bills, marketable securities, and commercial paper (short-term debt issued by corporates)

Inventory

| A company's stock of finished goods and raw materials
| Can be valued according to different conventions:
   ○ LIFO (last-in, first-out): The most recently produced items are recorded as sold first. In this case, the value of the inventory in the company's books will reflect the cost of the oldest stock of goods produced.
   ○ FIFO (first-in, first-out): The oldest inventory items are recorded as sold first. In this case, the value of the inventory will reflect the cost of the newest stock of goods produced.
   ○ The choice of LIFO or FIFO can materially affect the value of the inventory, particularly for companies whose raw material costs are very volatile, such as oil-related products.

Accounts receivable

| The money owed to a company by its clients.
| Related to the payment terms agreed upon. Usually, companies generate an invoice, and only later collect the cash.

Current assets — total

| Sum of the cash, inventory, and accounts receivable
| All assets that a company expects to convert into cash during the next 12 months

PPE (property, plant, and equipment)

| Fixed assets.
| Tangible assets that a company has bought and will use for a period of time. The PPE is depreciated each year according to the accounting standards in place.
| Every year the net PPE represents the difference between the historical cost of the fixed assets (gross PPE) and their associated cumulative depreciation.

Intangible assets

| Cannot be seen, touched, or physically measured.
| Acquisition or development of intellectual property, trademarks, and patents, as well as goodwill. Goodwill is the amount of money a company has paid to acquire another company, over the value of the net assets of that company.

1.2.2   Liabilities and Shareholders' Equity

The right-hand side of the balance sheet includes the liabilities and shareholders' equity. Below we describe the main categories.

Accounts payable

| The amount owed for the purchase of goods or services.
| Costs are recorded in accounts payable at the time an invoice is approved for payment, but no cash transaction has taken place yet.
| Also called *trade payable*.
| Varies according to the payment terms agreed upon with suppliers.

Short-term debt and current portion of long-term debt

| The amount owed to banks or other lenders that will fall due within one year of the balance sheet date

Current liabilities — total

| The sum of all the liabilities (for example, accounts payable and short-term debt) that will fall due within the next year

Long-term debt

| Represents the amount owed to banks or other lenders that will fall due more than one year after the balance sheet date

Shareholders' equity

| The difference between total assets and total liabilities.
| The book value of the equity interest that shareholders have in a company.
| Includes common equity, preferred stocks, minority interest, treasury stock, and retained earnings.
| Common equity represents the original paid-in capital invested by shareholders, including any additional offering of shares.
| Preferred stocks are a special type of equity security that have the properties of both an equity and a debt instrument. They usually carry no voting rights and offer a fixed dividend payment. They might also have priority over common shares in the case of bankruptcy. Dividends to common shareholders cannot be paid if a company has failed to pay dividends to preferred stockholders.
| Minority interest is also known as non-controlling interest. It represents the portion of a subsidiary's equity that is not owned by the parent company. In essence, minority interest is the part of a subsidiary that belongs to other non-controlling shareholders.
| Treasury stock exists when a company buys back its own stock. It is recorded at cost. The company can decide to cancel or sell these stocks.
| Retained earnings represent the accumulated profits a company has earned in the past and reinvested in the business.

1.3   THE MAIN FINANCIAL RATIOS AND THEIR USAGE

Financial ratios are indicators of a company's performance. All the following ratios can be calculated from information provided by the company's financial statements. In this section, we cover the main financial ratios and their interpretation.

When used in isolation, most ratios are useless. However, financial ratios can be helpful in

- Analyzing trends within the same company over different time periods. Looking at changes in the ratios over time provides useful information. It enables the identification of predictable patterns and prompts questions as to why the trends occur.

- Comparing a company with its industry peers. Financial ratios enable companies of different sizes to be compared. They help to identify potential problems and explain why different companies perform differently.

- Comparing different business units within the same company. It is often useful to analyze individual segments of a company. It is also useful to compare the same segment across different geographies.

The key financial ratios can be aggregated into the following categories:

1. Growth
2. Profitability
3. Operating efficiency
4. Financial leverage
5. Liquidity and solvency

1.3.1   Growth Rates

Profit growth

$$Profit\ Growth\ Rate = \frac{Profit_t}{Profit_{t-1}} - 1 = \frac{Profit_t - Profit_{t-1}}{Profit_{t-1}} \tag{1.1}$$

| Represents the percentage increase (or decrease) in net income (or profit) between two periods.

Sales growth

$$Sales\ Growth = \frac{Sales_t}{Sales_{t-1}} - 1 = \frac{Sales_t - Sales_{t-1}}{Sales_{t-1}} \tag{1.2}$$

| Represents the percentage growth in sales from one period to the next

EBITDA growth

$$EBITDA\ Growth = \frac{EBITDA_t}{EBITDA_{t-1}} - 1 \tag{1.3}$$

| Represents the percentage growth in EBITDA from one period to the next

All the growth rates can be analyzed annually or over a certain period. If the period is more than one year, it is common to use the compound annual growth rate (CAGR).

CAGR (compound annual growth rate)

$$CAGR = \left(\frac{ending\ value}{beginning\ value} \right)^{\left(\frac{1}{number\ of\ years} \right)} - 1 \qquad (1.4)$$

| It is the average (and steady) rate at which profits grow during a certain period.

Example: Computing CAGR of Profits over 5 years

Profits at 2005 end = 1000;   Profits at 2010 end= 1500

$$CAGR = \left(\frac{1500}{1000} \right)^{\left(\frac{1}{5} \right)} - 1 = 8.45\%$$

1.3.2 Profitability Financial Ratios

Profitability ratios include different measures of how successful a company is at generating profits. Trends of profitability over time (and within and across companies) are useful inputs for good decision making.

ROIC (return on invested capital)

$$ROIC = \frac{EBIT \times (1 - \%\ Tax\ Rate)}{Invested\ Capital} \qquad (1.5)$$

| Measures the return earned on a company's invested capital.
| Invested capital = long-term financial debt + short-term financial debt + equity. It represents all the capital raised from different suppliers of capital (shareholders and debt holders). It includes all interest-bearing debt raised by a company, whether it is short term or long term.

ROE (return on equity)

$$ROE = \frac{Net\ Income}{Shareholder\ Equity} \qquad (1.6)$$

| Measures the return earned on shareholders' equity
| Profits earned for each dollar invested in a company's equity capital

ROA (return on assets)

$$ROA = \frac{Net\ Income}{Total\ Assets} \tag{1.7}$$

| Measures the return earned on total assets
| Indicates how effectively assets are being used to generate profits
| Profits earned for each dollar of a company's assets

Profit margin

$$Profit\ Margin = \frac{Net\ Income}{Sales} \tag{1.8}$$

| Also called the *net margin, net profit margin,* or *net profit ratio.*
| The percentage return on sales: net profit as a percentage of the revenue.
| Shows the ability of a company to control all its costs relative to its level of sales.
| Can be related to a margin of safety: a low profit margin means a higher risk that a decrease in sales will wipe out profits.
| Varies widely across business models and product mixes.

Gross profit margin

$$Gross\ Profit\ Margin = \frac{(Sales - COGS)}{Sales} \tag{1.9}$$

| A measure of the gross profit earned on sales
| The percentage of money left over from revenues after accounting for the cost of goods sold
| Considers the cost of goods sold, but does not include other costs such as general expenses, taxes, interest, and depreciation
| Varies widely across business models and product mixes

EBITDA margin

$$EBITDA\ Margin = \frac{EBITDA}{Sales} = \frac{(Sales - COGS - SGA)}{Sales} \tag{1.10}$$

| Measures a company's operating profitability. It is equal to earnings before interest, tax, depreciation, and amortization (EBITDA) divided by the total revenue.

| Because EBITDA excludes depreciation and amortization, the EBITDA margin provides an investor with a clearer view of a company's operating profitability.
| Measures effectiveness because it ignores differences in accounting policy and capital structure.
| Is usually higher than the net profit margin and fluctuates less than it.

COGS to sales

$$COGS\text{-}to\text{-}Sales = \frac{COGS}{Sales} \qquad (1.11)$$

| An indicator of a company's margin
| The percentage of sales used to pay the direct costs of those sales

SGA to sales

$$SGA\text{-}to\text{-}Sales = \frac{SGA}{Sales} \qquad (1.12)$$

| An indicator of a company's overhead expenses
| The percentage of sales used to pay overhead costs

EPS (earnings per share)

$$EPS = \frac{Net\ Income}{Number\ of\ Shares} \qquad (1.13)$$

| An indicator of the net income attributable to each share.
| The denominator (Number of shares) can be calculated using
  ○ the number of shares at the end of the period.
  ○ the average number of shares over the reporting period.
  ○ the number of shares if all convertible securities were exercised (warrants, stock options, and convertibles outstanding), in which case it is called the *diluted EPS*.

1.3.3 Operating Financial Ratios

Operating ratios are metrics of the efficiency of management and a company's operations in utilizing its capital, including the working capital.

Asset turnover

$$Asset\ turnover = \frac{Sales}{Assets} \tag{1.14}$$

| Indicates how efficiently a company utilizes its assets.
| A higher turnover suggests more efficient use of assets or more efficient operations.
| Varies widely across industries and business models.

DSO (days sales outstanding)

$$DSO = \frac{Accounts\ Receivable}{Annual\ Credit\ Sales} \times 365 \tag{1.15}$$

| The average collection period or number of days that (credit) sales remain in accounts receivable before they are collected (cash received).
| The time a company takes to collect revenue after booking a sale.
| A high DSO means that a company gives high amounts of credit to its customers, and takes more time to collect the cash.
| A high DSO is not necessarily a bad sign, if the additional margin received compensates for the delay in collecting the cash.

DSI (days sales of inventory)

$$DSI = \frac{Inventory}{Cost\ of\ Goods\ Sold} \times 365 \tag{1.16}$$

| Also known as the *inventory period*, *days inventory*, or *inventory holding period*.
| The average inventory period, or number of days' worth of inventory.
| The amount of time a company holds inventory on average before selling it.
| A high DSI means that a company holds (and incurs costs) inventory for a large number of days' worth of sales.
| A high DSI is not necessarily a bad sign if the additional margin received compensates for the costs of holding the inventory (including capital costs).

DPO (days of payables outstanding)

$$DPO = \frac{Trade\ Payables}{Cost\ of\ Goods\ Sold} \times 365 \tag{1.17}$$

| Also known as the *payables period*.
| The average number of days' worth of credit from suppliers.
| A high DPO means that a company enjoys significant credit from its suppliers.

1.3.4 Financial Leverage Ratios

Financial leverage ratios are metrics pertaining to the sources of capital a company uses. They make it possible to analyze a company's capital structure and can be related to the long-term solvency of a company. Leverage ratios are often called *gearing ratios*, although this term represents different specific ratios for different companies. The following are the main ratios used to compute the leverage of a company.

Debt ratio

$$Debt\ Ratio = \frac{Total\ Debt}{Total\ Assets} \tag{1.18}$$

| Indicates the amount of short- and long-term debt as a percentage of the total assets.
| The proportion of a company's resources obtained through borrowing.
| A higher debt ratio corresponds to a greater financial risk.
| If the debt ratio is above 0.5, it means that the majority of a company's assets are financed with debt.

Debt-to-equity (D/E) ratio

$$D/E\ Ratio = \frac{Total\ Debt}{Equity} \tag{1.19}$$

| Indicates the relative magnitude of debt and equity financing used by a company.
| If the D/E ratio is below one, this means that the majority of the assets are financed by equity.
| A higher D/E ratio corresponds to a greater financial risk.

Interest coverage ratio

$$Interest\ Coverage\ Ratio = \frac{EBIT}{Financing\ Costs} \tag{1.20}$$

| Indicates how many times a company's earnings cover the interest payments on its debt.
| Indicates a company's ability to meet its interest obligations.
| Measures the amount of income available, relative to the interest expenses.
| Lower ratios mean more difficulty in meeting interest obligations.
| One of the key determinants of corporate ratings.

Debt-to-EBITDA

$$Debt\text{-}to\text{-}EBITDA \ = \ \frac{Total\ Debt}{EBITDA} \qquad (1.21)$$

| Indicates a company's ability to repay its debt.
| Can also be interpreted as the time that would be needed to pay off all of a company's debt if it used all the EBITDA for debt repayment (in which case the company will obviously not have any money left for capital expenditures).
| Lower ratios mean that a company can easily repay its whole debt.
| Another key determinant of corporate ratings.

1.3.5   Liquidity and Solvency Financial Ratios

Liquidity financial ratios show how solvent a company is based on its assets versus its liabilities. They show whether a company has the resources available to continue its normal operations, paying all its bills on time. Solvency financial ratios can also be related to the probability that a company will go bankrupt.

These ratios provide information on a company's ability to meet its short-term financial obligations. They are extremely useful for those granting short-term credit to a company, either through financing or through supplies of materials and services.

Current ratio

$$Current\ Ratio = \frac{Current\ Assets}{Current\ Liabilities} \qquad (1.22)$$

| Also known as the *working capital ratio*.
| The ratio of current assets to current liabilities.
| A ratio that is too low might indicate that a company could have difficulty meeting its short-term obligations.

| A ratio that is too high could indicate excessive holdings of cash, inventories, or customer credit (accounts receivable).
| Short-term creditors prefer a high current ratio.
| Varies substantially by industry.
| Companies in cyclical industries require a higher current ratio in order to remain solvent during downturns.

Quick ratio

$$Quick\ ratio = \frac{Current\ Assets - Inventory}{Current\ Liabilities} \qquad (1.23)$$

| Also known as the *acid test ratio*.
| Has a similar representation as the current ratio.
| An alternative measure of liquidity that does not include inventory in the current assets.
| Provides a more restrictive view of a company's liquidity, because it excludes inventories.

Interest coverage ratio

$$Interest\ Coverage\ Ratio = \frac{EBIT}{Financing\ Costs} \qquad (1.24)$$

| Indicates a company's ability to meet its interest obligations.
| Indicates how many times a company's earnings cover the interest payments on its debt.
| Measures the amount of income available relative to interest expenses.
| Lower ratios mean more difficulty in meeting interest obligations.
| One of the key determinants of corporate ratings.

What Is the Cost of Capital for My Company?

The cost of capital is one of the most important concepts in finance. It is the minimum acceptable rate of return that new investments must yield, and it represents the long-term opportunity cost of the funds used by a company. If management decides to invest in projects with expected returns above the cost of capital, the company's value goes up. Conversely, if a company invests in projects with expected returns below the cost of capital (even if the projects have positive accounting profitability), the company's value goes down. Also, the cost of capital is the discount rate that should be used in a discounted cash flow (DCF) analysis, in capital budgeting applications (chapter 4), and when valuing a company or a division (chapter 9), or an acquisition target (chapter 10).

The cost of capital is not fixed internally; rather, it must be estimated taking into account the rate of return required by the investors who finance a company. Investors who buy company bonds and stocks are looking for a return that compensates them for the risk in their investment, as well as the time value of money. Thus, the cost of capital can be interpreted, from the investors' point of view, as the opportunity cost of funds. And, of course, investors demand higher returns for riskier investments (risk-return principle).

In addition, the current cost of capital for a company may not be the appropriate parameter to use in an expansion project. If, for instance, a company is currently involved in electricity distribution and now wants to evaluate a new business opportunity in the media business, the past cost of capital is not an appropriate yardstick because the risks of the two businesses are not the same.

At the company level, the most important concept is the weighted average cost of capital (WACC). The WACC reflects not only the business risk but also the financial risk of the company being valued. The WACC must be estimated in the same currency as the cash flows, and it must incorporate the appropriate long-term target capital structure.

KEY LEARNING POINT ✓

The cost of capital represents the rate of return that the suppliers of capital (equity and debt) demand from a company.

The formula for the WACC is a weighted average of the equity and debt investors' required return (opportunity cost of capital for them) and is given by

$$WACC = \frac{debt}{debt + equity}(1-t)r_{debt} + \frac{equity}{debt + equity}r_{equity} \qquad (2.1)$$

| r_{debt} is the cost of debt, r_{equity} is the cost of equity, and t is the tax rate.
| *debt* is the sum of the short- and long-term financial debts.
| *equity* is the total value of the equity.

The WACC is the after-tax cost of funding for a company as a whole. It is computed as the weighted average of the cost of equity and the after-tax cost of debt, taking into account the appropriate mix of debt and equity. The costs of both equity and debt should be forward looking and reflect the cost demanded by the different sources of capital of a company (or the required return expected by investors given the risk of a company).

To compute the WACC:

1. Estimate the percentages of debt and equity financing. It is important that these be based on the market values of equity and debt. The book value and the market value of debt are not significantly different, unless the company is in financial distress.[1] However, the book value of equity is, for most companies, very different from its market value.

2. Estimate the cost of equity (r_{equity}) and the cost of debt (r_{debt}). These parameters must reflect the expectations regarding both the risk as well as the return required by investors. These costs (of equity and debt) must also reflect the appropriate capital structure of a company.

3. Estimate the WACC using the appropriate capital structure, which represents the target mix of the capital (debt and equity) of a company.

---

[1] Differences between the book and market value of debt arise when the company experiences large changes in its cost of debt (due to rating changes, or a large change in market interest rates) since the debt was originally issued. In this case, the face value of the loans or bonds will be different from their market value.

KEY LEARNING POINT ✓

The WACC is a market-value metric that management needs to know in order to make good decisions for a company's owners.

We will now look at how to estimate the required return for each source of capital: the cost of debt and the cost of equity.

2.1   RISK AND THE COST OF DEBT

To compute the WACC, the cost of debt must be forward looking, and it must reflect the expectations of both the risk as well as the return required by debt investors. It must also reflect the expected return on a long-term fixed-rate[2] loan (or bond) of a credit risk that is consistent with the capital structure ratios built into the WACC formula.

Companies can borrow from a bank by taking a loan. In this case, the cost of debt is the interest rate the bank charges a company.[3] Alternatively, a company can borrow directly from investors by selling bonds. In this case, the cost of debt is the current market rate or yield-to-maturity (YTM) required by investors to invest in the company's bonds.

Because a corporate bond has a certain probability of default, investors will always ask companies for interest rates that are higher than the risk-free rate. The cost of debt is then:

$$r_{debt} = r_f + Spread \qquad (2.2)$$

| r_{debt} is the corporate cost of debt, and r_f is the risk-free rate (the yield to maturity of similar maturity government bonds).

| The common practice is to consider the yield on a long-term (for instance, 10 years) government bond as the risk-free rate.

---

[2] Rates on floating-rate bonds or loans should not be used in cost-of-debt calculations. These have interest payments linked to a short-term benchmark rate, such as the LIBOR or Euribor (commonly used interbank offered rates), which can give a misleading estimate of the cost of debt over the long term. Even if a company has floating-rate debt, when calculating the WACC, we should consider the long-term fixed rate as the cost of debt.

[3] The rate a company pays to the bank is the before-tax cost of debt. It will then be multiplied in the WACC formula by $(1 - t)$. That is, if a company pays \$1,000 in interest costs and has a tax rate of 25%, taxes will be reduced by \$250 (owing to the deductibility of interest costs on the tax bill). Thus, the after-tax cost of debt is \$750.

| It is important to remember that this risk-free rate must be consistent with the currency in which the cash flows are estimated.
| The spread is the market estimate of a company's credit risk. Naturally, for riskier borrowers the spread (and thus the cost of debt) is higher than for safer ones.
| The cost of debt (r_{debt}) is then the yield to maturity that investors demand from debt instruments having a similar credit risk and maturity.

The *risk-free rate* is typically the yield to maturity of riskless government bonds. Ideally, the maturity of the bonds should exactly match the cash flows being discounted. In practice, it is common to use the yield to maturity on long-term government bonds (10 years or longer) as a measure of the risk-free rate. **Table 2.1** shows the range of yield to maturity of long-term government bonds (10 years' maturity) in different countries around the world.

TABLE 2.1:   Yield to maturity of 10-year government bonds

Country	Long-term rate
US	2.76%
UK	2.77%
Germany	1.69%
France	2.16%
Japan	0.61%
Netherlands	2.04%
Switzerland	0.88%

Source: Bloomberg, December 2013.

Credit ratings play an important role in helping investors make better-informed decisions and judge the risk of lending money to a given company. A credit rating is an evaluation of the creditworthiness of an issuer (or a specific bond).

KEY LEARNING POINT ✓

The cost of debt depends on the risk of the company to lenders. Credit ratings are a tool for assessing that risk.

The main global rating agencies are Moody's Investor Services (Moody's) and Standard & Poor's (S&P). **Table 2.2** shows their major rating categories.

TABLE 2.2: Rating categories for Moody's and S&P

	Moody's	S&P
	Aaa	AAA
	Aa	AA
Investment Grade	A	A
	Baa	BBB
	Ba	BB
	B	B
Junk Bonds	Caa	CCC
	Ca	CC
	C	C

Within each rating category, there are sub-categories — also called *notches*. Moody's uses numbers (1 for the safest tier, 3 for the riskier one), whereas S&P uses plus and minus signs. For instance, within the A category, there are three different tiers/notches: Moody's has A1, A2, and A3; S&P has A+, A, and A-.

Bonds with a rating equal to or above Baa3 (Moody's) or BBB- (S&P) are considered investment grade. Bonds with lower ratings are considered speculative grade — also called junk bonds, sub-investment grade, or high-yield bonds.

Given that ratings assess the potential default risk, lower ratings are associated with a higher cost of debt.[4] **Table 2.3** shows the average spread (above a risk-free bond with similar maturity) required by investors for different investment- and speculative-grade bonds.

Exxon Mobil has an AAA rating. Assuming that the risk-free rate equals 4%, we estimate Exxon's cost of debt to be

$$r_{debt} = r_f + Spread$$

The credit spreads in **Table 2.3** indicate that an AAA borrower[5], such as Exxon Mobil, pays on average 4.21% (risk-free rate of 4% + spread of 0.21%) for his debt.

---

[4] As an alternative to bond ratings, we can use a credit default swap (CDS) to estimate a company's credit risk (and thus the spread). A CDS is a special type of insurance that protects the buyer in case of a loan default. An annual premium has to be paid when a CDS is purchased. This is typically referred to as the CDS spread. In exchange for this premium, the buyer benefits from the insurance. In the case of the CDS market, the insurance is against the default of an issuer. Thus, the CDS spread can be interpreted as the market-based metric of the credit risk for a certain company.

[5] As of December 2013, only five corporate issuers had an AAA rating worldwide: Automatic Data Processing, Exxon Mobil, Imperial Oil, Johnson & Johnson, and Microsoft.

TABLE 2.3:   Credit spreads for different ratings

Investment grade			Junk bonds	
AAA	0.21%		BB+	2.18%
AA	0.34%		BB	2.41%
A+	0.48%		BB-	2.64%
A	0.56%		B+	3.14%
A-	0.88%		B	3.41%
BBB+	0.94%		B-	4.08%
BBB	1.13%			
BBB-	1.70%			

Source: Bloomberg, January 2014.

There is a world of difference between investment-grade and speculative-grade bonds. Indeed, speculative-grade bonds present several challenges to investors. Given the additional risk associated with these junk bonds, many institutional investors are by law forbidden (or severely limited) from investing in them. As expected, the difference in spreads between BBB and BB is large.

2.1.1   Credit Spreads Change over Time

Credit spreads are not constant. Thus, the rate at which a certain issuer can finance itself varies over time even if its credit rating does not change. **Figure 2.1** shows the evolution of the average credit spreads for issuers of different ratings. Also, from an investor's perspective, the prices of corporate bonds fluctuate as credit spreads widen or narrow. In general, corporate bond prices increase when spreads narrow.

All spreads increased significantly during the financial crisis of 2008/09. However, **Figure 2.1** also shows that the increase in spreads was not constant across the different rating categories. Indeed, the spreads increased mostly for issuers of lower credit quality.

The fact that credit spreads change over time has significant implications for a company. Indeed, even if a company stays within the same rating category, it can have very different costs of debt. For instance, a BB-rated company had a spread of close to 2% in 2007. But the same company, with the same BB rating, would have experienced spreads of more than 10% during 2008/09.

FIGURE 2.1: Credit spreads over time.

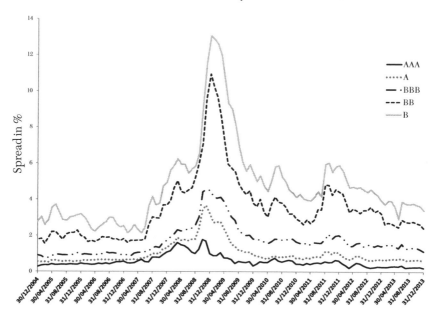

Source: Bloomberg, January 2014.

KEY LEARNING POINT ✓

The cost of debt can change over time even if the company's rating remains unchanged.

2.1.2   The Risk-Free Rate Changes over Time

The risk-free rate is not constant. **Figure 2.2** shows the evolution of the long-term government bond rates in different countries.

The data show a marked decrease in government bond rates over the last decade. Indeed, 2012–2013 marks the lowest point for risk-free rates over the past three decades.

KEY LEARNING POINT ✓

The cost of debt can change over time owing to changes in the risk-free rate.

FIGURE 2.2:   Long-term government bond rates over time.

Source: Datastream, January 2014.

2.2   RISK AND THE COST OF EQUITY

The return required by equity investors is proportional to the risk they face and depends on the risk of the company (or project) being valued. The capital asset pricing model (CAPM) is the traditional model used by analysts, investment banks, and best-in-class world corporations to estimate the cost of equity.

The CAPM model was developed by William Sharpe (Sharpe, 1964) and is used in the pricing of financial assets. In 1990 Sharpe received the Sveriges Riksbank Prize in Economic Sciences in Memory of Alfred Nobel, also known as the Nobel Prize in Economics, for his "pioneering work in the theory of financial economics." Indeed, Sharpe's work has shaped and impacted the world of financial economics for practitioners as well as academics. The model is widely applied, and research has shown that close to 75% of CFOs of international corporations use the CAPM to determine the cost of capital of their companies.[6]

---

[6] See Graham and Harvey (2001). Some alternative models to the CAPM have been gaining popularity. One clear contender is the Fama–French 3-factor model — see Fama and French (1993).

KEY LEARNING POINT

The CAPM is the standard model used to compute the cost of equity.

According to the CAPM, the cost of equity is equal to

$$r_{equity} = r_f + \beta \times (\text{Market Risk Premium}) \tag{2.3}$$

r_f is the risk-free rate (consistent with the currency of the cash flows), and β is the beta of a company, which represents the systematic risk of a company's common stock. It is important that this beta reflect an appropriate compensation for the business risk and also for the financial (capital structure) risk.

According to the CAPM, the main measure of risk is the beta coefficient. The beta is a measure of the systematic risk of a company's shares, which includes compensation for business and financial risk.

All companies and projects have their own beta coefficient.[7] The average beta is equal to one. A beta of one means that a company has an average risk, that is, a similar risk to that of the aggregate market or economy.

Betas above one indicate a higher-than-average risk. This suggests that a company is riskier than the average company in the economy. If a company has a beta higher than one, it is also an indication that its profits are sensitive to economic conditions and fluctuate substantially depending on the business cycle, competitive pressures, and technological innovation. For example, industries that typically have betas above one include IT and electronics and automobile manufacturing.

Betas below one indicate a below-average risk. This is common for companies with stable profits and cash flows. It indicates that a company's profits do not vary as much as the average company in the economy. It also suggests that a company is less sensitive to the business cycle than companies with higher betas. For instance, low betas are common in utilities industries and in the food and beverage sectors. See **Figure 2.3** for betas of different companies.

---

[7] For publicly traded companies, beta can be estimated as a regression of the returns on the share against the index return. Some free websites from which betas can be obtained include finance.yahoo.com, finance.google.com, and the *Financial Times* website. Reuters and Bloomberg (the main databases of financial data worldwide) also provide betas for publicly traded companies worldwide. For privately held companies, or for specific projects, the beta must be estimated using comparable companies as the reference point — see section 4.6.

KEY LEARNING POINT ✓

Beta is the key indicator of risk. Betas above one indicate a high risk; betas below one indicate a low risk. The average beta is one.

FIGURE 2.3: Betas of major global companies

Beta estimates for Euro Stoxx 50 Stocks

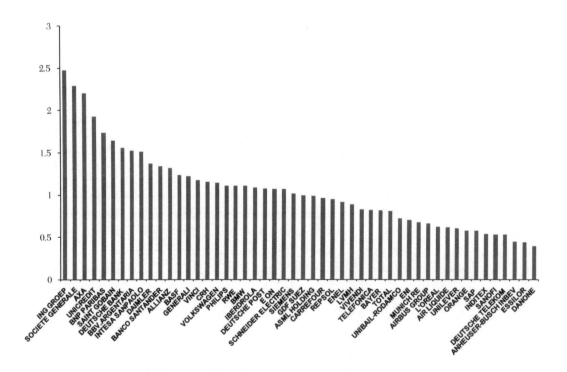

Beta estimates for Dow Jones 30 stocks

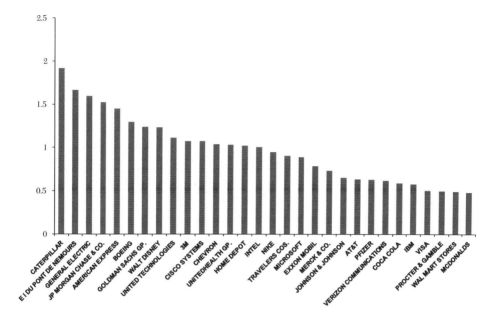

Beta estimates for Asia, Japan, and Latin America stocks

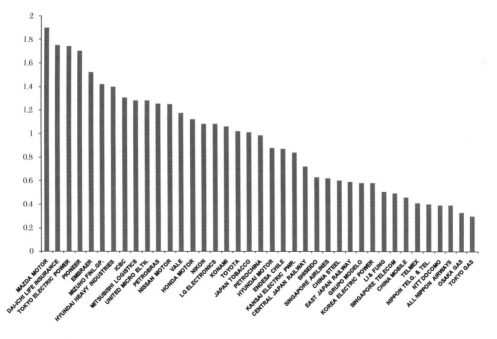

Source: December 2013, Datastream. Betas are estimated using monthly data on stock prices over five years (i.e., 60 monthly observations).

Two parameters are needed (in addition to beta) in order to estimate the cost of equity: the risk-free rate and the market risk premium. Note that these parameters are constant across companies. Only the beta coefficient varies and leads to changes in the cost of equity across different companies.

Theoretically, and according to the derivation of the CAPM, the market risk premium is the expected return above the risk-free rate on a portfolio that includes all the stocks in the market (market portfolio). There is no consensus among academics and practitioners on the "right" market risk premium. Estimates have been obtained from leading analysts, investment bankers, surveys of academics,[8] surveys of CFOs, aggregate data of the implied risk premium, and the long-term average of past realized returns in many different markets around the world. The different methods and data support a range for the market risk premium of 4% to 6%.

KEY LEARNING POINT ✓

The market risk premium is estimated to be 4% to 6%.

Table 2.4 shows the range of market risk premiums used by different investment banks.

TABLE 2.4: Investment bank market risk premiums

Investment bank	Market risk premium
Credit Suisse	6.00%
Morgan Stanley	5.00%
Santander	5.50%
JP Morgan	5.00%
Deutsche Bank	5.30%
Cheuvreux	4.00%

Source: IMD research, 2013.

---

[8] See Dimson, Marsh, and Staunton (2002) and Welch and Goyal (2008).

From now on in this chapter, we will use a point estimate of 5%.[9] This is also (approximately) the long-term average of the excess returns of equity markets over the risk-free rate for a wide range of countries since data has been available. A market risk premium of 5% can be interpreted as follows: investors demand 5% above the risk-free rate to hold a diversified portfolio of average risk (beta equals one).

Consider the betas for:

Alcoa	Disney	Pfizer
1.97	1.23	0.64

Assuming that the risk-free rate equals 4% and the market risk premium equals 5%, we would estimate their cost of equity to be

$$r_{equity} = r_f + \beta \times (\text{Market Risk Premium}) = 4\% + \beta \times 5\%$$

Company	Beta	Cost of equity
Alcoa	1.97	$4\% + \mathbf{1.97} \times 5\% = 13.9\%$
Disney	1.23	$4\% + \mathbf{1.23} \times 5\% = 10.1\%$
Pfizer	0.64	$4\% + \mathbf{0.64} \times 5\% = 7.2\%$

Companies with high betas such as Alcoa have a higher cost of equity. Conversely, companies with betas below one (such as Pfizer) have a lower (than average) cost of equity.

Given the data shown in **Figure 2.3** on Euro Stoxx, Dow Jones, and other global companies betas, the cost of equity of the majority of companies falls in the range 6% to 8% for very low-risk companies and 15% to 17% for high-risk ones.

2.3　PUTTING IT ALL TOGETHER — ESTIMATING THE COMPANY'S COST OF CAPITAL

Once we have estimated a company's after-tax cost of debt and the cost of equity, we can calculate the WACC.

$$WACC = \frac{debt}{debt + equity}(1-t)r_{debt} + \frac{equity}{debt + equity}r_{equity} \tag{2.4}$$

| r_{debt} is the cost of debt, r_{equity} is the cost of equity, and t is the tax rate.

---

[9] It is good practice to conduct a sensitivity analysis on the cost of capital using different numbers for its inputs.

In order to estimate the weighted average cost of capital for a company, we need to use the relative proportions of debt and equity financing. This is a very important step. The capital structure weights used to compute the WACC have to be calculated at market values.

The WACC is a market-based metric that management needs to know. Without this knowledge, they cannot make better decisions for a company's owners — bondholders and equity holders. When investors buy stocks or bonds, they expect — or rather demand — a return. This return is the cost of equity in the case of equity holders and the cost of debt in the case of debtholders. The WACC is just the weighted average of these two components, taking into account the relative proportions of the market values of debt and equity, which represent the capital structure of the company.

Because interest payments are tax deductible, the after-tax cost of debt is lower than the before-tax cost. Thus, in the WACC formula, we include the term $1 - t$ (one minus the corporate tax rate) to represent the tax shield obtained through interest payments. The correct tax rate of the WACC is the rate at which taxes will be reduced by interest deductions in the future. This may be the effective tax rate or the marginal tax rate depending on the circumstances.

The market value and the book value of equity are usually very different, so the market value should be used when computing the weights in the WACC formula (the market value of equity, also called *market capitalization*, is the share price multiplied by the number of shares).[10]

For debt, the book value can usually be used unless the company is in financial distress. In most situations, the market value of debt[11] is not significantly different from the book value. The book value of debt is the sum of all the financial (or interest-bearing) debt in the balance sheet (short and long term).

KEY LEARNING POINT

The market values of equity and debt should be used when computing the weights in the WACC formula. The book value of debt can be used unless the company is in financial distress.

---

[10] In the case of a privately held company, the market value of equity is obviously not observable. This is discussed in chapter 9, when the pure-play method is introduced.

[11] In order to compute the market value of debt, we need to discount the cash flows to be paid to debtholders at the market-based yield to maturity on the company's different debt instruments — bonds and bank loans. This is only feasible when all of the company's debt is through publicly traded bonds (which is not the case for most companies).

21st Century Fox has outstanding debt with a market value of $16 billion, and equity with a book value of $17 billion. The company has 2,281,806,390 shares outstanding, and the stock price is $33. It pays 30% taxes, has a beta of 1.5, and a rating of BBB+ (assume that the typical spread for BBB+ companies is 2%). Assuming a risk-free rate of 3% and a market risk premium of 5%, what is 21st Century Fox's WACC?

Step 1: Compute the cost of equity and the cost of debt:

$$r_{debt} = 3\% + 2\% = 5\%$$
$$r_{equity} = 3\% + 1.5 \times 5\% = 10.5\%$$

Step 2: Compute weights that reflect the appropriate capital structure of the company at market value:

The weights in the WACC formula are the fractions of 21st Century Fox financed with debt and financed with equity. These weights should be based on market values, because the cost of capital is based on investors' current assessment of the value of the company, and not on the historical accounting-based book values. For practical purposes, we can thus ignore the book value of equity.

Equity (at market value) = No. of shares outstanding × Current share price

$$= 2,281,806,390 \times \$33 = \$75 \text{ billion}$$

Total debt = $16 billion

The weight of equity is then 75/(16 + 75), which equals 82%, and the weight of debt is 18%.

Step 3: Compute the WACC:

$$WACC = \frac{debt}{debt + equity}(1-t)r_{debt} + \frac{equity}{debt + equity}r_{equity}$$

$$WACC = \frac{16}{16+75}(1-0.30) \times 5\% + \frac{75}{16+75} \times 10.5\% = 9.27\%$$

Table 2.5 shows the computed WACCs for a number of companies, taking into account their rating, beta, weights of debt and equity, and effective tax rate.

TABLE 2.5: WACC across different companies

	Caterpillar	Alcoa	Disney	Exxon Mobil	Pfizer	McDonald's
Beta	1.88	1.97	1.23	0.86	0.64	0.40
Cost of equity	13.4%	13.9%	10.1%	8.3%	7.2%	6.0%
Rating	A	BBB-	A	AAA	AA	A
Cost of debt	2.9%	4.9%	2.9%	1.5%	2.5%	3.8%
% of equity	57%	51%	89%	94%	89%	88%
% of debt	43%	49%	11%	6%	11%	12%
Effective tax rate	25%	25%	25%	42%	31%	32%
WACC	8.6%	8.9%	9.3%	7.8%	6.6%	5.6%

Source: Bloomberg, Datastream, December 2013.

Beta (the risk associated with equity) and rating (the risk associated with debt) impact the WACCs across companies. Riskier companies (typically, more cyclical companies such as Caterpillar) have a higher cost of capital. Conversely, companies with more stable businesses (such as Pfizer and McDonalds) tend to have lower WACCs. Finally, **Table 2.5** shows how the relative proportions of debt and equity also impact the WACC (the appropriate mix of debt/equity is addressed in chapter 5).

SUMMARY

All investors seek a return on their investment that compensates for the risk incurred. The WACC is thus a market-value metric that management needs to know in order to make sound decisions for a company's owners (or suppliers of capital). In this chapter, we have examined how to estimate the cost of capital and its two key components: the cost of debt and the cost of equity.

The cost of debt varies across companies and reflects the risk incurred by the company's creditors. Credit ratings provide an assessment of that risk. The cost of equity also varies; it reflects the variability of a company's profits. The CAPM is the model used worldwide to estimate the cost of equity. Companies with high betas have a higher cost of equity.

Note that the cost of capital is not dictated by management. The cost of capital is, rather, the rate of return demanded by the investors who finance a company by buying either company bonds (debtholders) or stocks (equity holders).

REFERENCES

Dimson, E., P. Marsh, and M. Staunton, 2002, *Triumph of the Optimists: 101 Years of Global Investment Returns*, New Jersey: Princeton University Press.

Fama, E.F., and K.R. French, 1993, Common Risk Factors in the Returns on Stocks and Bonds, *Journal of Financial Economics*, Vol. 33, Iss. 1:3–56.

Graham, J.R., and C.R. Harvey, 2001, The Theory and Practice of Corporate Finance: Evidence from the Field, *Journal of Financial Economics*, Vol. 60, Iss. 2:187–243.

Sharpe, W.F., 1964, Capital Asset Prices: A Theory of Market Equilibrium under Conditions of Risk, *Journal of Finance*, Vol. 19, Iss. 3:425–442.

Welch, I., and A. Goyal, 2008, A Comprehensive Look at the Empirical Performance of Equity Premium Prediction, *Review of Financial Studies*, Vol. 21:1455–1508.

A Managerial Framework for Value Creation

The overall goal of a company focused on value creation is to generate adequate returns on capital in a sustainable way. Companies raise cash from investors (debt or equity) and invest it in various projects and businesses. The key principle for companies is to create value by investing capital from investors and generating future cash flows that exceed the cost of capital.

3.1 A FRAMEWORK FOR VALUE CREATION

The framework for value creation proposed here is simply a way to identify, assess, compare, and measure the value created from new investments and existing assets (see **Figure 3.1**).

FIGURE 3.1:   The basic pillars of value creation.

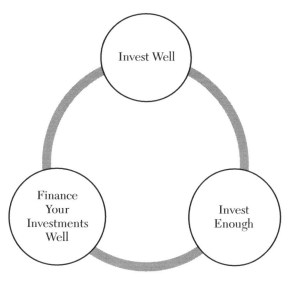

Value creation is thus achieved through an appropriate combination of

- Investment policies
- Financing strategies
- Payout policies: how much to reinvest and how much to pay back to investors

Various chapters of the book will cover these different topics. For instance, investment decisions for capital expenditure projects are covered in chapter 4, financing strategies are discussed in chapters 5 to 7, and payout or reinvestment policies are the focus of chapter 8.

In this chapter, we focus on the overall relation between returns on capital and the cost of capital. This is relevant whenever one wants to evaluate a company's performance as a whole, or the performance of its business units/segments.

3.2   RETURN ON INVESTED CAPITAL — WHEN DOES VALUE CREATION OCCUR?

The main formula to assess value creation by a company in a certain period is

$$\text{Return on Capital} > \text{Cost of Capital} \tag{3.1}$$

Return on Capital is a useful measure for comparing the relative profitability of companies after taking into account the amount of capital used. If the return on capital is higher than the cost of capital, this means that a company is using its capital at higher returns than it costs. Therefore, the company is creating value for its suppliers of capital. Also, the faster a company can grow and deploy capital at attractive rates of return, the more value it creates.

Three key concepts are required to compute the value created by a company over a certain period:

1. Net operating profit after tax (NOPAT)
2. Invested capital
3. Return on invested capital (ROIC)

NOPAT (net operating profit after tax)

$$\text{NOPAT} = \text{EBIT} \times (1 - \%\ \text{tax rate}) \tag{3.2}$$

| A company's after-tax operating profit for all investors
| Includes the after-tax profit available for shareholders and debtholders
| Equal to the net income if a company has no leverage

| A metric of operating performance that can be used to compare companies with different leverage policies

Invested capital

$$\text{Invested Capital} = \text{Long-Term Financial Debt} + \text{Short-Term Financial Debt} + \text{Equity} \qquad (3.3)$$

| Represents all the capital raised from different suppliers.
| The total cash investment made by shareholders and debtholders.
| Includes all interest-bearing debt raised by a company (short term or long term).
| The invested capital is then used in net working capital, property, plant and equipment, intangible assets, and other operating assets.

ROIC (return on invested capital)

$$ROIC = \frac{NOPAT}{Invested\ Capital}$$

$$\text{or} \qquad (3.4)$$

$$ROIC = \frac{EBIT \times (1 - \%\ Tax\ Rate)}{Invested\ Capital}$$

| Measures the return earned on a company's capital or how well a company utilizes the capital invested in the business.
| It can also be called ROCE, return on capital employed.[1]

KEY LEARNING POINT ✓

Whenever a company's capital is used in such a way that it provides higher returns than it costs, there is value creation. The basic rule for value creation is then:

Return on Invested Capital > Weighted Average Cost of Capital

---

Companies create value whenever they are able to generate returns on capital (ROIC) in excess of the cost of that capital (the WACC, as defined in chapter 2).

---

[1] Different industries and companies have different conventions regarding these terms. In this text, the terms Return on Capital, Return on Invested Capital (ROIC), or Return on Capital Employed (ROCE) are used interchangeably.

The following sections address how a certain ROIC is achieved, and the operational measures managers can employ to improve it.

3.3   EFFICIENCY AND PROFITABILITY — THE KEY DRIVERS OF VALUE CREATION

It is often useful to understand the sources of a certain ROIC. In particular, we often want to break down ROIC into two parts:

$$ROIC = \frac{EBIT \times (1 - \% \ tax \ rate)}{Sales} \times \frac{Sales}{Invested \ Capital} \qquad (3.5)$$

Or

$$ROIC = \text{Profit Margin} \times \text{Capital Turnover} \qquad (3.6)$$

Essentially, the ROIC equals the profit margin multiplied by the capital turnover. For example, if the margin increases, every sale brings in more money, resulting in a higher overall ROIC. Similarly, if the capital turnover increases, a company generates more sales for every unit of capital invested in it, again resulting in a higher overall ROIC.

KEY LEARNING POINT ✓

The ROIC is the product of Profitability and Efficiency.

Table 3.1 shows the return on invested capital that results from different combinations of profit margin and capital turnover.

TABLE 3.1:   The effects of profit margin and capital turnover on the ROIC

Profit margin	Capital turnover	ROIC
2%	600%	**12.0%**
10%	120%	**12.0%**
24%	50%	**12.0%**
60%	20%	**12.0%**

An ROIC of 12% can thus be achieved with very different combinations of profit margins. For instance, a supermarket will typically have a profit margin of 2%, but the rotation of stock is very high, so that the capital turnover equals 600%. In that case, even though each individual sale generates only a 2% margin, the volume of sales (relative to capital used) compensates for this.

The other extreme case is that of a luxury goods retailer. The profit margin on each item may be high (e.g., 60%), but the volume of sales is not high when compared to the invested capital. Thus, for a company with a 60% profit margin and 20% capital turnover, the ROIC is equal to 12%.

Splitting the ROIC into two parts makes it easier to understand changes in it over time and across companies. There are thus two ways of improving the ROIC:

Increasing profitability. The net margin measures the percentage profitability of each sale. Higher profitability can be achieved with a better product portfolio, better pricing, lower costs, or a combination of all of these.

Increasing efficiency in the use of capital. Capital turnover is a measure of how effectively a company converts its capital into sales. It can be improved through better utilization of the company's assets, including the net working capital. A company that is able to generate the same sales and margin with less capital provides a better ROIC to its suppliers of capital.

KEY LEARNING POINT ✓

Improvements in the ROIC are obtained by a combination of efficiency and profitability improvements.

3.4   HOW MANAGERS CAN IMPACT THE ROIC

Figure 3.2 shows some of the levers that managers can use to impact their company's ROIC.

FIGURE 3.2:   Levers that affect the ROIC.

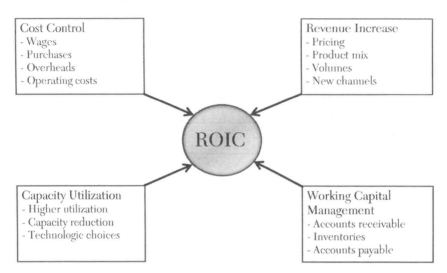

3.4.1   Efficiency Improvements

Even when the profit margin is small, companies can enjoy a high ROIC if they use capital efficiently. As seen in **Table 3.1**, a company with a low profit margin (2%) can achieve a 12% ROIC if its capital turnover is equal to 6× (that is, its revenues are six times their invested capital).

Therefore, in order to improve the ROIC, companies may need to be more effective in their utilization of capital. This in itself can be achieved by many different alternative routes:

• Sell excess equipment.

• Reduce or outsource inventory.

• Collect receivables (that is, reduce the DSO — days sales outstanding).

• Reduce inventory.

• Renegotiate payment terms with suppliers.

• Identify alternative uses of available capacity.

All these measures reduce the need for invested capital. Indeed, when a company has lots of receivables outstanding (client invoices that have not yet been paid), it still needs to fund its operations somehow — either with additional debt or equity. Thus, if a company can improve the collection of receivables, it will reduce its need for external capital — and at the same time improve its ROIC.

3.4.2 Profitability Improvements

Alternatively, the ROIC can be improved by working on the profitability side:

- Ensure that the company is compensated for all services provided.
- Pursue additional service/product offerings.
- Ensure cost control on operating costs, wages, purchases, and overheads.
- Secure high utilization of the available capacity.
- Seek lower-cost sourcing with adequate quality.
- Increase revenues by improving the product mix and pricing.

3.4.3 Excel — Decomposition of the ROIC

We are interested in computing the ROIC of a company with:

- Revenues = $20,000
- Cost of goods sold (COGS) = $15,000
- EBIT margin = 14.5% (which means EBIT = $2,900)
- The effective tax rate = 25%
- Fixed assets = $13,000
- Inventory = $2,500
- Accounts receivables = $2,700 (approximately 49 days' sales outstanding)
- Inventory = $2,500
- Accounts payables = $3,000 (approximately 73 days of payables outstanding)

The invested capital of this company can be obtained by adding the fixed assets and the net working capital:

Invested Capital = Fixed Assets + (Accounts Receivable + Inventory − Accounts Payables)

Invested Capital = $13,000 + ($2,700 + $2,500 − $3,000) = $15,200

We thus obtain for this company an ROIC of

$$\text{ROIC} = \frac{\$2,900 \times (1 - 25\%)}{\$15,200} = 14.3\%$$

What would the ROIC be if this company maintains the tax rate and the EBIT, but introduces the following measures:

- Sells $1,000 worth of fixed assets
- Collects money faster from customers: reduces the DSO by 10 days, to 39 days
- Holds less inventory: reduces days of inventory by 10 days, to 51 days
- Extends payment terms to suppliers by 10 days, to 83 days.

Under these conditions, the new ROIC would equal 17%, almost 3% higher than the original one.

Figure 3.3 shows the calculations of the initial ROIC in Excel, as well as a model for simulation of the company's ROIC under different assumptions for different items.

FIGURE 3.3:   Excel decomposition of the ROIC.

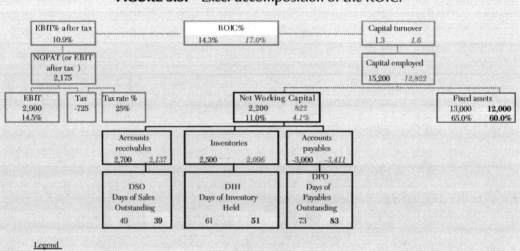

In this particular example, the ROIC increased from 14.3% to 17%, which was entirely achieved by a higher capital turnover (or efficiency), because the NOPAT (EBIT after tax) was assumed to be constant. In this case, as a result of the various measures introduced in the company, the capital employed was reduced to $12,822 (from $15,200). This reduction in capital needs translated into a higher capital turnover (1.6 versus the original 1.3), and thus a higher ROIC.

3.5	**ACHIEVING A CULTURE OF VALUE — RIGHT INCENTIVES FOR EACH LEVEL OF THE ORGANIZATION**

The ROIC measures profitability in relation to invested capital. It is nowadays a commonly used measure of performance for companies worldwide. In particular, it is the standard for many capital-intensive companies in sectors from telecoms, utilities, chemical, heavy industries, oil and gas, food and beverages, tobacco, etc. Analysts frequently use ROIC metrics to compare the performance of companies within the same industry, and identify whether or not companies can afford their cost of capital. It is thus highly correlated with stock prices.

At the top level of an organization, it may be appropriate to focus on the ROIC, and even link remuneration levels to it. However, at lower levels, the ROIC can be seen as too "intangible," and giving ROIC metrics for all employees may not be appropriate in all circumstances.

The alternative is to think about the drivers of the ROIC. As the decomposition in the previous section (section 3.4) shows, the ROIC is essentially a combination of efficiency and profitability, and each one of these is impacted by different levels of staff in an organization.

KEY LEARNING POINT

Not all employees should have incentives or targets related to the ROIC. The targets should be tailored to the level of impact of each employee in the company.

When a company is focusing on improving its ROIC, it can implement various measures, as discussed in section 3.4. It is important that these measures be eventually translated into key performance indicators (KPIs) that each employee can impact herself.

For instance, if salespeople are rewarded on booked sales, they have no incentive to help manage customer payables. Thus, in order to reduce working capital needs and thereby improve the ROIC, rewards for salespeople should depend not just on sales, but also on collection. Similarly, a supply chain manager could have targets related not only to the cost of raw materials, but also to the amount of inventory levels. The overall principle is that each employee should be able to focus on a sub-component of the ROIC that is under her level of control.

KPIs and incentive schemes used in practice

- Reward salespeople for sales growth as well as for receivables.
- Reward operations managers for utilization of assets: This aims to increase efficiency by improving the utilization rates of tools and equipment.
- Implement immediate invoicing. Track delay in invoicing, or incorrect invoices that are returned by the customer and will thus delay payment until a properly filled invoice is sent.
- Collect receivables due throughout the year, not just on the last days of December.
- Monitor and resolve overdues (customers who are late on their payments) on a regular basis.
- Improve communication between sales and inventory managers. This frequently allows for lower levels of inventory without compromising on the availability of goods to deliver.

3.6   THE VALUE–GROWTH MATRIX

Figure 3.4 presents a framework that can be applied to a company as a whole, or to its different business units or segments.

FIGURE 3.4:   The value–growth matrix.

	LOW RETURN	HIGH RETURN
HIGH GROWTH	KILLERS	JEWELS
LOW GROWTH	SLOW KILLERS	CASH COW

On the vertical axis, we have growth, which can be high or low. On the horizontal axis, we have returns, which can be high or low (relative to the relevant cost of capital). The matrix has the following categories:

Killers: These are business units that have high growth and low returns. If their performance continues to fall in this quadrant, they can destroy a company owing to the constant need for additional investment (high growth needs investment), with low returns.

Slow Killers: These are business units that have low growth and also low returns. This is probably the most dangerous quadrant. Indeed, businesses or segments in the Slow

Killer quadrant are often not subject to enough managerial attention. Because the growth is low, no additional capital is needed for this business, and it can stay put, underperforming, for a long time.

Jewels: This is the best possible quadrant, provided enough financing is available. Here, the business shows high growth and also delivers high returns. It is an important source of value creation.

Cash Cows: This quadrant includes businesses with low growth but high returns. Because the growth is low, there is very limited need for additional investments. Together with the high returns, this means that these businesses release large amounts of cash, which is available for different uses: dividends, buyback, or reinvestment (see chapter 8 for a thorough analysis of the optimal payout policies).

Companies create value when they enjoy high returns, and this is true whether the growth is high or low. The matrix also shows how high growth with low returns can destroy value.

Many companies have historically been very focused on growth targets, with a lack of control on the capital side. Many of these ventures have ended in disaster. It is critical that managers realize that growth can be good or bad: Good growth delivers returns above the cost of capital. But not all growth is good. If the returns on capital continue to be below the cost of capital, the company is better off stopping growth projects and returning the money to its shareholders (see chapter 8).

SUMMARY

Many managers have a strong focus on growth. Often, however, growth of accounting profits does not translate into value. The important factor is that growth must be profitable, which means that it should deliver returns on capital above the cost of capital. This is essential for value creation — having a positive accounting profitability is not enough.

The tools in this chapter highlight the fact that it is critical to consider not just the profits on the income statement, but also the balance sheet, or the capital side of the company. When a company grows but delivers mediocre returns on capital, it is effectively destroying value.

We have examined some of the managerial drivers of value creation. Some of the most important ones include efficiency in operations and profitability. It is the combination of these two elements that leads to a certain return on invested capital.

Value creation depends on different financial policies (Financing, Investment, and Payout). These must be executed appropriately, in a holistic manner. In subsequent chapters, we will analyze each of these in detail.

Selecting the Right Investment Projects — Capital Budgeting Tools

This chapter focuses on the main methods used to value investment projects. It covers concepts such as

- The discounted cash flow (DCF) method
- The estimation of cash flows
- Appropriate discount rates and cost of capital
- Project valuation in privately held companies and in a different industry
- NPV and additional project valuation metrics

The tools in this chapter can greatly enhance decisions, be it a new product launch, the purchase of assets, investment in a new market, or any other kind of investment project. Additionally, the methods can be used to evaluate brands, as well as royalty interest. Importantly, these tools take into account a company's overall cost of capital and allow the company to select only those projects that create value for shareholders.

4.1   PROJECT VALUATION USING DISCOUNTED CASH FLOWS

The value of an investment depends on the cash flows it generates. This is valid whether it is a capital expenditure, a new product launch, entry into a new market, or replacement of a machine. There is an old saying, "Cash is a fact, profit is an opinion." When analyzing a project, it is thus important to distinguish between profits and cash flows.

Income (or profit) is different from cash flow. For instance, booking a sale usually translates into more income. Usually, however, customers obtain trade credit, and only after some time is the cash actually collected. One other major difference between cash flow and income is the way fixed assets are treated. In accounting terms, the value of a car (or any kind of fixed asset) depreciates over time. Thus, each year there is an accounting item that reflects how much depreciation the accounting tables allow for those fixed assets. However, in reality, cash is paid when the car is bought. And from then on there are no cash flows related to the acquisition of the car. This implies that when computing cash flows, we have to undo several accounting statement entries to eliminate virtual transactions that have no cash flow implications.

The most common method of valuation using discounted cash flows (DCF) is the *free cash flow to the firm (FCFF) method*. Under this method, we attempt to determine the project value by discounting[1] all the cash flows over the life of the project, without including any financing aspect in the cash flows.[2]

The end result of a project evaluation using the DCF method is the net present value (NPV). In order to arrive at it, we perform the following steps:

1. Estimate the free cash flow to the firm (FCFF) generated by the proposed investment project. This is done for each year of the project's useful life.

2. Compute the weighted average cost of capital (WACC). The WACC must reflect the riskiness of the project's cash flows.

3. Discount cash flows to obtain the net present value of the project.

$$NPV = -Investment_0 + \sum_{t=1}^{T} \frac{FCFF_t}{(1+WACC)^t} \qquad (4.1)$$

| NPV is the project's net present value.

| $\sum_{t=1}^{T} \frac{FCFF_t}{(1+WACC)^t}$ represents the present value of all the FCFFs of the project that are discounted at the WACC (weighted average cost of capital).

| $Investment_0$ is the initial investment required for the project.

The resulting NPV is today's value (in monetary terms) of the project, taking into account the future stream of cash flows. All cash flows are discounted to take into account the time value of money and the riskiness of the cash flows. And cash flows further in the future are automatically more discounted than the short-term ones.

KEY LEARNING POINT ✓

The NPV is a tool that takes into account cash flows, and their timing and risk.

---

[1] The terms *discounting* and *present value* are used interchangeably.

[2] Alternatively, we can use the free cash flow to equity method (FCFE), which is only a slight modification of the FCFF method described here. At the end of this chapter, we provide a brief description of the FCFE method and highlight how it is different from the FCFF method.

Once a company has obtained the NPV and performed rigorous security checks, it can decide whether to invest in a project. Projects with a positive NPV are recommended. An NPV > 0 implies that, over time, the project will be able to recover all the investment, besides generating an appropriate (higher than the cost of capital) return on the invested capital.

An NPV < 0 implies that, in today's terms and after adjusting for risk, the project's positive cash flows will not be enough to compensate for the initial investment.[3] Indeed, many projects may show a positive accounting profitability, and yet the NPV may indicate that they still destroy value (see section 4.3).

4.1.1   Defining Free Cash Flows to the Firm (FCFFs)

The FCFF represents the cash generated by a project that is available after taxes have been paid and the project's investment needs have been met. It can be used to return money to shareholders (either through dividends or share buybacks), repay debt, acquire other companies, provide extraordinary bonuses to key employees, invest in new projects, and so on.

The FCFF is also called the *unlevered cash flow* because it represents the total amount of cash available for distribution to all suppliers of capital, including debtholders. It can also be interpreted as the free cash flow that a project without debt (an unlevered or all-equity project) would have.[4]

KEY LEARNING POINT ✓

The FCFF, or free cash flow to the firm, is the cash flow that a project without any debt generates.

The FCFF is defined for each year as

$$FCFF = EBITDA - \Delta NWC - Taxes - CAPEX \qquad (4.2)$$

or

$$FCFF = Unlevered\ Net\ Income + Depreciation - CAPEX - \Delta NWC \qquad (4.3)$$

---

[3] Whether having a project with an NPV exactly equal to 0 is good or bad is a subject for a long philosophical discussion. In practice, we do not really find NPVs that equal exactly zero, and if we do, this means that the project delivers exactly the cost of capital. Whether delivering to shareholders exactly the return they want is good or bad is a topic for another philosophical discussion … But most likely, the answer is yes — zero is still good!

[4] Interest payments are tax deductible from pre-tax income, which effectively lowers the cost of debt (tax shields). The tax advantage of debt is intentionally excluded from the FCFF calculation. In this way, we avoid double-counting the tax shields, because they are already incorporated in the WACC.

| *EBITDA* is the earnings before interest, taxes, depreciation, and amortization generated by the project.
| *ΔNWC* is the annual change in the net working capital.
| *Taxes* is the amount of taxes to be paid, assuming there are no debt-related tax shields. *Taxes = EBIT × Tax rate*. *EBIT* is the earnings before interest and taxes.
| *CAPEX* is the capital expenditure required by the project each year.
| *Unlevered net income* is equal to *EBIT × (1 – Tax rate)*. The unlevered net income is also called the net operating profit after taxes (NOPAT).
| *Depreciation* includes all the non-cash operating expenses used for tax purposes, including depreciation, depletion, and amortization.

In the FCFF method, we do not include any debt-related payment in the cash flows generated by the project. The cost of debt and its associated tax shields are considered in the cost of capital. Therefore, debt payments and their tax shields do impact the project valuation, through the discount rate (or cost of capital).

There are thus two alternative routes (and potential variants) to reach the FCFF. Using formula (4.2), we start with the EBITDA and subtract ΔNWC to obtain the operating cash flows. We then need to subtract the taxes to be paid as well as the necessary capital expenditures to arrive at the FCFF.

With formula (4.3), we start with the unlevered net income[5] and then add back the depreciation expenditures, because they are non-cash expenses recognized only for tax purposes. Then, as with formula (4.2), we still need to subtract the capital expenditures during the period, as well as the additional investments in the net working capital. The results will be exactly the same when both methods are used correctly.

4.1.2 Forecasting Future Cash Flows in Capital Budgeting Applications

In order to estimate the future FCFF, we need to generate pro forma accounting statements for future years. Given the definition of the FCFF, we need to prepare projected income statements and balance sheets so that we can compute the different items needed for the FCFF.

It is common to start with sales. Forecasting sales for future years requires market research as well as competitive positioning analysis, which allows us to project sales growth rates into the future. The project manager would need to obtain estimates of unit volume and prices of the product/service under consideration in order to calculate the operating revenues for each year.

---

[5] The unlevered net income represents the profit generated by a project if it does not have any debt-related payments (or the associated tax shields on debt). It equals *EBIT × (1 – % Tax rate)*.

Then, assumptions related to the operating profit margin must be made. We must forecast the evolution of the various costs (cost of goods sold and general expenses) over the lifetime of the project. It is sometimes assumed that these costs represent a certain percentage of sales. It is also important to consider that margins might be higher or lower than in the past for fundamental reasons, such as

- Capacity utilization
- Unit labor cost
- Raw material costs
- Competition — local and foreign— and its impact on margins

With these assumptions regarding sales and various costs, we can compute the forecasted EBITDA for each year.

The net working capital also needs to be estimated. It can be defined as a percentage of sales, a fixed amount per customer, or in monthly terms (e.g., one month of credit to customers, two of inventories). It is important always to look at *changes in the net working capital* from one year to the next.

Although depreciation is not a cash item, it must also be estimated as it will impact taxes. Depreciation reflects the past capital expenditures made by the company and the average useful life of equipment.

Another key item of the FCFF is the amount of capital expenditures. It is typical to assume that projects have an initial investment, followed by a series of positive cash flows. However, in many cases the initial investment is not enough, and the project requires capital expenditures in different years (and not just at time 0). These must be included in the FCFF calculation.

Overall, we need to have forecasts for each year for each of the components of the foregoing FCFF formulas. The cash flow forecasts should be based on sound industry and company analysis and should reflect industry trends, market research data, competitive pressures, and company strategy. Obviously, the quality of the inputs determines the accuracy of FCFF forecasts and, ultimately, a trustworthy NPV.

LH Incorporated, a soft drinks manufacturer, is considering investing in a new line of drinks. In order to enter this new business, the company needs to acquire a new machine that costs $10,000. The business development team has compiled the following data on this project:

- First year revenues = $10,500. These are expected to grow at 4% and 3% over the next two years, respectively.

- The variable costs of production are approximately equal to 50% of the selling price of the new drink. This includes all the raw materials (fruit, bottles, plastic, etc.) needed to sell the drinks. We can thus compute the cost of goods sold (COGS) = 50% of sales.
- The marketing expenses, energy, labor costs, and other administrative expenses, amount to 15% of the sales price. We thus compute selling, general, & administrative expenses (SG&A) = 15% of sales.
- The effective tax rate = 30%.
- Net working capital requirements = 5% of sales.
- During the lifetime of the project, additional capital expenditures are required as shown in the following table:

	XXX1	XXX2	XXX3
CAPEX	$1,500	$1,470	$1,420

- Depreciation rate = 10%. Assume that this depreciation rate is the same for initial investments as well as for subsequent CAPEX.

Given the above capital expenditures and the annual depreciation rate (10%), the fixed assets of the project will be as follows:

(in $)	XXX0	XXX1	XXX2	XXX3
Fixed assets	10,000	10,500	10,920	11,248
CAPEX	10,000	1,500	1,470	1,420
Depreciation		1,000	1,050	1,092
Depreciation rate	10%	10%	10%	10%

The original investment in the project is $10,000. But every year, the project still requires additional investments. During year 1, the project requires additional capital expenditures of $1,500. The original value of the assets is $10,000, but 10% is depreciated every year. Thus, at the end of the first year, the fixed assets are given by

$$\text{Assets year 1} = \text{Assets year 0} - \text{depreciation in year 1} + \text{new CAPEX in year 1}$$
$$= \$10,000 - \$1,000 + \$1,500 = \$10,500$$

In year 2, the depreciation is higher than in year 1. This is due to the higher amount of assets at the end of year 1: $10,500.[6]

The first step in any project valuation using the NPV is to estimate the cash flows generated by the project. Regardless of the method chosen to compute the FCFF, we must always prepare a pro forma income statement in order to determine the amount of taxes to be paid, as well as other important components of the FCFF.

---

[6] For practical purposes, it is assumed that an asset starts being depreciated in the year following its acquisition. For instance, in year 1, the total assets are $10500 after the depreciation in that year, and the new CAPEX. Thus, in year 2, the depreciation is going to be equal to 10% of that: $1050.

In this case, given the above assumptions, revenues grow at 4% and 3%, respectively, and the income statement will be as follows:

(in $)	XXX1	XXX2	XXX3
Revenues	10,500	10,920	11,248
COGS	5,250	5,460	5,624
SG&A	1,575	1,638	1,687
EBITDA	**3,675**	**3,822**	**3,937**
Depreciation	1,000	1,050	1,092
EBIT	**2,675**	**2,772**	**2,845**
Taxes (*EBIT* × *tax rate*)	803	832	853
Unlevered net income	**1,873**	**1,940**	**1,991**

Given that the company will always require 5% of sales in working capital, the working capital requirements for each year are as follows:

(in $)	XXX1	XXX2	XXX3
Net working capital (NWC)	525	546	562
Changes in NWC (ΔNWC)	–525	–21	–16

For project valuation, only the yearly changes in the NWC account are relevant. If the NWC increases from one year to the next, that means an additional investment must be made (and hence the negative sign). For instance, in the first year of the project, the company needs to invest $525 in the NWC. In year 2, the project needs $546 of the NWC (5% of year 2 sales). This means that there is an additional investment of $21 in the NWC. Similarly, in year 3, the required NWC equals $562, which means an annual change in the NWC of –16.

Under formula (4.2), the FCFF can be computed as follows:

(in $)	XXX1	XXX2	XXX3
EBITDA	3,675	3,822	3,937
Changes in NWC	–525	–21	–16
– Taxes	–803	–832	–853
– CAPEX	–1,500	–1,470	–1,420
FCFF	**848**	**1,499**	**1,647**

We start with the EBITDA as per the forecast income statement. Then, to get to the FCFF, we must subtract the additional capital expenditures, taxes, and changes in the NWC.

Alternatively, with formula (4.3), the FCFF can be computed as follows:

(in $)	XXX1	XXX2	XXX3
Unlevered net income	1,873	1,940	1,991
+ Depreciation	1,000	1,050	1,092
− CAPEX	−1,500	−1,470	−1,420
Changes in NWC	−525	−21	−16
FCFF	**848**	**1,499**	**1,647**

Both methods arrive at exactly the same FCFF result of $848, $1,499, and $1,647 for years 1, 2, and 3, respectively. It is important to note that we do not include (or subtract) interest payments, because the objective is to compute the FCFF, which is the cash flow available to pay all owners (or suppliers of capital). All interest- and debt-related costs are included in the discount rate — the WACC. Thus, the FCFF is independent of the amount of debt in the capital structure of the company. Changes in capital structure, and consequently the tax shield implications of debt, are incorporated in the WACC calculation.

4.1.3   Which Cash Flows Should We Consider?

It is important to remember why we perform project valuations: we are trying to decide whether it is profitable for the company's owners to invest in a certain project.

Often, there are lengthy discussions within companies on which are the right cash flows to discount. To solve these issues, it is useful to think about two scenarios:

1. Cash flows that the company is going to generate *with the project.*
2. Cash flows that the company is going to generate *without the project.*

Thus, the relevant cash flows and CAPEX that should be analyzed are all those that occur as a consequence of the project — incremental or differential cash flows. And these cash flows should always be considered on an after-tax basis. This concept of differential or incremental cash flows is far-reaching and has important implications for decision making.

For instance, we should not consider sunk costs. Sunk costs are costs already incurred in the past and cannot be recovered, for instance:

*   Past software installation expenses
*   Past advertising expenses
*   Specialized equipment bought and installed, but for which there is no liquid resale market, given that it is so specific to the company

Because these costs (sunk costs) will be incurred with or without the project, there is no difference between the two scenarios (with and without the project), and thus they should not be included in the project valuation.

Some projects have certain cash flows that are incurred in the last year because of clean-up costs after the project is over, for instance. Also, sometimes equipment can be sold at the end of the project's lifetime — *residual value*. In both cases, these cash flows are clearly incremental and should be included in the project analysis. But once again, it is the after-tax value of the cash flows that is relevant.

Another typical discussion relates to the use of assets or facilities already held by the company. In this case, we must always consider that assets frequently have alternative uses — for example, they can be sold or rented. It is, once again, the differential cash flow relative to the alternative use that is relevant for project valuation purposes and optimal decision making. For instance, when analyzing a project for a new hotel, the company may in the past already have acquired the necessary land. With the new project, the land will be used to build the hotel. Without the project, the land could be sold for $10 million (after tax). Thus, the differential cash flow, comparing with/without the project, is $10 million.

In essence, only differential cash flows (that is, cash flows that are different because of the project) should be included in a project valuation based on the DCF. Other factors may be relevant for something else, but not for the Go/No Go decision.

KEY LEARNING POINT ✓

Only differential cash flows should be considered in a project analysis.

4.1.4   Projects with an Unknown But Very Long Horizon — Terminal Value

The FCFF method computes the value of a project based on the discounted cash flows to the firm over the life of the project. For some very long-term projects, it is sometimes assumed that a project has an infinite life.[7] In this case, the valuation is split into two components: the explicit period (also called *the forecast period*) and the terminal value.

---

[7] If we know the lifetime of the project in years, this infinite life assumption is obviously not used. We merely forecast cash flows for the actual maturity of the project. Also, in some specific cases related to concessions over a certain number of years, this infinite life assumption is obviously not used.

For the explicit period, we compute forecasts of the FCFF for each year. The length of the recommended explicit period varies. There is no absolute truth here. The explicit period depends on our scenario for growth; that is, the length of time that we believe the new project will be able to grow at a fast rate. But eventually, every project reaches a mature stage. At this stage, the terminal value can be computed.

The terminal value is estimated in the last year of the explicit cash flow period and represents the sum of all the future cash flows that the project is going to generate, in the steady state, thereafter.

KEY LEARNING POINT ✓

The terminal value should be used only for very long-term projects for which there is no defined maturity.

The standard formula for the terminal value is

$$TV_t = \frac{FCFF_{t+1}}{WACC - g} = \frac{FCFF_t(1 + g)}{WACC - g} \tag{4.4}$$

| TV_t is the terminal value expressed at time t. <u>It is important to remember that it should still be discounted to the present.</u>
| $FCFF_t$ represents the free cash flow to the firm at time t.
| $WACC$ is the weighted average cost of capital.
| g is the constant growth rate that is expected in perpetuity.

The terminal value is equal to the present value of all the cash flows occurring after the explicit forecast period ends. In perpetuity, it is assumed that the project's cash flows will grow at a constant rate (it can also be negative, if we assume a perpetual decline in the FCFF).

4.2   PROJECT VALUATION — AN APPLICATION

The first step in a project valuation is to estimate the cash flows for each year. Second, we must have a clear measure of the cost of capital. Indeed, the FCFFs are all estimated for different times (t) and must thus be discounted to the present.

It is important to remember that the cash flows being discounted are the FCFFs. These are the cash flows available to all providers of capital, i.e., equity and debt. Then we must subtract the full investment expenditures (regardless of how they are financed) to obtain the project's net present value (NPV).

$$NPV = -Investment_0 + \sum_{t=1}^{T} \frac{FCFF_t}{(1+WACC)^t}$$

| NPV is the project's net present value.

| $\sum_{t=1}^{T} \frac{FCFF_t}{(1+WACC)^t}$ represents the present value of all the FCFFs of the project, which are discounted at the weighted average cost of capital.

| $Investment_0$ is the initial investment required for the project.

LH Incorporated, a soft drinks manufacturer, is considering investing in a new line of drinks. In order to enter this new business, the company needs to acquire a new machine that costs $10,000. The business development team has compiled the following data on this project:

- First year revenues = $10,500
- Estimated revenue growth = 4%, 3%, 2%, and 2% over the next 4 years, respectively
- Cost of goods sold (COGS) = 50% of sales. This includes all the raw materials (fruit, bottles, plastic, etc.) needed to sell the drinks.
- Selling, general, & administrative expenses (SG&A) = 15% of sales. This includes marketing expenses, energy, labor costs, and other administrative expenses.
- The effective tax rate = 30%
- Net working capital requirements = 5% of sales
- Besides the initial investment, several other capital expenditures are planned during the project's lifetime. For the first 5 years, capital expenditures are planned according to the following table:

(in $)	XXX1	XXX2	XXX3	XXX4	XXX5
CAPEX	1,500	1,470	1,420	1,350	1,377

- Depreciation rate = 10%. Assume this depreciation rate is the same for initial investments as well as for the subsequent CAPEX.
- After year 5, the FCFF is expected to grow in perpetuity at 2% per year.
- The appropriate WACC for this project is 10%.

The first step in a project valuation is the estimation of the cash flows. We estimate the FCFF for the 5-year forecast period, using the above inputs:

(in $)	XXX1	XXX2	XXX3	XXX4	XXX5
EBITDA	3,675	3,822	3,937	4,015	4,096
Changes in NWC	−525	−21	−16	−11	−11
− Taxes	−803	−832	−853	-867	−885
− CAPEX	−1,500	−1,470	−1,420	−1,350	−1,377
FCFF	848	1,499	1,647	1,787	1,823

This specific project is assumed to have an infinite life.[8] We compute the terminal value in year 5, assuming the company will then grow at a constant rate of 2% and that the WACC is 10%:

$$TV_5 = \frac{FCFF_6}{WACC - g} = \frac{FCFF_5 \times (1+g)}{WACC - g} = \frac{1,823 \times 1.02}{10\% - 2\%} = 23,243$$

The terminal value is estimated at \$23,243. This terminal value, in the final year of the forecast period (year 5), capitalizes all the future cash flows occurring thereafter.[9] It is important to remember that this value is, however, computed in year 5 and thus must also be discounted by five years to be expressed in present value terms. In this case, the present value of the terminal value (in year 5) equals \$14,432.[10]

With the terminal value computed, we can proceed to the full NPV calculation by discounting all the cash flows (FCFF) at the WACC of 10% and subtracting the year zero investment expenditures:

(in \$)	XXX0	XXX1	XXX2	XXX3	XXX4	XXX5
FCFF	−10,000	848	1,499	1,647	1,787	1,823
Terminal value						23,243
Present value FCFF + TV	−10,000	770	1,239	1,237	1,220	15,564

Thus, the NPV of the project is the sum of the present values of each of the cash flows above: [11]

$$NPV = -10,000 + \frac{848}{(1+0.10)^1} + \frac{1,499}{(1+0.10)^2} + \frac{1,647}{(1+0.10)^3} + \frac{1,787}{(1+0.10)^4} + \frac{1,823+23,243}{(1+0.10)^5}$$

$$= -10,000 + 770 + 1,239 + 1,238 + 1,221 + 15,564$$

$$= +10,032$$

---

[8] If we knew the lifetime of the project in years, we would not use the terminal value here. We would simply discount each year's cash flows. In reality, no project lasts forever. However, the terminal value calculation is used whenever we have projects with very long lifetimes, where no concrete estimate of the final year of the project can be determined. It is important to perform sensitivity checks on the final NPV — that is, examine how it changes given different assumptions for the terminal value calculation.

[9] We can, if using Excel, avoid using terminal values by simply extending the number of columns/years of the project for an additional 1,000 years, for instance. The discounted value of those 1,000 additional years would be almost the same as the terminal value using this formula (which assumes an infinite lifetime).

[10] The present value of \$23,243 received in five years $= \dfrac{23,243}{(1+0.10)^5} = \$14,432$

[11] When using Excel to compute the NPV, we can use the NPV (rate; cash flows) formula. It is important to watch out for the timing specifications used by Excel. Specifically, the first cash flow introduced in the formula will be discounted one year, the second two years, and so forth. This means that in order to compute an NPV, the initial investment at time 0 must be subtracted from the NPV formula and not be included in it (otherwise we would discount the initial investment by one year).

After discounting all the FCFFs — together with the terminal value — and considering the initial CAPEX, the value of the project (NPV) equals + $10,032. This means that this project will create value for the company, because it covers its cost of capital (10%) and also generates an additional value, in present value terms, of $10,032.

A positive NPV means that the investment earns the cost of capital and makes an additional value contribution (through the amount of the NPV). Having an NPV > 0 means that over time, the project will be able to recover all the investment and generate an appropriate (higher than the cost of capital) return on the invested capital as well. Therefore, after performing rigorous sensitivity checks, the recommendation is for companies to invest in projects with a positive NPV.[12]

4.2.1   What Is the Growth in Perpetuity?

The free cash flow used in the terminal value formula must be a steady-state cash flow for the year after the forecast period ends. The assumption then is that this cash flow will grow at a constant steady-state rate in perpetuity.

When we use a terminal value calculation, we are assuming that all the cash flow items will grow at the expected constant steady-state rate. For instance, the CAPEX in the steady state must maintain a certain growth. First, it is necessary to replace assets that are being depreciated. Second, if we assume a certain long-term growth rate for sales, then the assets of the company also have to grow over time. It is common to assume a certain constant long-term assets/sales ratio, which implies that in the steady state, the operating efficiency of the assets will be maintained. Another commonly used alternative is to specify a certain ratio of the CAPEX to sales that will be maintained in perpetuity. Alternatively, if we assume growth in revenues when calculating the FCFF but do not allow for growth in the CAPEX, we would be assuming an infinite improvement in the efficiency of the assets in place. The same applies to the NWC. If a certain growth is assumed across the company, then the working capital items will also need to grow over time. It is common to assume a certain long-term relation between the NWC and sales: For instance, the NWC is expressed as a certain percentage of sales, which is maintained constant in the long term.

Every investment eventually reaches the stage of maturity. At this point, long-term growth is moderate, and g is likely to be close to the inflation rate with some small adjustments for other factors.

---

[12] See the worksheet Ch 4-DCF project for a sensitivity analysis performed on the cost of capital, growth rates, COGS, taxes, and working capital requirements.

KEY LEARNING POINT

When computing the terminal value, long-term growth should be low — it is difficult to justify long-term growth above the inflation rate.

It is important to remember that small changes in the growth rate produce large changes in the terminal value. **Table 4.1** shows the present value (that is, the value already discounted to time 0) of the terminal value of the above example, using various growth rates.

TABLE 4.1: Present value of the terminal value for various growth rates

(in $)	1.00%	1.50%	2.00%	2.50%	3.00%
Present value of the TV	12,703	13,517	14,432	15,470	16,656

Under the base case scenario, where the long-term growth rate is assumed to be 2%, the present value of the terminal value equals $14,432. However, if the long-term growth rate is 1.5%, the terminal value goes down to $13,517. Alternatively, if the long-term growth rate equals 2.5%, the terminal value increases to $15,470.

KEY LEARNING POINT

The terminal value (when used) is a key determinant of the value of a project.

It is thus advisable to dedicate a substantial amount of time to computing the steady-state growth rate. In perpetuity, no project can grow faster than the overall economy. This means that the growth rate can never be higher than the nominal GDP growth (in the long term). In many cases, it is common to assume long-term growth rates of 1% to 2%, that is, close to the inflation rate. But in some sectors (such as fixed-line telecoms), where markets are mature and competitive pressures keep driving margins down, it is sometimes reasonable to assume negative long-term growth rates.

4.2.2   Inflation and Project Valuation

Inflation affects the prices and costs of different products and services. The recommended way of dealing with inflation is to consider it (or only part of it) in the cash flows. That is, when estimating the different components of the cash flows (revenues, costs of goods sold, wages, etc.), we must think about what their evolution over time will be. For instance, inflation may have an impact on the selling price of our product. But it may not be a linear impact. Indeed, many products and services cannot increase their pricing at the same rate as inflation. Nominal cash flows are cash flows that take into account all potential impacts of inflation. And they should be discounted at the nominal WACC, as defined in chapter 2.

An alternative way of dealing with inflation is to perform the entire project valuation in real terms. In that case, we need real cash flows, and a real discount rate. Real cash flows are obtained if we assume a constant selling price and production costs over the lifetime of the project (thus, the only way to increase revenues or costs is by increasing the volume). In this case, we must have the cost of capital also in real terms (i.e., the return investors would want if there were no inflation in the economy). Our normal estimates of WACC, cost of debt, and cost of equity already include a compensation (or premium) for inflation (they are also called *nominal discount rates*). So if we want to obtain real discount rates, we must remove inflation from the previously estimated WACC. The real discount rate (or real WACC) is

$$Real\ discount\ rate\ =\ \frac{1\ +\ nominal\ discount\ rate}{1\ +\ inflation\ rate}\ -\ 1 \qquad (4.5)$$

The important point is to handle inflation consistently. If inflation is ignored when computing cash flows (real cash flows), then it should be removed from the discount rate (real rate). On the other hand, if inflation is included in the cash flows, then it should also be present in the discount rate — nominal cash flows and the nominal discount rate.

Projects should usually be evaluated based on nominal rates and cash flows. Using real cash flows and the real WACC is only recommended if one is considering a project in a very high-inflation environment.

4.3   PROFIT MARGIN OR VALUE?

Some projects may look great from an accounting point of view, but ultimately destroy value for the company. This is why it is so important to analyze projects using the tools introduced in this chapter, namely, the NPV metric.

Stealth Corporation, a furniture manufacturer and retailer, is analyzing a possible entry into a new Asian market. This requires investments in setting up a new factory, retail outlet, and machinery for a total of $80,000,000, to be depreciated over 10 years (the lifetime of the project). According to the local team's projections, this new market would generate $30,000,000 sales per year. Given the forecasted costs, this means a $7,000,000 additional margin per year, representing a 23.3% sales margin. Furthermore, the local government has granted the company exemption from income taxes. The cost of capital for the company is 15%, and there are no taxes. The financials of this project are as follows:

(in $ 000s)	XXX1	XXX2	XXX3	XXX4 ... XXX10
Revenues	30,000	30,000	30,000	30,000
COGS and SG&A	−15,000	−15,000	−15,000	−15,000
Depreciation	−8,000	−8,000	−8,000	−8,000
Net income	7,000	7,000	7,000	7,000
Return on sales	**23.3%**	**23.3%**	**23.3%**	**23.3%**

Thus, from an accounting point of view, this seems like a promising business, with an adequate margin. It delivers an EBIT (or net income, because there are no taxes) of $7 million, representing 23.3% of revenues.

However, when we analyze the project from a value creation point of view, taking into account the risk and the time value of money, a different picture emerges. In order to compute the NPV, we first need to calculate the FCFF for each year. At time zero, there is a negative cash flow of $80,000,000, which is the original investment. And then, every year there is a positive cash flow of $15,000,000.[13]

We can compute the NPV of this project as follows:

$$NPV = -80,000,000 + \frac{15,000,000}{(1+0.15)^1} + \frac{15,000,000}{(1+0.15)^2} + ... + \frac{15,000,000}{(1+0.15)^{10}} = -4,718,470$$

Taking into account the cost of capital, the risk, and the time value of money (all of which is done when we use the NPV), the NPV is −$4.7 million, which suggests the project destroys significant value.

The above example shows how accounting profitability metrics ignore the difference between cash and profits, the timing of cash flows, the risk of the project, and the appropriate remuneration for the capital invested in the project. Only by using an NPV analysis will we be able to say whether or not a specific project creates value.

---

[13] Because there are no taxes, this can be computed as the revenues minus the costs, or the net income with depreciation added back.

> ## KEY LEARNING POINT ✓
>
> *A project with high accounting margins does not necessarily add value. Margins can be high, but the NPV can still be negative.*

4.4   DECISION MAKING AND THE USE OF THE NPV

The concept of *present value* is routinely used in the analysis of projects to make a selection. It essentially uses variously distributed incomes and costs by "discounting" them to their present value. That is, a cash flow at a future date has a lower certainty than an immediate cash flow, and this is incorporated through the assumed rate of risk — the cost of capital (WACC). The key criterion is typically whether or not the NPV is bigger than 0. Besides the Go/No Go utilization of this tool, there are many other settings where it can be useful.

4.4.1   Expansion Projects

The NPV is well suited for the evaluation of expansion projects. The decision of whether or not to go ahead should be based on the NPV, or potential value creation from the project, taking into account its cash flows, risk, and time value of money.

Rio Tinto and the old mine

Rio Tinto is considering an investment that would extend the life of one of its iron ore mines in Pilbara (Western Australia) for five years. The project would require investment in equipment of $500 million. The equipment will be depreciated via the straight-line method over that period. At the end of the five years, Rio Tinto expects to sell the used equipment for $100 million.

If this project is approved, over the next five years, Rio Tinto expects annual sales of $200 million, and mining costs and operating expenses of $40 million, per year. Rio Tinto does not anticipate any net working capital requirements for the project, and it pays a corporate tax rate of 30%.

Based on the above information, Rio Tinto expects annual after-tax operating cash flows of $142 million per year from this mine (EBITDA equals $200m – $40m = $160m. Depreciation equals $100m (20% of the original investment, as it is depreciated over 5 years). Thus, the earnings before tax are $60, and the taxes to be paid are 30% of that: $18 million. Thus, the annual cash flow equals $200m – $40m – $18m = $142m)

In the final year, the equipment will be resold for $100 million. Because at that time it will be fully depreciated, its book value is zero. When selling an asset for $100 million whose book value is lower (in this case zero), additional taxes will need to be paid on the capital gains. In this case, taxes on capital gains are $30 million. Thus, the effective cash flow from reselling the used equipment is $70 million.

	1	2	3	4	5
After-tax operating cash flow	142	142	142	142	142
Residual Value after tax					70
FCFF	142	142	142	142	212

Using this information, and assuming that the market risk of the project associated with extending the life of the mine is the same as for Rio Tinto's overall business, we can use Rio Tinto's WACC of 8% to compute the NPV of the project:

$$NPV= -500+\frac{142}{(1+0.08)^1}+\frac{142}{(1+0.08)^2}+\frac{142}{(1+0.08)^3}+\frac{142}{(1+0.08)^4}+\frac{142+70}{(1+0.08)^5}=+115$$

Given the up-front cost of extending the life of the mine, the cash flows it generates, and the residual value, this project is a good idea, and results in an NPV of $115 million for Rio Tinto.[14]

4.4.2 New Product Launches

Danone and the new yogurts

Danone is considering introducing a new ultra-light yogurt with ten calories to be called Danone Angels. The company believes that the new yogurt will appeal to calorie-conscious consumers. The cost of bringing the new yogurt to market is €800 million. Danone expects first-year incremental free cash flows from Angels to be €150 million and to grow at 2% per year thereafter. Should Danone go ahead with the project?

We can use the NPV method shown in Equation 4.1 to value Angels. We will need Danone's WACC, which was estimated as 10%. The cash flows for Angels are a growing perpetuity,[15] and so

[14] See the book's Excel file for more details on each of the examples in this section.

[15] The present value of a growing perpetuity is the cash flow after the first period divided by the difference between the discount rate and the growth rate. It can be shown that this is mathematically equivalent to the sum of all the growing cash flows to the present:

$$\frac{CF_1}{WACC-g}=\frac{CF_1}{(1+WACC)^1}+\frac{CF_1\times(1+g)}{(1+WACC)^2}+\frac{CF_1\times(1+g)^2}{(1+WACC)^3}+...+\frac{CF_1\times(1+g)^n}{(1+WACC)^{n+1}}$$

we have:

$$NPV = -I + \frac{CF_1}{WACC - g} = -800 + \frac{150}{10\% - 2\%} = +1,075$$

The Angels project has a positive NPV and adds value to the company. It has a positive NPV of $1,075 million because it is expected to generate a return on the €800 million invested that is far in excess of Danone's WACC of 10%.

4.4.3 Mutually Exclusive Projects

In the case of two mutually exclusive projects, the one with the higher NPV should be chosen.

Which machine?

A specialized chemical manufacturer needs to choose between two alternative technologies for a new plant. One technology is more expensive initially, but has lower maintenance costs. The other technology requires a lower initial investment, but higher operating costs afterward. The NPV tools can easily be applied to this situation. We must estimate the cash flows (in this case, only costs and investments) of both technologies and identify the one that leads to a higher NPV.

4.4.4 Cost Reduction Projects

The tools in this chapter can be applied to analyze potential cost reduction initiatives that require an initial investment.

To Buy or Lease?

An industrial company needs to choose between acquiring a new compressor or leasing it. Leasing versus buying decisions can be analyzed through their NPV. Leasing requires a certain annual lease payment. Buying requires an up-front investment. In order to decide between the two alternatives, we must estimate the cash flows (taking into account the tax implications of leasing) and identify the one that leads to a higher NPV.

4.4.5 Valuing Brands and Royalties

The principles of project valuation can be applied to brand valuation, as well as the valuation of a stream of royalty payments.

For *brand valuation*, typical methodologies (for instance, the one used by Interbrand) use the incremental cash flow method. Brands have value because they allow for a certain price premium to be charged, and/or allow for extra volumes to be sold. In practice, the value of a brand can be computed as the present value of the incremental cash flows that are attributable to the brand. That is, the cash flows to be discounted are the extra cash flow in a branded business when compared to a comparable unbranded business.

Levi's Brand

Levi's, a clothing manufacturer widely known for its jeans, wants to evaluate the value of its brand. Levi's analyzed its sales, and concludes that the brand allows them to sell their products at a 30% price premium relative to unbranded ones. They also estimate that the sales are 80% higher than they would be without the brand. Thus, the Levi's brand impacts cash flows through the price and volume premiums. Of course, the brand requires additional investments every year to maintain its power. If they became an unbranded producer, they would save money on these investments, so their overall cost structure would be lower. Based on these inputs, the Levi's team prepared an estimate of their cash flows with the brand, and also if they did not have the brand name "Levi's" behind their products (all in million USD):

	XXX1	XXX2	XXX3
With the brand	800	830	850
Without the brand	450	460	475
Difference in CF attributable to the brand	350	370	375

The value of the brand is the present value of the differential cash flows, that is, the extra cash flow in Levi's branded business when compared to an unbranded clothing manufacturer selling the same lines of products. Assuming a 10% cost of capital, and a growth after the 3rd year of 1%,[16] the value of the brand is $4,067 million.

$$Brand\ Value = \frac{350}{(1+0.10)^1} + \frac{370}{(1+0.10)^2} + \frac{375+4,208}{(1+0.10)^3} = +4,067$$

4.4.6   Royalty Interest

Royalty interest is the right to collect a stream of future royalty payments. This is frequently used in the entertainment industry, as well as in the oil and gas industry. In the oil and gas industry, royalty interest refers to ownership of a fraction of the resource or revenue that is

---

[16] The terminal value computed as in formula (4.4) equals 4,208.

produced. Typically, it is paid to the government of the country that granted rights of production in a certain field. The owner of the royalty interest does not bear any of the costs of the operations needed to produce the resource, but it still owns part of the revenues produced. Royalty interest can be valued by calculating the present value of the cash flows to be received.

Pharmaceutical royalties

CCP, a research and development limited partnership, has provided seed capital to the research and development of a new drug called Myotrophin. In exchange for that, CCP will receive royalty payments of 10% of the sales of Myotrophin for 10 years. The sales are estimated to be $10 million in the first year, $20 million in the second, and then $35 million per year for the remaining years 3 to 10. The value of this royalty, computed as the present value of the cash flows to be received by CCP (10% of the revenues) discounted at a cost of capital (assumed) of 12%, equals $16 million:

$$NPV = \frac{1}{(1+0.12)^1} + \frac{2}{(1+0.12)^2} + \frac{3.5}{(1+0.12)^3} + \frac{3.5}{(1+0.12)^4} + \ldots + \frac{3.5}{(1+0.12)^{10}} = 16$$

4.5 SENSITIVITY ANALYSIS

After any project valuation model is prepared, it is important to complement it with sensitivity analysis. The goal of sensitivity analysis is to gain insight into which assumptions are critical.

The value of the Rio Tinto project analyzed in section 4.4.1 depends on a number of economic factors, such as selling price, quantities sold, operating cost estimates, useful life of the project, growth rates, and so on. The original NPV was $115 million. Sensitivity analysis involves varying these inputs in order to understand how the investment value varies with these factors — **Figure 4.1** shows the results. For instance, if operating costs are higher by 10%, the NPV is reduced to $103 million. Similarly, if sales are lower by 10%, the NPV is reduced to $59 million. This analysis was performed by manually changing different inputs of the model (see the book's Excel worksheet "Ch 4 – Rio Tinto" for details, including an example using the Excel Table Function to compute the NPV with different "what-if" scenarios).

Another possible analysis focuses on threshold values (or the breakeven). Here, we are interested in knowing what are the limiting values of key input variables that still justify going ahead with the project, that is, an NPV greater than 0. For instance, in the Rio Tinto

FIGURE 4.1:   The impact of key variables on the NPV of the Rio Tinto Project.

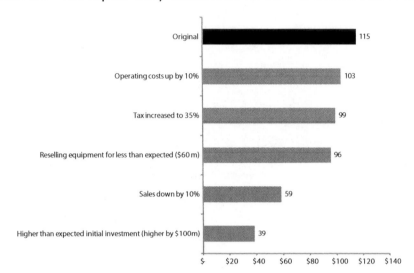

mine case, we might be interested in knowing the maximum value of operating costs that still yields a positive NPV. The Excel Goal Seek tool allows us to perform this analysis.

Assigning zero to the cell with the NPV (C54) and changing the cell with the operating costs (D10) results in the value $78 million for operating costs. Our base case is that the operating costs are going to be $40 million. However, this sensitivity analysis tells us something else. We now know that if the operating costs rise above $78 million, the project destroys value for Rio Tinto.[17]

Sensitivity analysis thus allows managers to

– Understand the relationship between key variables and the NPV of the project
– Identify the critical variables that impact the project

---

[17] Sensitivity analysis can be performed by changing one variable at a time, or by simultaneously changing combinations of variables, creating scenarios. The excel tool Data Table is useful to simulate the impact on the NPV of changing two variables simultaneously. If more variables are to be changed simultaneously, an alternative is Monte Carlo simulation. Several Excel add-ins can perform this analysis.

- Know the ranges of the input variables that lead to a positive outcome (in this case, a positive NPV)
- Make a more informed decision, taking into account the scenarios studied

But besides helping the decision maker, sensitivity analysis is also important after the decision is made. By performing these rigorous checks, we improve our understanding of the economics of the project and identify the key variables that may impact its success. Thus, managers can, ex-post, focus their attention on a certain number of key inputs that are known to significantly impact the project's value creation potential.

4.6 WHAT TO DO WHEN THE PROJECT IS IN A DIFFERENT INDUSTRY — THE PURE PLAY METHOD

Up to this point, we assumed that the risk and the leverage of the project under consideration matched the risk and leverage for the company as a whole. This assumption allowed us to assume that the cost of capital for a project matched the company's cost of capital (see chapter 2 on how to compute the cost of capital (WACC) for each company). Often, however, specific projects differ from the average investment made by the company. Consider Siemens, a large company with many divisions that operate in completely different lines of business. Projects in Siemens's health care division are likely to have a different risk than projects in its Automation division, or in the Financial Solutions divisions. In this section, we show how to calculate the cost of capital when a project's risk differs from the company's overall risk. Specifically, we introduce here the *pure play method*.

A "pure player" is a company that is traded on the stock exchange and that operates in a single line of business or industry. The pure play method can be used as a benchmark for calculating the cost of capital for a proposed new venture or product line.

4.6.1 Privately Held Companies

Beta calculations exist only for publicly traded companies. Thus, for privately held companies, we need to use the pure play method. For instance, how would you compute the cost of equity for a coffee shop that also sells ice creams and is located by the beach?

It is important to consider the risks in the business we are interested in evaluating. Then we must find pure players (companies that operate exclusively in the same line of business) and obtain their betas. This will give a good indication of the appropriate beta for our cost of equity estimation. In the case of the beach bar, the appropriate comparison group could be restaurants or ice cream companies. We could also envision a scenario (for instance, if the bar is in the Caribbean) in which the relevant risks for the beach bar are correlated with the airline industry or the hotel business. In this case, we would obtain betas of players that are exposed to the same sorts of risks as our company or project.

KEY LEARNING POINT ✓

The beta can be obtained by analyzing a sample of pure players in the line of business we are interested in.

The way a company balances its financing between equity and debt has an impact on its cost of equity and its beta — in particular, the use of debt financing increases risk. This is obviously true for debtholders — the cost of debt goes up for higher levels of debt use — but it is also true for equity holders. It is important to remember that equity is always the residual claimant on a company's cash flows. The volatility of a company's earnings also increases when a company has a significant amount of leverage. Thus, the cost of equity increases as the company uses higher percentages of debt financing. Conversely, a company without debt is less risky for its equity owners than a highly leveraged company.

Thus, when using the pure play method, we must recognize that different companies may have different mixes of debt and equity. When we use other companies' benchmarks to obtain a beta (or cost of equity) for a specific investment valuation, it is important to remember that debt increases a company's risk (see chapter 5), which partly explains the variation in betas across companies in the same business.

The following formula shows the relation between leverage and cost of equity:

$$r^L_{equity} = r^U_{equity} + \frac{D}{E} \times (r^U_{equity} - r_{debt}) \tag{4.6}$$

| r^L_{equity} is the cost of equity of a leveraged company, r^U_{equity} is the cost of equity of an all-equity company (unleveraged, no debt), r_{debt} is the corporate cost of debt, and D/E is the ratio of debt to equity, at market value.

In practice, formula (4.6) states that the cost of equity of a leveraged company includes compensation for the normal business risk (cost of equity of an unleveraged company) plus compensation for the additional risk that leverage brings to shareholders.

The same relation can be seen in terms of CAPM betas[18]:

$$\beta_{equity}^{L} = \beta_{equity}^{U} \times \left(1 + \frac{D}{E}\right) \tag{4.7}$$

or, reversing it:

$$\beta_{equity}^{U} = \frac{\beta_{equity}^{L}}{1 + \dfrac{D}{E}} \tag{4.8}$$

| β_{equity}^{L} is the beta of a leveraged company, β_{equity}^{U} is the beta of an all-equity company (unlevered beta), and D/E is the ratio of debt to equity, at market value.

According to formula (4.7), the cost of equity is higher for companies with higher levels of debt. The formula[19] can be reversed to estimate an unlevered beta — formula (4.8) — if the observed levered betas for different companies are known,[20] as well as the amount of their outstanding debt.[21]

When valuing a project in a privately held company, we must use *the pure play method* to find appropriate benchmarks for the discount rate to use:

1. Find publicly traded companies that operate in the same line of business as the project we are interested in evaluating.

2. Obtain their cost of equity (or betas).

3. Unlever the observable betas (from the pure players) to remove the effect of their specific capital structure. Average these unlevered betas of the comparable companies to obtain a cleaner estimate of the true business risk of the industry to which our project belongs.

4. Re-lever the industry level beta (from 3), using the target capital structure we envision, to obtain the cost of equity for this new project — using our own financing mix — and

---

[18] The complete formula includes a component related to the beta of debt. A common assumption in practice is that the beta of debt is zero, and thus we can obtain formula (4.9).

[19] Alternative formulas exist, using $(1 - t)$ for the computation of levered and unlevered betas. The justifications are more theoretical than practical. Different formulas than the ones recommended here rely on different assumptions about the risk of the debt tax shields, as well as about the value of debt. In practice, the differences are not very relevant. Indeed, if we use the same formulas consistently for leveraging and unleveraging the betas, the end result is very similar, regardless of whether $(1 - t)$ is used or not. (*For a discussion of the merits of different formulas, refer to the references at the end of this chapter.*)

[20] Betas for stocks can be obtained from various financial services. These betas are levered betas and thus reflect both the business risk and the financial risk of a company based on the company's debt. Some free sites from which betas can be obtained include finance. yahoo.com; finance.google.com; and the *Financial Times* website. Reuters and Bloomberg (main databases of financial data worldwide) also provide betas for companies worldwide.

[21] In practice, we never observe unlevered betas because almost all companies have some amount of debt.

its risk implications (namely, what will the cost of debt and equity be if this capital structure is used).

5. Compute the WACC, using the capital structure used in point 4 and the corresponding costs of equity and debt.

In summary, the capital structure of the company must be reflected in the cost of equity, as well as in the weights (of debt and equity) used in the WACC.

4.6.2   Projects in Different Industries

It is important to consider risks in the business we are interested in evaluating. Indeed, the basic principle of discounting is that the discount rate should compensate investors for the risk involved in the cash flow forecasts. For many projects, the cost of capital of the company is the most appropriate discount rate to use. But sometimes it is not — if the riskiness of the project's cash flows is very different from the company's risk. This is likely to happen in many expansion projects outside the core industry of the company. If, for instance, a company is currently involved in electricity distribution and now wants to evaluate a new opportunity in the media business, its current cost of capital is not appropriate, because the risks of the two businesses are not the same.

In these cases, we must also use the pure play method described in section 4.6.1. We must first unlever the betas of comparable companies, then finally re-lever the estimated industry beta to obtain the relevant cost of capital for our own project.

Huawei, a Chinese telecommunications company, is evaluating the possibility of selling cloud computing services to companies. Huawei's WACC is 9%. Cloud computing is a new line of business for Huawei, however, so the risk of this business likely differs from the risk of Huawei's current telecom's business. As a result, the assets invested in this new business should have a different cost of capital. In order to find the cost of capital for the cloud computing business, we need to identify companies operating in Huawei's targeted line of business — pure players. Then we follow the steps 1–5 to compute the appropriate cost of capital for Huawei to use in the analysis of this new project.

KEY LEARNING POINT

The appropriate discount rate may be different from the company-wide rate if the project is outside the company's core business.

Even when projects are within the same industry, some companies use different hurdle rates for different types of projects. For instance, a company with a WACC of 10% might use:

- A discount rate of 7% when analyzing replacement of assets in existing product lines, for cost improvement reasons
- A discount rate of 10% for expansion projects for current product lines
- A discount rate of 14% for new product development proposals

In these cases, the recommendation is that, on average, the discount rate across the different proposals should not differ much from the company's WACC of 10%. There is a certain rationale for applying different hurdle rates for projects within the same company and industry: cost improvement projects are often less risky than new product launches. But we should be careful about using different hurdle rates within the same industry. Indeed, the approach presented above (7% to 14% discount rates) makes it harder for new product development projects to get approved and makes it easier for cost improvement projects to meet the NPV > 0 goal. This may be a strategic aim of the company — to reduce costs. But it is important to bear in mind the unintended consequences that this approach might have: It could stifle innovation and, in the end, make the company's managers (who then apply the NPV tools to their investment proposals) focus primarily on reducing costs on current products, rather than on growth alternatives (new product launches).

KEY LEARNING POINT ✓

Using different hurdle rates within the same industry may have unintended consequences.

In summary, when looking at projects outside the core industry of the company, different discount rates should be used, and for that we must look at benchmarks from other pure players in those industries. But for projects within the same industry, the company's WACC is usually the most appropriate rate to use.

4.7   ALTERNATIVE PROJECT VALUATION TECHNIQUE — THE FCFE METHOD

Up to now, we have focused on the FCFF method, which uses all the cash flows generated by the project, without any funding considerations. That is, we do not include any debt-related payments in the cash flows, because the debt and its after-tax cost (reflecting the tax shield generated by debt) are included in the WACC.

An alternative to this is to use the free cash flow to equity method (FCFE). In this method, we must focus on the <u>cash flows to equity holders after all debt-related cash flows have been deducted (interest and amortization of debt).</u>

The FCFE is defined for each year as

$$\text{FCFE} = \text{Net Income} + \text{Depreciation} - \text{CAPEX} - \Delta\text{NWC} \\ + \text{New Debt} - \text{Debt Repayments} \tag{4.9}$$

| Net Income equals EBIT – Interest – Taxes.
| Depreciation includes all non-cash operating expenses used for tax purposes, including depreciation, depletion, and amortization.
| CAPEX denotes capital expenditures.
| ΔNWC denotes the change in the net working capital.

The main difference between the FCFE and the FCFF relates to the debt repayments (and new debt issued), as well as the annual interest payments (and associated tax shield), which are now explicitly considered in the cash flows, namely, in the net income calculation. It is important to use the equity holders' investment, not the total investment expenditure in the project. <u>When using the FCFE, all the cash flows, including the early investments, must be the net movements in cash from the equity holders' perspective.</u>

The FCFE is then discounted at the cost of equity.[22] It is important that the cost of equity reflect the appropriate business and financial risk. It should also be remembered that whenever a project is partially financed with debt, the discount rate must reflect that fact (see section 4.6.1). We know that higher leverage implies more risk to equity holders.

Thus, the NPV using the FCFE method is given by

$$NPV = -Investment_0^{equity} + \sum_{t=1}^{T} \frac{FCFE_t}{(1 + r_{equity}^L)^t} \tag{4.10}$$

| NPV is the project's net present value.

| $\sum_{t=1}^{T} \dfrac{FCFE_t}{(1 + r_{equity}^L)^t}$ represents the present value of all the FCFEs of the project, which are discounted

at r_{equity}^L — the cost of equity of a leveraged company.

| $Investment_0^{equity}$ is the equity holders' investment in the project.

---

[22] For consistency, the cash flows must always be discounted at a rate that reflects their risk. When using the FCFF method, we must focus on the company level risk, and its appropriate compensation, which is the WACC. When we discount the FCFE, we must focus on the risk of equity holders alone, which is the cost of equity.

Computed correctly, the NPV of a project does not depend on the method used; the result using the FCFE method should equal exactly that obtained with the FCFF method.

4.8 OTHER PROJECT VALUATION METRICS

As described in this chapter, companies should invest in projects that deliver a positive NPV. However, when valuing a project, it is common to compute additional investment metrics, as well as the NPV.

Below we list some of the common typical alternative metrics. They will all be applied to a potential investment project that has the following annual cash flows:

	XXX0	XXX1	XXX2	XXX3	XXX4
Cash flows	$ –10,000	$3,500	$5,000	$4,000	$4,000

4.8.1 Internal Rate of Return (IRR)

The Internal Rate of Return (IRR) is the discount rate at which the NPV equals zero.

We know that the IRR must make the NPV equal zero. We know the cash flows of the project, so we can find the IRR by solving the equation:

$$0 = -10000 + \frac{3500}{1+IRR} + \frac{5000}{(1+IRR)^2} + \frac{4000}{(1+IRR)^3} + \frac{4000}{(1+IRR)^4}$$

Thus, the IRR equals 23% (using the Excel IRR formula).

When using the IRR as a criterion, we focus on projects whose IRR is above the cost of capital.

4.8.2 Payback Period

The payback period is the number of years until the cash inflows match the cash outflows. It can also be computed using all cash flows expressed in present value terms (that is, discounted to time 0); this is called the *adjusted payback*.

4.8.3 Return Index (RI)

The return index, also called the *profitability index, value-to-investment ratio* (VIR), is computed as

$$Return\ Index = \frac{PV(+CF)}{Investment} \tag{4.11}$$

| $PV(+CF)$ represents the present value of the project's cash flows, after the initial investment at time zero.
| Investment is the initial CAPEX investment in the project.

Assuming a 10% cost of capital, we compute the RI as

$$RI = \frac{\left[\dfrac{3500}{1+10\%} + \dfrac{5000}{(1+10\%)^2} + \dfrac{4000}{(1+10\%)^3} + \dfrac{4000}{(1+10\%)^4}\right]}{10000} = 1.3051$$

When using the RI as a criterion, we should focus on projects whose RI is above 1. These projects generate, in present value terms, more cash flows than their original investment.

4.8.4 Why We Should Focus on NPV

It must be highlighted that the NPV is the ultimate metric reflecting the value that a specific project creates for the company. First, it provides an analysis that takes into account the time value of money over the full life of the project. In addition, the NPV takes into account risk, which is explicitly incorporated into the discount rate. Higher-risk projects should have higher discount rates (WACC) than lower-risk ones. As a consequence, the cash flows of riskier projects are more discounted (that is, they make lower contributions toward the final NPV) than lower-risk ones. Finally, the NPV is a monetary value metric, not a percentage (as IRR and RI are). Ultimately, what concerns shareholders the most is how much value is created in monetary terms by the companies in which they invest.

KEY LEARNING POINT ✓

The NPV is the ultimate metric that analyzes how much value — in monetary terms — is created by a specific project.

SUMMARY

The tools in this chapter are relevant whenever a company needs to take resource allocation decisions and is interested in what a particular decision is worth.

The fact that a project generates an expected accounting profit in future years is not enough reason to approve it. Indeed, even if a project seems to generate a promising margin, it may be destroying value. Accounting profitability metrics ignore the difference between cash and profits, the timing of cash flows, the risk of the project, and the appropriate return for the capital invested in the project.

In this chapter, we have focused on the discount cash flow method. This is the recommended method for project valuation and results in the NPV. The NPV has the advantage of being a forward-looking metric that focuses on cash flow but also recognizes the time value of money as well as risk.

After computing the NPV and performing rigorous sensitivity checks, a company should only invest in projects with returns that are higher than the cost of capital, which happens whenever the NPV is greater than 0.

The NPV takes into account risk through the discount rate/cost of capital/WACC. The WACC is the after-tax cost of funding for a company as a whole, as it currently is, that is, with the current capital structure and business risks. This last point is often forgotten. The WACC should be consistent with the risk of the business being analyzed and thus its cash flows. Different industries have different costs of capital (and risk). In addition, different capital structures imply different WACCs. Thus, sometimes we must use comparable companies as a benchmark in order to obtain the appropriate discount rate for a particular project.

No valuation is right in an absolute sense, but there are countless wrong ones. Many assumptions underlie any valuation. For managerial decision making, it is vital to know the impact of those assumptions as well as what drives value in an investment project, through sensitivity analysis. The DCF method allows for an understanding of the economics of an investment project. If required, we can incorporate different business models, efficiency gains, and special insights on different items explicitly into the valuation. Ultimately, this allows for a thorough evaluation of the merits of various managerial actions and approaches to the project.

REFERENCES

Harris, R.S., and J.J. Pringle, 1985, Risk-Adjusted Discount Rates: Extensions from the Average Risk Case, *Journal of Financial Research*, Vol. 8, Iss. 3:237–244.

Miles, J., and J. Ezzell, 1980, The Weighted Average Cost of Capital, Perfect Capital Markets and Project Life: A Clarification, *Journal of Financial and Quantitative Analysis*, Vol. 15, Iss. 3:719–730.

Modigliani, F., and M. Miller, 1963, Corporate Income Taxes and the Cost of Capital: A Correction, *American Economic Review*, Vol. 53, Iss. 3:433–443.

Deciding between Different Sources of Capital — The Capital Structure Decision

Capital structure policy deals with the right-hand side of the balance sheet, that is, with a company's financing activities. A company can choose from among many different capital structure possibilities. It can issue large amounts of debt or very small amounts. It can issue fixed-rate debt or floating-rate debt. It can have off-balance-sheet debt,[1] such as lease financing, or normal-balance-sheet debt, such as bank loans or bonds.

The most important step in any kind of financing decision is to decide how much external capital is required. Once the amount of external capital has been determined, the next step is to select and design the instruments to be sold, namely, loans and bonds (chapter 6) or equity issues (chapter 7).

In this chapter, we will examine the latest thinking on capital structure, with a focus on the trade-offs that it involves and also its links to company strategy. We start by introducing the advantages of having debt, followed by a consideration of its disadvantages. Ultimately, we will show how capital structure is very relevant, and has significant implications for a company's risk, value, and operations. Evidence of how financial markets look at capital structure decisions is presented, as well as empirical evidence based on CFO surveys, research results, and actual capital structures across many different companies and industries.

5.1 THE ADVANTAGES OF DEBT — TAX BENEFITS

Merton Miller and Franco Modigliani's influential work won each of them a Nobel Prize in Economics. In what was probably their most important paper, "The Cost of Capital,

---

[1] *Off balance sheet* refers to an asset or debt not on the company's balance sheet. In the case of debt, some of the most important sources of off-balance-sheet debt are operating leases. In an operating lease, the asset is kept on the lessor's balance sheet, and the lessee only reports the required rental expense for use of the asset every year on its income statement. However, given the contractual commitment, these rental expenses are considered (under both US GAAP and International Financial Reporting Standards) to be a liability — off-balance-sheet debt. Other examples of off-balance-sheet debt include unfunded deficits in pension plans and financial obligations of unconsolidated subsidiaries.

Corporation Finance, and the Theory of Investment" published in *The American Economic Review*, they concluded that "the market value of any firm is independent of its capital structure."[2]

Modigliani and Miller demonstrated that when operating cash flows are constant and there are no taxes, a company's value is not affected by the amount of debt it carries. And if company value is independent of the debt–equity choices, then Modigliani and Miller concluded that capital structure is irrelevant. However, they arrived at this conclusion for a world without taxes, financial distress costs, asymmetric information, and several other transaction costs. More importantly, their key assumption was that investment and financing decisions are independent decisions. That is, the way a company is financed has no impact on its investment strategy. Their reasoning was as follows: The company's assets are the real source of value creation because they generate cash flows. As long as the expected cash flows produced by the assets do not change, the value of the company will remain unchanged.

Therefore, one of Modigliani and Miller's most important contributions is that financing choices that affect cash flows, and thus shareholder value, will also affect company value. Their work has inspired researchers to study why in reality we observe different capital structure choices and to explore whether there are optimal capital structure choices that maximize company value.

The key Modigliani–Miller theorem (the value of a company is independent of the capital structure) was conceptualized in a world without taxes. In reality, when a company carries debt, it incurs interest charges that are tax deductible.[3] As a result, it pays less tax to the government.

In a world with taxes, companies can be viewed as a partnership between shareholders and government (through the taxes the companies pay on their pre-tax profits). The graph on the left of **Figure 5.1** illustrates the value of an all-equity company with a tax rate of 33.3%, which means that 33.3% of the company's pre-tax profits belongs to the government, which can then be considered to own one-third of the pie. On the right of **Figure 5.1** we show the pie chart for a leveraged company. Here, there are three claims on the company's profits: shareholders (stock), debtholders (for instance, bonds), and government taxes.

---

[2] Modigliani and Miller (1958).

[3] This occurs because the tax code treats interest differently than it does earnings to shareholders. Thus, interest is tax deductible, whereas dividends are not.

FIGURE 5.1: Tax shields.

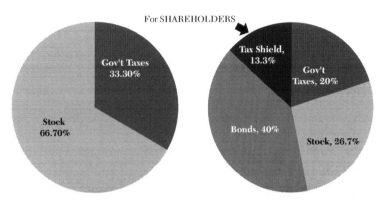

The graph on the right illustrates that when a company introduces debt in its balance sheet, it will pay less taxes, thus increasing the company's value. The tax advantage of debt is related to cash flows. As debt increases, taxes decrease (because the interest charges are tax deductible), thus increasing the cash available for distribution to owners and creditors.

Because the value of a company is the combined equity and debt values, the company's value increases as taxes decrease. And the tax shield (less tax is paid to the government) is actually money that belongs to shareholders.[4]

KEY LEARNING POINT ✓

Leverage can increase firm value because interest on debt is tax deductible (also called tax shields).

5.1.1 Valuing the Tax Savings from Debt

A company has a corporate tax rate of 30% and expects an EBIT of $10 million per year. Its entire earnings after taxes are paid out as dividends. The company is considering two financing alternatives:

$A \rightarrow$ No debt in its capital structure
$B \rightarrow$ $4 million of debt with interest costs of 10% per year

---

[4] It is important to remember that when a firm has more debt, shareholders need to invest less of their own money in the company.

Under alternative B, more cash flow reaches the suppliers of capital to the company (shareholders and bondholders). The difference between the two scenarios is because of the lower taxes paid (debt financing) under alternative B.

	A	B
EBIT	$10,000,000	$10,000,000
Interest	$0	$400,000
EBT	$10,000,000	$9,600,000
Tax	$3,000,000	$2,880,000
Net income	$7,000,000	$6,720,000
Dividends	$7,000,000	$6,720,000
Dividends + interest	$7,000,000	$7,120,000

That is, with debt (alternative B) the taxable income is $400,000 lower, which implies a reduction in corporate taxes paid of $120,000 (30% × $400,000).

If *debt is perpetual*, only interest expenses are paid each year; the full amount of the debt is never repaid. In this case, the interest paid yearly is $4 million × 10% = $400,000. This implies a tax saving of $400,000 × 30% = $120,000 every year.

The present value of the tax shield (PVTS) is the present value of all these cash flows. Because this is a perpetual saving of cash flows, it can be represented by the following formula[5]:

$$\text{Present Value of Tax Shields} = \text{Tax rate} \times \text{Debt}$$
$$= 30\% \times \$4,000,000 = \$1,200,000 \tag{5.1}$$

Therefore, $4 million of perpetual debt (i.e., debt that will remain on the balance sheet of the company forever or debt that is constantly rolled over) contributes $1.2 million to firm value because lower taxes are paid to the government.[6]

We will now compute the value of debt, i.e., the tax savings, when *debt levels change over time*. Suppose the company has issued debt equal to $4 million to be repaid over four years at $1 million per year. As before, the cost of debt equals 10%, and the tax rate equals 30%.

In this case, the debt matures over time, because the $4 million will be fully repaid in four years. Because the company is amortizing its debt each year, both the interest expenses and the tax shield will decrease over time.

---

[5] It is obtained by discounting to the present all the yearly tax savings. The discount rate used to discount these cash flows is the cost of debt.

[6] This results from the present value of the yearly tax savings ($120,000) that will occur in perpetuity, discounted at the cost of debt. That is, $120,000/0.10 = $1.2 million.

	Debt outstanding at beginning of year	Interest paid yearly (financial costs) = debt × cost of debt	Debt amortized at end of year	Yearly tax saving
1	$4,000,000	$400,000	$1,000,000	$120,000
2	$3,000,000	$300,000	$1,000,000	$90,000
3	$2,000,000	$200,000	$1,000,000	$60,000
4	$1,000,000	$100,000	$1,000,000	$30,000
5	$0	$0		$0

In this case, the value of the tax shields is the present value of the yearly tax savings:

$$PVTS = \frac{\$120,000}{(1+0.10)^1} + \frac{\$90,000}{(1+0.10)^2} + \frac{\$60,000}{(1+0.10)^3} + \frac{\$30,000}{(1+0.10)^4} = \$249,040$$

As expected, the value of the tax shield is lower in this case, because the debt (and associated tax shield) is being reduced over time. But the main point is still valid. Having debt on the balance sheet of a company, even if it is repaid over a certain period, contributes to a higher firm value because of the lower taxes paid to the government.

5.2   HOW CAN A COMPANY CHANGE ITS CAPITAL STRUCTURE RELATIVELY QUICKLY?

Companies frequently change their capital structure when new investment or merger opportunities arise. They must decide on the financing required for these investments and often rethink their capital structure decisions. One of the most common ways for companies to effect major changes in their capital structure is through a debt-financed share buyback program (also called *leveraged recapitalization*). This implies an increase in debt and a reduction in equity. As a result of the debt increase, the tax shield is higher and so is the firm value.

Debt-financed share buyback — immediate change in the capital structure

Suppose a company has a 25% tax rate and 200 shares outstanding that are valued at $25 each. The total market value of equity is $5,000. Originally the company has no debt; thus, the value of the company is $5,000 as well. The company then announces an issue of $2,000 in debt that will be used to buy back shares. After this announcement, shareholders (and creditors) know that the company will pay less tax, thus generating a tax shield.[7] Assuming the $2,000 debt funding is permanent, the present value of the interest tax shield (PVTS) is $500 (2,000 debt × 25% tax rate). Thus, the market value of the company is equal to $5,500.

After the buyback program is announced, the share price exceeds the prior share price by the per-share amount of the PVTS. Therefore, the share price goes up to $27.50. At that price, the $2,000 of debt will allow the repurchase of 72.72 shares.[8]

	Before: 100% equity financed	After buyback announcement , but before actual buyback	After buyback
Number of shares	200	200	127.2727
Price per share	$25	$27.50	$27.50
Market value of equity	$5,000	$5,500	$3,500
Debt	$0	$0	$2,000
Value of company	$5,000	$5,500	$5,500
Debt/market value of equity	0	0	57%

In the end, the company is left with 127.27 shares (the original 200 minus the 72.72 bought back). The value of equity equals $3,500, and the value of debt equals $2,000. The overall value of the company is equal to $5,500. Once again, the source of value creation is the interest tax shield.

5.3   THE ADVANTAGES OF DEBT — MONITORING AND COMMITTING

Another advantage of debt is the added discipline it enforces upon the company and its managers. In most cases, the managers are not the owners of the company. This separation between management and ownership raises the possibility that managers may maximize their own wealth and benefits rather than that of shareholders.[9]

Debt makes managers more disciplined because they must make sure the company delivers on the fixed debt payments (either interest only, or a combination of interest and debt repayment). Also, issuing debt may be a positive signal about the company's future strength, because managers are confident that the company will not become bankrupt and will be able to meet all debt-related payments.

---

[7] This assumes there is no additional operational impact of the buyback program; i.e., nothing will change in terms of product mix, sales, costs, capital expenditures, etc. It is a purely financial transaction, whereby the debt will be raised and paid back to shareholders.

[8] $2,000 of debt available to repurchase shares valued at $27.50.

[9] This is called *the principal-agent problem*.

This is based on the "free cash flow hypothesis" originally introduced by Michael Jensen,[10] which states that when managers are flush with too much cash (relative to all the NPV > 0 projects they have available), they will tend to use the cash in negative-NPV projects. Indeed, this negative aspect of "too much cash available" explains why diversification programs (and unrelated M&As) are likely to destroy value and why bidders that pay cash tend to experience abnormally poor performance after the takeover announcement (see chapter 10).

Thus, an additional benefit of debt is that it reduces the agency costs of free cash flows because it forces managers to further optimize the company's resources, committing them to operate more efficiently (or face bankruptcy). Indeed, this benefit of debt underlies the majority of leveraged buyouts (LBOs) used in the private equity sector. By leveraging the company, shareholders obtain two benefits:

- Their own equity investment is reduced.
- There are strong incentives for managers to perform well and deliver on the debt's scheduled payments

5.4   HOW MUCH TO BORROW — LEVERAGE AND RISK

The above examples suggest that the value of a company increases with the amount of debt it incurs, and they illustrate how value creation can occur on the right-hand side of the balance sheet. Provided all other factors are constant, higher tax shields as a result of interest payments increase shareholder wealth. However, the real world is much more complex, and there are also many costs associated with debt, which we will explore in this and the following sections.

5.4.1   Cost of Debt Goes Up with Leverage

Modigliani and Miller assumed a constant cost of debt. In reality, because corporate bonds have a certain probability of default, investors will always ask companies for interest rates higher than the risk-free rate. The cost of debt is then

$$r_{debt} = r_f + Spread \tag{5.2}$$

| r_{debt} is the corporate cost of debt, and r_f is the risk-free rate (the yield-to-maturity of similar maturity government bonds).

| The spread is the market estimate of a company's credit risk.

---

[10] Jensen (1986).

The spread (and thus the cost of debt) is higher for riskier borrowers than it is for safer ones.[11] Credit ratings play an important role in helping investors make better-informed decisions and judge the risk of lending money to a given company. A credit rating is an evaluation of the creditworthiness of an issuer (or a specific bond). Bonds with a rating equal to or above Baa (Moody's) or BBB (S&P) are considered investment grade. Bonds with lower ratings are considered speculative grade — also called junk bonds, sub-investment grade, or high-yield bonds.[12]

Many factors are used by rating agencies when determining a company's credit rating, such as cash flow generation, cyclicality of sales, product differentiation, geographical diversification, and asset tangibility. **Table 5.1** shows some indicators of companies in the different rating categories.

TABLE 5.1: Key ratios for global companies

	Operating margin (%)	EBIT/ Interest expense	Debt/EBITDA	Debt/Equity (%)
Aaa	20.3	21.6	1.0	24.7
Aa	13.1	9.6	1.7	35.4
A	11.2	6.9	2.2	43.5
Baa	10.9	4.2	2.9	47.0
Ba	11.1	3.0	3.3	51.1
B	8.0	1.4	5.1	72.3
C	2.7	0.4	7.6	98.1

Source: Moody's Financial Metrics Key Ratios for Global Non-Financial Corporations: December 2010.

The data in the third and fourth columns (debt/EBITDA and debt/equity) clearly show how ratings fall as debt increases. Also, as a company's ability to pay the interest costs decreases (EBIT/Interest Expense), its rating tends to decrease, as creditors identify a higher risk of not being repaid.

---

[11] Bond spreads also reflect liquidity. See section 6.4.6.

[12] An AAA rating suggests that the issuer has an extremely strong capacity to meet its financial obligations. A BBB rating suggests that the issuer has adequate resources to honor its commitments. However, this rating also suggests a weakened capacity to meet its obligations in an adverse economic environment. A company with a BB rating is grappling with major ongoing issues, which could hamper its capacity to meet its financial commitments.

Given that ratings assess the potential default risk, lower ratings are associated with a higher cost of debt.[13] **Table 5.2** shows the average spread (above a risk-free bond with similar maturity) required by investors for different investment-grade and speculative-grade bonds.

TABLE 5.2: Credit spreads for different ratings

Investment grade		Junk bonds	
AAA	0.21%	BB+	2.18%
AA	0.34%	BB	2.41%
A+	0.48%	BB-	2.64%
A	0.56%	B+	3.14%
A-	0.88%	B	3.41%
BBB+	0.94%	B-	4.08%
BBB	1.13%		
BBB-	1.70%		

Source: Bloomberg, January 2014.

KEY LEARNING POINT

The cost of debt is not constant, and increases in debt will lead to increases in the cost of that debt.

5.4.2 Cost of Equity Goes Up with Leverage

Debt levels are also related to the cost of equity. Under normal conditions, equity holders of leveraged companies have higher expected returns than holders of unleveraged companies; however, they also incur greater risks.

---

[13] As an alternative to bond ratings, we can use a credit default swap (CDS) to estimate a company's credit risk (and thus the spread). A CDS is a special type of insurance that protects the buyer in case of loan default. An annual premium has to be paid when a CDS is purchased. This is typically referred to as the CDS spread. In exchange for this premium, the buyer benefits from the insurance. In the particular case of the CDS market, the insurance is against the default of an issuer. Thus, the CDS spread can be interpreted as the market-based metric of the credit risk for a certain company.

Debt and risk — three scenarios

A company has assets of $10,000 and no debt. This company has 400 shares outstanding, and each share is worth $25 (equity = $10,000 = $25 × 400).

Consider three possible scenarios for the future: a normal scenario, a recession scenario, and an expansion scenario. Under normal conditions, the company will generate a return on assets (ROA) of 15%. In a recession scenario, the ROA equals 5%; in an expansion scenario, the ROA equals 25%.

Under these conditions, the following table shows what the profit and earnings per share (EPS) are under each scenario:

	Recession	Normal	Expansion
Assets	$10,000	$10,000	$10,000
Debt	$0	$0	$0
Equity	$10,000	$10,000	$10,000
Return on assets (ROA)	5%	15%	25%
Earnings	$500	$1,500	$2,500
Return on equity (ROE)	5%	15%	25%
Earnings per share (EPS)	$1.25	$3.75	$6.25

Because the company has no debt, the ROE equals the ROA for all cases. The table clearly shows how the company's EPS will vary according to each scenario. In the recession scenario, the EPS is $1.25. In the normal scenario, it equals $3.75, and it equals $6.25 in an expansion scenario.

Suppose now that this company wants to change its capital structure to 50% debt financed and 50% equity financed.

How can the company do that? If there are no additional investment opportunities, the company cannot simply borrow $5,000 from the bank, keep the cash, and show it on its balance sheet. This would be an inefficient use of capital because the company would be paying the interest to the bank on the money it borrowed. An alternative solution is to borrow $5,000 and use it to repurchase (buy back) shares from shareholders. If we ignore taxes and assume that the company's share price will remain unchanged after the buyback is announced, the share price will still be $25. This means that the company will be able to repurchase 200 shares ($25 × 200 shares = $5,000.)

Following this buyback plan, the company will have 200 shares outstanding and will have a debt of $5,000. The interest cost on debt is equal to 10%. The following table represents the earnings and the EPS that the company with debt will have under the above three scenarios.

	Recession	Normal	Expansion
Assets	$10,000	$10,000	$10,000
Debt	$5,000	$5,000	$5,000
Equity	$5,000	$5,000	$5,000
Return on assets (ROA)	5%	15%	25%
Earnings before interest	$500	$1,500	$2,500
Interest	−$500	−$500	−$500
Earnings after interest (net income)	$0	$1,000	$2,000
Return on equity (ROE)	0%	20%	40%
Earnings per share (EPS)	$0	$5	$10

The table clearly shows how debt is risky for shareholders. In a normal scenario, in which the ROA is 15%, the company will still generate earnings before the interest of $1,500. After deducting the interest costs (we are ignoring taxes in this example), the net income will be $1,000.

Because the company now has only 200 shares outstanding, the EPS will be equal to $5 per share. The ROE will now equal 20%. This is above the operating ROA of the company of 15%, and the source of the difference is the leverage. Equity holders now have less money invested in the company, but they will generate a higher rate of return on that money.

However, in a recession scenario, things are very different. The net income will be $0 and so will the EPS. Conversely, in the expansion scenario, the company will have an even higher EPS and ROE than in the normal scenario. Overall, across the three scenarios, we see how the ROE varies between 0%, 20%, and 40% (higher risk), and the EPS varies between $0, $5, and $10.

The above example shows how leveraged shareholders have better returns in good times and worse returns in bad times. This clearly shows that a leveraged company is riskier for its equity holders. Therefore, the cost of equity of a leveraged company must be higher than that of an unleveraged company:

$$r_{equity}^{L} = r_{equity}^{U} + \frac{D}{E} \times (r_{equity}^{U} - r_{debt}) \tag{5.3}$$

| r_{equity}^{L} is the cost of equity of a leveraged company, r_{equity}^{U} is the cost of equity of an all-equity company (unleveraged, no debt), r_{debt} is the corporate cost of debt, and D/E is the debt-to-equity ratio at market value.

Formula (5.3) states that shareholders' required return (cost of equity) will be higher when the company uses higher levels of debt.

The same relation can be seen in terms of the capital asset pricing model (CAPM) betas[14]:

$$\beta^{L}_{equity} = \beta^{U}_{equity} \times \left(1 + \frac{D}{E}\right) \tag{5.4}$$

| β^{L}_{equity} is the beta of a leveraged company, β^{U}_{equity} is the beta of an all-equity company (unlevered beta), and D/E is the ratio of debt-to-equity, at market value.

Formula (5.4) shows how the beta of a leveraged company is higher than that of an all-equity (or unleveraged) company.

KEY LEARNING POINT ✓

The cost of equity of a company depends not only on the company's business risk but also on the financial risk that leverage poses to shareholders.

5.4.3 Overall — Cost of Debt and Equity

Higher debt poses a greater risk to equity holders and lenders, who will then incorporate that risk into their expected returns (or cost of capital). In other words, as a company increases its debt level, the cost of debt and equity both increase. This helps to explain why companies should not be overleveraged.

KEY LEARNING POINT ✓

Higher leverage increases risk and leads to higher costs of debt and equity.

---

[14] The complete formula includes a component related to the beta of debt. A common assumption in practice is that the beta of debt is zero, and thus we can obtain formula (5.4).

5.5   HOW MUCH TO BORROW — DISTRESS COSTS

Financial distress costs are one of the most important factors in understanding capital structure decisions. These costs have two components: direct and indirect costs.

The direct costs of financial distress are the legal and administrative costs of bankruptcy or liquidation. These costs are small as a percentage of firm value; estimates vary between 1% and 5%.[15] Essentially, these costs are the fees paid to courts, lawyers, and accountants who work on the settlement of the bankruptcy or liquidation proceedings.

Much more important are the indirect costs of financial distress. Indeed, companies in financial distress find it difficult to do business. Indirect costs can be internal to the company, for example, lost business opportunities as management needs to cut back on investments, R&D, and marketing to conserve cash, or they can be external costs, such as lost sales and adverse commercial conditions from suppliers that will increase operating costs. The company may also lose market share, forcing it to sell some assets inefficiently (at fire-sale prices) to raise capital to meet debt obligations.

One of the biggest mistakes in terms of capital structure decision making is to assume that the only costs due to financial distress are the legal costs of bankruptcy or liquidation. In practice, many factors will come into play in addition to these legal costs. As a company becomes financially distressed, several stakeholders may change their relationship with the company. These changes will translate into operational impacts that may significantly affect future cash flows.[16]

5.5.1   Customers and Financial Distress Costs

The financial distress of a company plays a very important role in customers' decision making, particularly when they are looking for a long-term relationship with a company. Therefore, the fact that a company may be sliding into financial distress may mean that it will start losing customers that value a long-term and stable relationship.[17] Customers usually face switching costs if a company is liquidated. These costs are particularly high when there is a strong bilateral relationship, such as when unique products or assets are involved.[18]

---

[15] Median expenses as a percentage of the pre-bankruptcy assets. *Sources:* Altman (1984); Warner (1977); Weiss (1990); Bris, Welch, and Zhu (2006).

[16] For instance, customers may stop buying from the firm. Suppliers may stop supplying the firm or change their trade credit arrangements. Also, employees might start fleeing the firm as their jobs come under threat.

[17] This effect is completely absent in a Modigliani–Miller world, because their key assumption is that the investment, and therefore the operational performance of the firm, is independent of the financing decision.

[18] Opler and Titman (1994) find that financially distressed firms lose substantial market share to their competitors.

Would you want to buy a long-term asset, with significant service and warranty implications, from a company that is so highly leveraged that it may become financially distressed? Furthermore, would you want to buy pre-paid services (like insurance or other services) from a financially distressed company that may not be around to deliver on those services when you need them?

5.5.2   Suppliers and Financial Distress Costs

Suppliers are important stakeholders that also consider financial distress when making decisions. Suppose you are supplying a company that is going into financial distress (or that you fear might go into financial distress, given its high debt levels). You may think twice about whether you will continue to do business with this company. Moreover, if you do continue dealing with it, you will probably want to change the payment terms or, in extreme circumstances, collect cash on delivery. When suppliers change their operating behavior because a company is possibly going to go into financial distress, this generates substantial costs for the company.

This is particularly important when there is a strong customer–supplier relationship and where several relationship-specific investments have to be made. For instance, if your company is a supplier to an auto manufacturer, you need to invest a significant amount of money in production lines that may be specific to the company or the car model. If you learn that your customer (the auto manufacturer) is headed for financial distress, you will think twice about committing additional investments in the relationship.

The same holds true when a company supplies only a few big customers. For instance, if a supplier is greatly dependent on a customer (for example, it accounts for 80% of its sales), then the customer's liquidation (or possible financial distress) is a matter that is of great interest to the supplier. As a result, in many durable goods industries, only companies in sound financial health can persuade their suppliers to invest in relation-specific assets.

5.5.3   Overall — Financial Distress Summary

Financial distress costs are much more damaging than legal bankruptcy costs. If clients, suppliers, or employees leave the company when it enters (or is headed for) financial distress, this is even more damaging to the company's operational and financial value. Additional costs of financial distress can arise owing to the behavior of employees. Indeed, in a distressed company, employee retention is difficult, and it is likely that employees will start looking for other jobs. Also, the management becomes extremely focused on short-run financial issues, and not so much on managing the business.

All these financial distress costs are notoriously difficult to measure. Some estimates suggest they can be higher than 20% of firm value,[19] but they vary widely across industries.

KEY LEARNING POINT ✓

Financial distress can lead to a substantial decline in firm value due to lost customers, employees, and suppliers.

FIGURE 5.2: Percentage erosion of company value owing to financial distress.

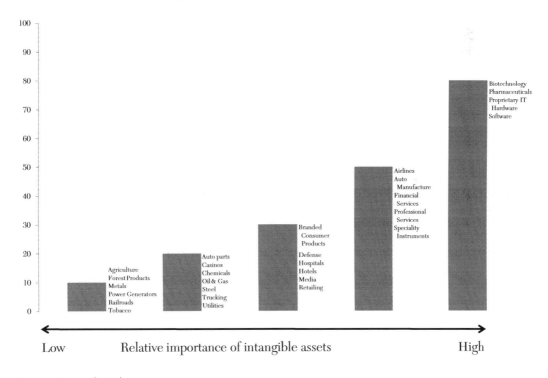

Source: Passov (2003).

---

[19] These financial distress costs represent the present value of future cash flows that are lost owing to financial distress. *Sources:* Andrade and Kaplan (1998) and Korteweg (2010).

Figure 5.2 clearly shows how financial distress costs vary across sectors. High financial distress costs usually occur in industries with a high percentage of intangible assets such as pharmaceuticals. In these industries, up to 80% of the firm value is lost in times of financial distress, whereas in utilities or food-related industries, financial distress costs are relatively low because customers and suppliers are not as concerned about the possible financial distress of these companies. For instance, imagine you are a consumer of McDonald's burgers. If you read in the newspaper that the company's debt situation is dangerous — if it cannot refinance its bonds next year, it will go into financial distress — will you stop eating McDonald's burgers because of its potential financial distress? Most McDonald's customers would not!

However, in sectors in which long-term relationships are important for customers, such as automobiles, the financial distress costs are very high. Suppose you are considering buying a new BMW and you read in the newspaper that BMW is highly indebted and might not be able to pay all its debts in the coming years. You would probably decide to choose a different make of car. Most consumers value a long-term relationship with their car manufacturer (because of warranty and maintenance implications). This means that they would be reluctant to buy a BMW today if they come to know that the company is in financial distress.[20]

KEY LEARNING POINT ✓

Financial distress can destroy 20% of firm value on average, but significant cross-industry variation exists.

As we will see later in this chapter, financial distress costs are key to understanding capital structure choices. Companies in industries with relatively high financial distress costs typically have less leverage than other companies.

5.6   HOW MUCH TO BORROW — MANAGERIAL FLEXIBILITY

Companies with low amounts of debt have the flexibility to raise additional capital from the market. Access to capital markets varies substantially depending on a company's rating.

---

[20] Note that in this example BMW is not bankrupt; it is still technically solvent. But the news may make things worse on the product market front, because customers who were considering buying a BMW would shift to another brand.

For instance, companies that are rated AAA or AA have very easy access to money markets or short-term corporate borrowing. As the rating decreases, companies have less and less access to these markets. If a company's rating changes from BBB (investment grade) to BB (junk bonds), its ability to raise appropriate funding in debt capital markets is substantially reduced.[21]

Financial flexibility has huge value for corporations and is another important determinant of companies' debt choices. In particular, this additional factor leads companies to limit their use of debt. Too much debt constrains their financial flexibility, which can result in lost investment opportunities and a consequent reduction in firm value.[22] Conversely, having reasonable amounts of debt and a high rating gives companies the strategic flexibility to make major strategic moves. This means that if an interesting growth project or a promising M&A opportunity materializes, they can raise debt to finance these new ventures. As is to be expected, the value of flexibility is different for different companies. And, once again, this is an important factor in understanding different capital structure choices across sectors.

KEY LEARNING POINT ✓

Excessive leverage may destroy financial flexibility.

5.7   PUTTING IT ALL TOGETHER — THE TRADE-OFFS BEHIND THE FINANCING MIX

We have seen that a key advantage of debt is the interest tax shield it generates. However, debt also results in various costs for the company. First, the cost of both debt and equity will increase with high amounts of leverage. Second, financial distress costs are an important factor that prevents companies from being overleveraged. Finally, financial flexibility is an important determinant of a company's capital structure. Too much debt reduces the company's freedom to make major strategic moves.

---

[21] Given the additional risk of junk bonds, many institutional investors are by law forbidden from investing in them (or severely limited in their ability to do so).

[22] For instance, Campello, Graham, and Harvey (2010) report that constrained firms backed out of or postponed attractive investment opportunities in the aftermath of the 2008 credit crisis, when they were unable to borrow externally.

Unfortunately, no single formula determines the optimal capital structure, but all of the above factors must be taken into consideration. This means that companies with higher financial distress costs should have lower amounts of leverage. Similarly, companies for which financial flexibility is important, for instance, high-growth companies, should have lower amounts of leverage. Finally, companies that have high taxes should have higher debt levels, because the tax shield effects are stronger for these companies. As debt increases, the tax shield increases the value of the company. This relationship can be seen in **Figure 5.3**.

FIGURE 5.3: Positive effects of debt — tax shields.

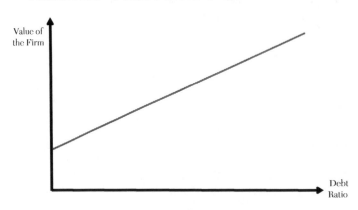

However, as debt increases, the company's financial distress costs increase, and financial flexibility decreases. These two factors contribute to a lower firm value as shown in **Figure 5.4**.

FIGURE 5.4: Negative effects of debt — financial distress and lost flexibility.

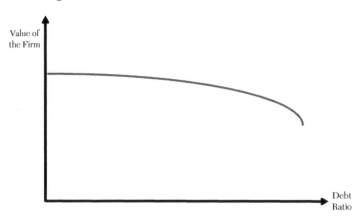

Figures **5.3** and **5.4** suggest that there is an optimal amount of debt that maximizes the value of the company. This optimal amount of debt occurs when the tax shield is maximized relative to the costs of financial distress and lost flexibility. **Figure 5.5** represents the relationship between firm value and the debt-to-equity ratio when these two offsetting factors are combined.

FIGURE 5.5: Combining all effects — optimal capital structure.

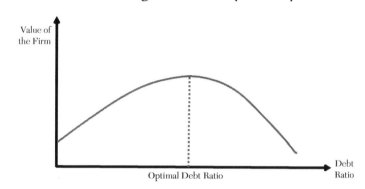

Figure **5.5** suggests that for low levels of debt, financial distress costs are small, financial flexibility still exists, and thus firm value increases with debt levels (owing to the tax shields). However, after a certain point, the costs of financial distress and lost flexibility outweigh the additional benefits of having more debt. At this point, the company has reached its maximum firm value, and thus this is the "optimal" capital structure.

This picture varies for different industries — the trade-offs are different across industries. This means that there is not a single optimal target debt-to-equity ratio. Rather, the appropriate balance between debt and equity differs across sectors, as **Figure 5.6** shows.

FIGURE 5.6: Combining all effects — optimal capital structure for different industries.

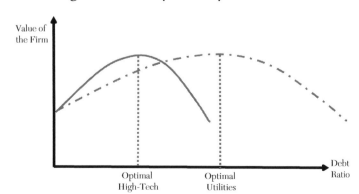

For instance, in the utilities sector, financial distress costs tend to be low. In this case, the optimal capital structure includes significant amounts of debt. In other sectors, such as pharmaceuticals, the optimal debt ratio is significantly lower. In this case, the financial distress costs are high and so is the value of financial flexibility.

KEY LEARNING POINT ✓

The optimal capital structure varies across companies owing to different tax savings, financial distress costs, and values of flexibility.

5.7.1 Optimal Capital Structure and the Cost of Capital

As indicated above, the company's optimal capital structure is the debt ratio that maximizes the company's value. A similar relationship can be seen when the WACC formula is used. With corporate taxes, we can define the weighted average cost of capital (WACC) as

$$WACC = \frac{debt}{debt + equity}(1-t)r_{debt} + \frac{equity}{debt + equity}r_{equity} \qquad (5.5)$$

| r_{debt} is the cost of debt, r_{equity} is the cost of equity, and t is the tax rate.

Overall, debt is always less risky than equity capital, so the cost of debt must always be below the cost of equity. This is because equity holders are always the residual claimants on a company's cash flow. First, the company must pay the bank and bondholders, and then if anything is left, it can distribute money back to its shareholders (as either dividends or stock buybacks).

The WACC is the after-tax[23] cost of funding for a company as a whole. It is computed as the weighted average of the cost of equity and the after-tax cost of debt, taking into account the appropriate mix of debt and equity. The costs of both equity and debt should be forward looking and reflect the cost demanded by the different sources of the company's capital (or the required return expected by investors given the company's risk).

---

[23] Because interest payments are tax deductible, the after-tax cost of debt is lower than the before-tax cost. Thus, in the WACC formula, we include the term $1 - t$ (one minus the corporate tax rate) to represent the tax shield obtained through interest payments. The correct tax rate of the WACC is the rate at which taxes will be reduced by interest deductions in the future. This may be the effective tax rate or the marginal tax rate depending on the circumstances.

Figure 5.7 shows how the WACC can be reduced with a higher reliance on debt only up to a certain point. Until that point, a company lowers its cost of capital by increasing its leverage[24] because of the tax advantage of debt relative to equity and the fact that interest is deductible (the tax shield).

FIGURE 5.7:   Optimal capital structure and cost of capital.

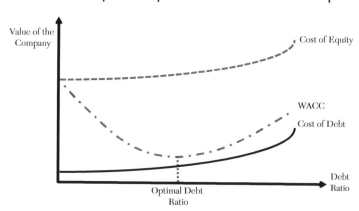

However, as debt increases, the costs of both equity and debt go up. The cost of debt increases because of the higher risk to debtholders, who will then charge higher rates when lending money to the company. The higher cost of equity occurs because of the added risk that financial leverage brings to equity holders.

After a certain point, the increase in the costs of debt and equity is such that a company will not be able to reduce its cost of capital by using more debt. The value of the leverage ratio that minimizes the WACC (which is also the value that maximizes firm value) is then the optimal capital structure.

5.8   EMPIRICAL EVIDENCE FROM AROUND THE WORLD

The empirical literature has surveyed practitioners to analyze how they make financial decisions in a practical setting.

---

[24] The value of the firm is its future cash flows discounted at the weighted average cost of capital (WACC). Therefore, a WACC decrease corresponds to an increase in firm value.

FIGURE 5.8: Importance of different factors in deciding on company debt levels.

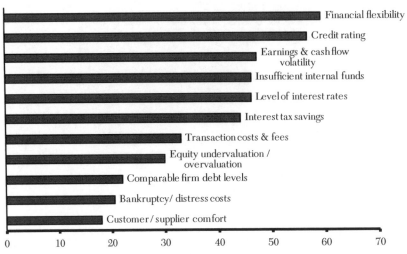

Percentage of CFOs identifying factor as important or very important

The survey results[25] (see **Figure 5.8**) show that CFOs rely on several factors when choosing the capital structure. The most important are financial flexibility and a good credit rating. Companies are very concerned about their credit ratings, which can be interpreted as an indication of their concern about financial distress. Cash flow stability is also important. As expected, companies with more stable cash flows can have higher leverage, because they have lower chances of falling into financial distress. Companies with very volatile cash flows tend to have lower leverage to avoid the risk of falling into financial distress in a bad year. The corporate tax advantage of debt is also, as expected, an important factor in capital structure decisions.

When CFOs were asked whether their companies had an optimal debt–equity ratio target or range, only 19% of respondents said they did not have a target debt ratio or range. More than 80% said they had a target, which could be a fixed number or, more likely, a range (see **Figure 5.9**).

---

[25] See Graham and Harvey (2001).

FIGURE 5.9:   Debt–equity targets in companies.

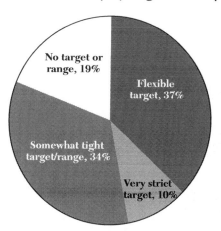

Overall, these numbers provide support for the notion that companies trade off the costs and the benefits of debt to derive an optimal debt ratio.

Companies in different industries have very different capital structure patterns. **Figure 5.10** presents the debt ratios of major global companies; the debt ratio here is defined as the total debt as a percentage of the total capital (the sum of debt and equity).[26]

FIGURE 5.10:   Debt ratios of major global companies.

Total debt as a percentage of total capital for Euro Stoxx 50

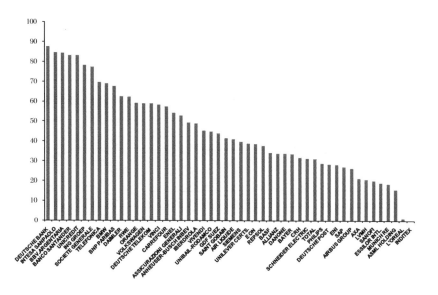

---

[26] It is also common to present debt ratios using net debt (total debt minus cash) as a percentage of the total capital.

Total debt as a percentage of total capital for DJ30

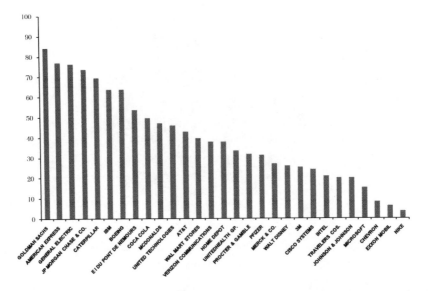

Total debt as a percentage of total capital for Asia, Japan, LATAM

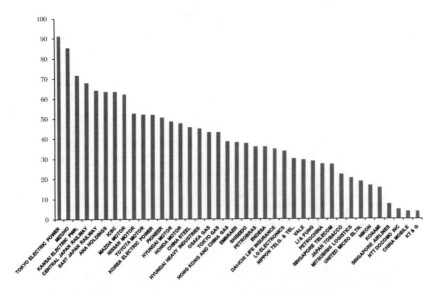

Source: Computed as of February 2013, using data from Datastream.

The data presented in **Figure 5.10** suggest that significantly different capital structure choices exist across sectors. Financial companies are always highly leveraged, but there are also several other sectors (for instance, utilities and infrastructure) that tend to have significantly higher leverage ratios. Consistent with the theories presented in this chapter, on the right-hand side of the graph, we typically find high-tech companies, pharmaceuticals, etc. In these sectors, the value of financial flexibility, as well as the cost of financial distress, outweighs any possible tax benefit of debt. Consequently, companies have low levels of debt.

Research studies have also applied regression techniques to a large number of global companies in order to understand the determinants of capital structure. Based on data from more than 30,000 non-financial companies across developed and emerging markets (companies), several determinants have been identified. **Table 5.3** summarizes the regression results.

TABLE 5.3: Determinants of capital structure in emerging and developed markets

	Emerging	Developed
Tangibility	**0.1300**	**0.2408**
Size	**0.0281**	**0.0203**
Return on assets (ROA)	**−0.0058**	**−0.0009**
Growth potential	**−0.0691**	**−0.0092**
Age	0.0002	**0.0003**
Risk (volatility of earnings)	0.0381	**−0.0107**
Observations	63,171	209,213
Adjusted R-squared	0.35	0.22

Source: Fernandes (2011).[27]

Overall, across developed and emerging markets, similar factors seem to impact the debt–equity choices.[28] Specifically, the results in **Table 5.3** (the most statistically significant coefficients are in bold font) suggest that certain factors favor higher leverage ratios:

---

[27] **Table 5.3** reports estimates of coefficients of the annual time-series cross-sectional firm-level regression of leverage ratios. The sample period is from 1990 to 2007. All specifications use standard errors corrected for heteroskedasticity and are clustered at the country level. A bold font means that a coefficient is significant at the 5% levels.

[28] Rajan and Zingales (1995), Booth, Aivazian, Demirgüç-Kunt, and Maksimovic (2001), and Frank and Goyal (2009) also find that tangibility, growth potential, and size are important determinants of capital structure choices. Claessens, Djankov, and Xu (2000), Allayannis, Brown, and Klapper (2003), and Bris, Koskinen, and Pons (2004) address firms' capital structures around the time of the Asian financial crisis of 1997–1998. Some other studies of international capital structure include Rajan and Zingales (1995), Giannetti (2003), Harvey, Lins, and Roper (2004), Mahajan and Tartaroglu (2008), and Fan, Titman, and Twite (2012).

- *More tangible assets:* Companies with more tangible assets are in general more valuable in case of bankruptcy or liquidation. Conversely, companies that are heavily invested in intangible assets and human capital are more difficult to liquidate without substantial costs, and they face higher costs in times of financial distress. The results show that companies and industries with relatively more tangible assets tend to have higher debt ratios.

- *Low growth:* Companies with higher growth opportunities prefer lower leverage, consistent with the idea that excessive leverage may force companies to pass up profitable investment opportunities. This highlights the empirical importance of financial flexibility.

- *Larger companies:* Larger companies tend to have higher leverage. Indeed, it is widely known that larger companies can weather recessions better, and they have more diversified revenue streams, which reduces the likelihood of their falling into financial distress. Apart from the lower probability of bankruptcy, larger companies also face lower (as a percentage) costs in the event of default. As a result, large companies, in comparison with smaller ones, can use larger amounts of leverage.

- *Lower volatility of earnings:* The negative coefficient suggests that companies with higher volatility have, as expected, lower levels of debt. That is, companies that are more volatile have a higher probability of becoming financially distressed and thus choose to have lower leverage. In contrast, companies with more stable cash flows typically raise more debt. Thus, companies in industries that are not very cyclical can have more debt. This is typically the case for utility companies (and **Figure 5.10** does indeed show that most utilities have high amounts of debt).

The regression results in **Table 5.3**, together with the empirical data on companies (**Figure 5.10**), suggest that leverage depends significantly on some key company-level characteristics. Indeed, leverage is impacted by a company's business model and also by the overall type of assets and revenue streams of the company.

Finally, the capital structure choice is also influenced by the shareholder structure of the company, and their subjective preferences. In particular, companies with shorter-term shareholders tend to favor higher leverage. For instance, it is common for publicly traded companies to act upon recommendations from shareholders such as mutual funds to increase leverage, and at the same time return money to shareholders through a share buyback (see chapter 8). Conversely, companies with long-term investors (such as pension funds, family owners, sovereign wealth funds) typically favor lower leverage. These long-term shareholders are often more interested in the company having a solid balance sheet (thus assuring the long-term survival of the company) rather than short-term optimization of its cost of capital and short-term returns to shareholders.

SUMMARY

Capital structure and the choices related to it are important decisions for a company. If a company's owners increase debt, they need to invest less of their own capital in the company. However, they will incur additional financial risk, because the volatility of company's returns will increase.

This chapter highlights that there are costs associated with being underleveraged and overleveraged, and that companies must try to achieve an optimal capital structure that maximizes firm value yet still allows for financial flexibility. Capital structure must thus be aligned with the company's investments and strategic direction.

The framework introduced in this chapter suggests that companies must balance the advantages and disadvantages of debt. Higher debt means lower taxes (a positive effect), but it also means higher risk, a greater likelihood of financial distress, and lower financial flexibility (negative effects). When a company is affected by financial distress, it may suffer important losses of customers, suppliers, employees, and other stakeholders. Also, management efforts are focused on overcoming the financial distress and thus diverted from important business decisions. Conversely, too little debt means the company must resort to using the most expensive source of capital (equity) and could thus be leaving "money on the table."

The optimal capital structure is achieved when the additional benefits of debt are offset by the different costs of having leverage. At this point, the company reaches its maximum value and minimum cost of capital. We have analyzed how different factors vary across industries and companies, and their impact on optimal capital structure choices. The empirical evidence shows how companies with higher taxes, lower financial distress costs, and less need for flexibility tend to have higher amounts of debt.

REFERENCES

Altman, E.I., 1984, A Further Empirical Investigation of the Bankruptcy Cost Question, *Journal of Finance*, Vol. 39, Iss. 4:1067–1089.

Allayannis, G., G. Brown, and L. Klapper, 2003, Capital Structure and Financial Risk: Evidence from Foreign Debt Use in East Asia, *Journal of Finance*, Vol. 58, Iss. 6:2667–2709.

Andrade, G., and S.N. Kaplan, 1998, How Costly Is Financial (Not Economic) Distress? Evidence from Highly Leveraged Transactions that Became Distressed, *Journal of Finance*, Vol. 53, Iss. 5:1443–1493.

Booth, L., V. Aivazian, A. Demirguc-Kunt, and V. Maksimovic, 2001, Capital Structures in Developing Countries, *Journal of Finance*, Vol. 56, Iss. 1:87–130.

Bris, A., Y. Koskinen, and V. Pons, 2004, Corporate Financial Policies and Performance around Currency Crises, *Journal of Business*, Vol. 77, Iss. 4:749–796.

Bris, A., I. Welch, and N. Zhu, 2006, The Costs of Bankruptcy, *Journal of Finance*, Vol. 61, Iss. 3:1253–1303.

Campello, M., J.R. Graham, and C.R. Harvey, 2010, "The Real Effects of Financial Constraints: Evidence from a Financial Crisis." *Journal of Financial Economics*, Vol. 97, Iss. 3:470–487.

Claessens, S., S. Djankov, and L.C. Xu, 2000, Corporate Performance in the East Asian Financial Crisis, *World Bank Research Observer*, Vol. 15, Iss. 1:23–46.

Fan J., S. Titman, and G. Twite, 2012, An International Comparison of Capital Structure and Debt Maturity Choices, *Journal of Financial and Quantitative Analysis*, Vol. 47, Iss. 1:23–56.

Fernandes, N., 2011, Global Convergence of Financing Policies: Evidence for Emerging-Market Firms, *Journal of International Business Studies*, Vol. 42, Iss. 8:1043–1059.

Frank, M.Z., and V.K. Goyal, 2009, Capital Structure Decisions: Which Factors Are Reliably Important?, *Financial Management*, Vol. 38, Iss. 1:1–37.

Giannetti, M, 2003, Do Better Institutions Mitigate Agency Problems? Evidence from Corporate Finance Choices, *Journal of Financial and Quantitative Analysis*, Vol. 38, Iss. 1:185–212.

Graham, J.R., and C.R. Harvey, 2001, The Theory and Practice of Corporate Finance: Evidence from the Field, *Journal of Financial Economics*, Vol. 60, Iss. 2:187–243.

Harvey, C., K. Lins, and A. Roper, 2004, The Effect of Capital Structure When Expected Agency Costs Are Extreme, *Journal of Financial Economics*, Vol. 74, Iss. 1:3–30.

Jensen, M.C., 1986, Agency Costs of Free Cash Flow, Corporate Finance and Takeovers, *American Economic Review*, Vol. 76, Iss. 2:323–329.

Korteweg, A., 2010, The Net Benefits to Leverage, *Journal of Finance*, Vol. 65, Iss. 6:2137–2170.

Mahajan, A., and S. Tartaroglu, 2008, Equity Market Timing and Capital Structure: International Evidence, *Journal of Banking and Finance*, Vol. 32, Iss. 5:754–766.

Modigliani, F., and M.H. Miller, 1958, The Cost of Capital, Corporation Finance, and the Theory of Investment, *American Economic Review*, Vol. 48, Iss. 3:261–297.

Opler, T.C., and S. Titman, 1994, Financial Distress and Corporate Performance, *The Journal of Finance*, Vol. 49, Iss. 3:1015–1040.

Passov, R., 2003, How Much Cash Does Your Company Need?, *Harvard Business Review*, Vol. 81, Iss. 11:119–125.

Rajan, R., and L. Zingales, 1995, What Do We Know about Capital Structure? Some Evidence from International Data, *Journal of Finance* Vol. 50, Iss. 5:1421–1460.

Warner, J.B., 1977, Bankruptcy, Absolute Priority, and the Pricing of Risky Debt Claims. *Journal of Financial Economics*, Vol. 4, Iss. 3:239–276.

Weiss, L.A., 1990, Bankruptcy Resolution: Direct Costs and Violation of Priority of Claims, *Journal of Financial Economics*, Vol. 27, Iss. 2:285–314.

Borrowing from Banks and Capital Markets

What is the difference between bank loans and bonds? What is the impact on a company when it obtains financing through the bond market? How is the risk-free rate arrived at? How are financing costs determined? And how do investors assess bonds with different characteristics?

This chapter addresses these and other questions and discusses the main principles underlying debt financing. We start by defining bonds and the risk-free rate. Then we analyze the risks of bond investing. We show that even if the credit risk is zero, investing in bonds still involves risk, which depends on the bonds' maturity.

Finally, we address the question of how companies can use debt markets to finance their operations.[1] We cover corporate bonds and their role, and also provide examples of the costs of financing for different companies. We discuss the differences between bank loans and bonds, and also describe recent advances in retail bonds and hybrid instruments.

6.1   VALUATION OF BONDS AND YIELD TO MATURITY

A bond is a security that establishes a credit relationship between the purchaser of the bond and the issuer. The purchaser pays a certain amount of money up front to the issuer, and in exchange expects to receive the principal at the end of the life of the bond, as well as coupon payments over the life of the bond. All payments (principal and coupons) are stipulated in the bond contract, which is why bonds are also called *fixed income* securities.

The *principal* is the face amount of the bond, also called its *nominal value*, *face value*, or *par value*. These terms are used interchangeably and represent the value the investor will receive upon redemption of the bond at maturity.

---

[1] The question of how much debt to have or the appropriate amounts of debt and equity in a company are not discussed here. For a complete coverage of this topic, see chapter 5.

The *coupon* rate of a bond is the stated rate of interest that the bond will pay. This contractual rate is then applied to the face value of the bond to determine the amount to be paid in coupons (for instance, if the coupon rate is 5% and the face value is €100, then the coupon is €5). The term *coupon* came into use as in the early stages of this market, the physical bond had coupons attached to it. The holder of the bond would tear off a coupon on the assigned date and collect the promised coupon payment in exchange.

In this section, we focus on risk-free government bonds. We first show how zero-coupon bonds are priced, then we discuss coupon bonds. Finally, we introduce the concept of the yield curve.

6.1.1 Zero-Coupon Bonds

Bonds for which no coupon is paid are referred to as *zero-coupon bonds*. The only payment the issuer makes to the purchaser of the bond is at the maturity date.

Consider a zero-coupon bond with a face value of €1,000 and a five-year maturity. Assume it is a *risk-free* government bond, for which repayment of the principal is guaranteed after five years. **Figure 6.1** illustrates the profile of cash flows that the bond provides for its holder.

FIGURE 6.1:   Cash flows on a zero-coupon bond with five-year maturity.

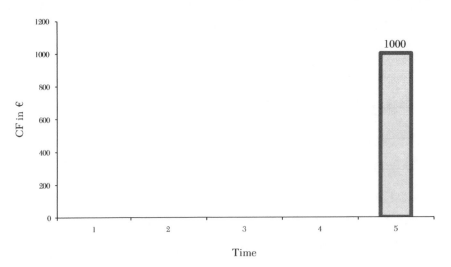

KEY LEARNING POINT ✓

Zero-coupon bonds are financial instruments that provide only a single fixed payment at maturity.

Bond prices are computed as the present value of the cash flows the bond provides for its holder or investor. The appropriate discount rate at which the cash flows are discounted is called the *yield to maturity* (**YTM**). It is also called the *current market interest rate* or *market yield*. It represents the rate of return that investors require in order to invest in a particular bond, given the alternatives available in the market.

We can determine a bond's price based on its YTM. If investors demand a 6% yield, or rate of return, to lend money to the issuer for five years, then the price of the bond (with a face value of €1,000) is

$$P = \frac{1,000}{(1+0.06)^5} = 747.26$$

If an investor buys the five-year zero-coupon bond now for €747.26, keeps it for five years, and then collects the final payment of €1,000, the effective annual return will be exactly 6%.

KEY LEARNING POINT ✓

The yield-to-maturity (YTM) is the interest rate at which a certain bond is traded in the market. It represents the rate of return investors require in order to invest in that bond.

Similarly, we can determine the YTM of a bond based on its price. For instance, assume that a five-year zero-coupon bond is currently priced at €750. What is the YTM of this bond? We use the following bond pricing formula to find the appropriate YTM:

$$750 = \frac{1000}{(1+YTM)^5}$$

Thus, YTM = 5.92%.

For a particular bond, therefore, knowing its YTM or its price amounts to the same thing. If we know one of them, we can compute the other.

There is a negative relationship between bond prices and the YTM. When the YTM changes, there is no corresponding change in the cash flows that the bond provides for the investor, and thus the bond price has to adjust correspondingly. If the investor were to demand a higher YTM, the price of the bond today would have to be lower in order to generate the required YTM.

If the YTM is 7%, the bond price is

$$P = \frac{1,000}{(1+0.07)^5} = 712.99$$

This means that if an investor buys the five-year zero-coupon bond right now for €712.99, keeps it for five years, and then collects the final payment of €1,000, its annual return would be 7%.

Similarly, if the YTM is 5%, the bond price is

$$P = \frac{1,000}{(1+0.05)^5} = 783.53$$

Figure 6.2 shows the negative relationship between the YTM and bond prices.

FIGURE 6.2: The price of a five-year zero-coupon bond with a face value of €1,000 for different YTMs.

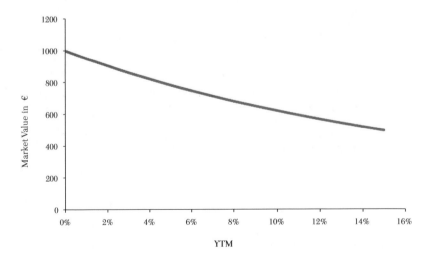

In a hypothetical scenario in which investors do not require any return for lending their money, the YTM is zero. In this case, the price of the bond would be €1,000, the same as its nominal value. As the YTM increases, the present value of the fixed bond cash flows (in this case, only one cash flow of €1,000 in five years' time) decreases. Thus, we obtain a negative relation between current interest rates (the YTM) and bond prices.

KEY LEARNING POINT ✔

There is a negative relationship between bond prices and the YTM.

6.1.2   Coupon Bonds

In the case of coupon bonds, in addition to the repayment of the principal at maturity, fixed coupon payments are made at regular intervals.

Consider a five-year, 8% coupon bond with a face value of €1,000. **Figure 6.3** shows the profile of the cash flows that the bond provides for its holder.

FIGURE 6.3:   Cash flows on an 8% coupon bond with five-year maturity.

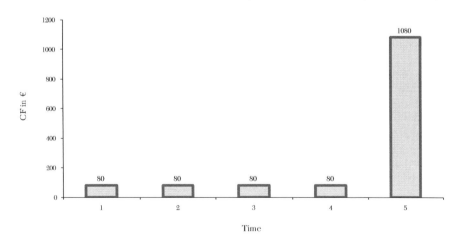

We see that each year the bondholder receives a coupon of 8% (which, given the nominal value of €1,000, is equal to €80) plus, in the final year, the reimbursement of the nominal value of the bond (€1,000).

As usual, the price of the bond is given by the present value of all the cash flows the bond provides for its holder. If investors demand a 6% YTM, the price of the bond is

$$P = \frac{80}{(1+0.06)^1} + \frac{80}{(1+0.06)^2} + \frac{80}{(1+0.06)^3} + \frac{80}{(1+0.06)^4} + \frac{1,080}{(1+0.06)^5} = 1,084.25$$

Given the YTM of 6%, the current price of the five-year 8% coupon bond should be €1,084.25. This bond is considered to be trading *above par*.[2] This means that investors are willing to pay more than €1,000 for the bond, because it will provide them, over the next five years, with a coupon rate of 8% (that is, €80 per year), yet they require only 6% to invest in it. Indeed, by investing €1,084.25 today and then receiving €80 coupons each year for five years plus the reimbursement of the €1,000 nominal value in the fifth year, investors are guaranteed a 6% return (which is their required yield).

KEY LEARNING POINT ✓

Bonds are said to be trading above par whenever the coupon rate is higher than the YTM.

With coupon bonds, as with zero-coupon bonds, there is a negative relationship between bond prices and the YTM. Indeed, if investors demand a higher interest rate (of 7%, for instance), this does not translate into a change in the cash flows. The issuer will still pay €1,000 to the bondholder after five years, plus €80 every year. Specifically, if the yield is 7%, the bond price equals €1,041:

$$P = \frac{80}{1+0.07} + \frac{80}{(1+0.07)^2} + \frac{80}{(1+0.07)^3} + \frac{80}{(1+0.07)^4} + \frac{1,080}{(1+0.07)^5} = 1,041.00$$

The price of the bond today has to be lower in order to provide investors with the required 7% rate of return.

Alternatively, if the YTM is 5%, then the price of the bond will be higher (€1,129):

$$P = \frac{80}{1+0.05} + \frac{80}{(1+0.05)^2} + \frac{80}{(1+0.05)^3} + \frac{80}{(1+0.05)^4} + \frac{1,080}{(1+0.05)^5} = 1,129.88$$

---

[2] The par value of the bond is its nominal value of €1,000.

If the YTM is 10%, then the price of the bond is equal to €924.18 (the sum of the cash flows from this bond, discounted at 10%). The bond is now considered to be valued *below par* (924 < 1,000). This occurs whenever the coupon rate is insufficient to provide investors with their required yield. In this case, the price of the bond today has to be below par.

If the YTM is equal to 8%, the price of the bond is equal to exactly €1,000. In this case, the bond is considered to be valued *at par*, because its market price (€1,000) equals the nominal value of the bond (also €1,000). By investing €1,000 today, and receiving an €80 coupon each year for five years, plus the reimbursement of the €1,000 nominal value in the fifth year, investors are guaranteed an 8% return or YTM.

In summary, bonds trade above/at/below par, when

Below par	Coupon rate < YTM
Above par	Coupon rate > YTM
At par	Coupon rate = YTM

6.2   RISKS OF INVESTING IN BONDS — MATURITY AND PRICE RISK

The negative relationship between bond prices and the YTM is more pronounced for longer-maturity bonds. Consider several bonds (all with a par value of $1,000) with different maturities — 1-, 5-, 10-, and 20-year bonds — all of which have a 6% coupon rate. If their cash flows are discounted at a YTM of 4%, we obtain the prices in the first row of **Table 6.1**. All these bonds are trading above par as expected because in each case the coupon rate (6%) is higher than the YTM (4%).

TABLE 6.1:   Price of 6% coupon bonds for different YTMs

	1-year	5-year	10-year	20-year
Price (YTM = 4%)	€1,019.23	€1,089.04	€1,162.22	€1,271.81
Price (YTM = 5%)	€1,009.52	€1,043.29	€1,077.22	€1,124.62
Change in price	–€9.71	–€45.74	–€85.00	–€147.18
% Change in price	–0.95%	–4.20%	–7.31%	–11.57%

If interest rates increase and the YTM rises to 5%, the price of these bonds will be lower (second row of **Table 6.1**). However, the reduction in price is not the same for all of the bonds. The price of the 1-year bond decreased by €9.71, from €1,019.23 to €1,009.52, which represents a 0.95% negative return. As the maturity of the bonds lengthens, the price changes increase. For instance, the 20-year bond sees its price fall by 11.57%, from €1,271.81 to €1,124.62.

The opposite happens as interest rates fall. Thus, if the YTM were to decrease from 4% to 3%, the prices of all the bonds would increase (see **Table 6.2**).

TABLE 6.2: Price comparison of 6% coupon bonds when the YTM decreases

	1-year 6% coupon bond	5-year 6% coupon bond	10-year 6% coupon bond	20-year 6% coupon bond
YTM = 4%	€1,019.23	€1,089.04	€1,162.22	€1,271.81
YTM = 3%	€1,029.13	€1,137.39	€1,255.91	€1,446.32
Change in price	€9.90	€48.35	€93.69	€174.52
% Change in price	0.97%	4.44%	8.06%	13.72%

As the YTM decreases, bond prices increase, with longer-term bonds exhibiting the most pronounced increase. For instance, the 10-year bond sees its price rise by 8.06%, from €1,162.22 to €1,255.91, and the 20-year bond's price goes up by 13.72%.

We can see, then, that long-term bonds are more sensitive to changes in interest rates and market yields, and their price fluctuations are more pronounced than those of short-term bonds. So, from an investor's point of view, and with all else being equal, it is riskier to hold a long-term bond than a short-term one, even in the absence of any credit risk concerns.

KEY LEARNING POINT ✓

Long-term bonds are more sensitive to changes in market interest rates.

6.2.1 Price Changes Depend on the Coupons

The coupon rate does not change during the life of a bond. Thus, the bond provides fixed cash flows to investors over its life. However, the price of the bond fluctuates as the coupon rate's attractiveness varies relative to other interest rates available at different times in the market. This exposes investors to risk.

We have seen that as interest rates go down, bond prices go up, and the magnitude of the price change depends on the maturity of the bond, with long-term bonds being more sensitive to changes in yield than short-term ones. However, the magnitude of the price changes also depends on the coupons paid by the bonds.

A comparison of the price evolution between coupon bonds and zero-coupon bonds when the YTM equals 4% and 5%, respectively, is revealing (see **Table 6.3**).

TABLE 6.3:   Price comparison: 6% coupon bond and zero-coupon bond with face values of €1,000

	One-year	Five-year	Ten-year	Twenty-year
6% Coupon bond				
YTM = 4%	€1,019.23	€1,089.04	€1,162.22	€1,271.81
YTM = 5%	€1,009.52	€1,043.29	€1,077.22	€1,124.62
% change in price	**−0.95%**	**−4.20%**	**−7.31%**	**−11.57%**
Zero-coupon bond				
YTM = 4%	€961.54	€821.93	€675.56	€456.39
YTM = 5%	€952.38	€783.53	€613.91	€376.89
% change in price	**−0.95%**	**−4.67%**	**−9.13%**	**−17.42%**

Comparing the results, we notice that changes in bond prices are greater for the zero-coupon bond, especially at longer maturities. The value of a coupon bond is determined by all its cash flows, whereas for a zero-coupon bond, the only cash flow is at maturity when the issuer repays the nominal value to the bondholder. The value of a zero-coupon 20-year bond is based solely on its final cash flow of €1,000, which occurs after 20 years, whereas the value of a coupon bond is based on the sum of all the discounted cash flows that occur during its life, i.e., €60 per year for the first 19 years and €1,060 in year 20.

Thus, when the yield increases, the 20-year zero-coupon bond is hit harder, and its price drops more steeply. This reflects the fact that longer-term cash flows are more affected by discount rate changes than shorter-term cash flows.

In conclusion, long-term bond prices fluctuate more than short-term bond prices. Also, if interest rates change, the price of bonds with higher coupons changes less than the price of those with lower coupons.

6.2.2   Returns to Bondholders — Changes in Bond Prices over Time

Even though the coupon and repayment of the principal are guaranteed with risk-free government bonds, this does not mean that investors who purchase such bonds do not incur any risk.

The total return for investors depends on the initial price paid, the coupons received, and the final selling price. The return for a holding period of one year is given by

$$return = \frac{(P_1 - P_0) + Coupon_1}{P_0} \qquad (6.1)$$

| P_1 is the selling price after holding the bond for one year, P_0 is the initial price paid, and $Coupon_1$ is the coupon received at the end of one year.

| The investor's total return is a combination of the coupon received and the change in price (selling price − buying price).

Consider a 10-year 4% coupon bond with a face value of €1,000. Assume that an investor buys the bond today at par for €1,000 (which implies a YTM of 4%) and holds it for one year.

One year from now, if the investor sells the bond in the market (after cashing in the first €40 coupon), the bond will have become a 9-year bond. But the price at which the investor will sell this bond (in one year) is not known today. However, we do know what cash flows the bond will provide: €40 for eight years and €1,040 in the final year (the ninth year).

If the YTM is still equal to 4% when the investor sells after a year, the price of the bond (which then has nine years of cash flows left) will be €1,000. In this case, there is no change in the price of the bond (bought and sold for €1,000), and the investor receives a €40 coupon payment at the end of the first year. Thus, the investor obtains a one-year return of 4%, which is exactly equal to the YTM expected when the bond was purchased.

However, the YTM available in the market one year from now is not guaranteed or known in advance. **Table 6.4** shows the price of the bond (which has become a 9-year bond with a coupon rate of 4%) one year from now, under different possible YTM values ranging from 2% to 6%.

TABLE 6.4: Price of a 9-year 4% coupon bond with a €1,000 face value with different YTMs

YTM (%)	Price (in €) of a 9-year 4% coupon bond with a face value of €1,000
2.00	1,163.24
3.00	1,077.86
4.00	1,000.00
5.00	928.92
6.00	863.97

This means that an investor who buys a 10-year bond with a one-year investment horizon can sell the bond (after one year) for a wide range of prices, depending on the YTM at the time of the sale.

The investment returns can differ significantly from the original 4% YTM. If interest rates go up during the year, and if the YTM in the market becomes 6% (up from 4%), then when the investor sells the bond, the selling price would be €863.97. Thus, the investor would have obtained a negative return on this one-year investment, even though it was a risk-free government bond. Indeed, in this case, the investor sells the bond for €863.97, thus effectively facing a capital loss of €136.03 (because the bond was originally bought for €1,000). The coupon received only partially alleviates this loss. In the end, the total return for holding the bond for one year is negative: −9.6%.[3]

Conversely, if interest rates go down during the year and the YTM in the market becomes 3%, by the time the investor sells the bond, the selling price will be €1,077.86. In this case, the investor will receive a return of 11.78%,[4] which is significantly higher than the original YTM.

For different YTMs after one year, the one-year holding-period returns are shown in **Table 6.5**.

---

[3] The return is given by $(863.97 - 1000 + 40)/1000 = -9.60\%$.

[4] The return is given by $(1077.86 - 1000 + 40)/1000 = +11.78\%$.

TABLE 6.5: Returns after one year for different YTMs

YTM at time of selling the bond (%)	Selling price (€)	Coupon received (€)	Selling price + coupon received (€)	Initial investment (€)	% Return (%)
2.00	1,163.24	40.00	1,203.24	1,000.00	20.32
3.00	1,077.86	40.00	1,117.86	1,000.00	11.79
4.00	1,000.00	40.00	1,040.00	1,000.00	4.00
5.00	928.92	40.00	968.92	1,000.00	–3.11
6.00	863.97	40.00	903.97	1,000.00	–9.60

If the bond is held for two or more years, the same principle applies. The investor's holding-period return will depend on the cash flows received (coupons) as well as the final selling price (which is always negatively related to the YTM at the time of selling).

The evidence in this section shows how, even with risk-free government bonds, investors can incur substantial risk if they invest in bonds with maturities that are different from their investment horizon.

6.3 YIELD CURVE AND RISK-FREE RATES

Interest rates in a particular country are not determined by any institution. Indeed, the commonly referred ECB (European Central Bank) or FED (Federal Reserve System) rates are just overnight rates, i.e., the rates that investors will receive for depositing their money with an institution for one night. In reality, the relevant interest rates for companies and investors are often the long-term rates. And long-term interest rates are determined by the price of long-term government bonds.

Every government bond with a different maturity has a distinctive YTM. The yield curve is the graphic representation of the required yields for bonds of different maturities.

Consider the following bonds issued by the UK government (also known as Gilts):

Maturity (years)	1	2	3	4	5	7	10
Coupon rate	2.75%	4.50%	2.00%	1.75%	5.00%	3.75%	2.25%
Price (£)	1021.50	1070.40	1018.10	1002.80	1145.50	1093.70	945.40

Because we know the prices of the above bonds (from December 2013), we can compute the YTM for each one by solving the individual bond pricing equations. For instance, for the one-year bond, which has a coupon rate of 2.75% and one year to maturity (meaning that in one year, investors will be paid the face value of £1,000, plus the coupon of £27.5), the YTM is given by

$$1021.5 = \frac{1027.5}{(1+Y_1)}$$

| Y_1 is the YTM of this one-year bond. In this case, $Y_1 = 0.59\%$.

For the 10-year bond, priced at £945.40, we have

$$945.40 = \frac{22.5}{(1+Y_{10})^1} + \frac{22.5}{(1+Y_{10})^2} + \frac{22.5}{(1+Y_{10})^3} + ... + \frac{1022.5}{(1+Y_{10})^{10}}$$

| Y_{10} is the YTM of this 10-year bond. In this case, $Y_{10} = 2.89\%$.[5]

Repeating the procedure for each of the above bonds, we obtain the *yield curve* shown in **Figure 6.4**. The yield curve (also called the *term structure of interest rates*) depicts the relationship that prevails at a given time in the marketplace between bond interest rates and maturities.

FIGURE 6.4: Yield curve for UK bonds with one- to ten-year maturities, December 2013.

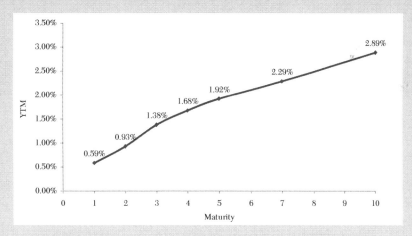

Because we are considering risk-free UK government bonds, the end result is a set of risk-free interest rates for different maturities. And each YTM reflects the rate demanded by investors in exchange for lending money to the UK government.

---

[5] This is equivalent to the internal rate of return (IRR). We know that the net present value (NPV) of the bond is its current price. We also know its cash flows over time: coupon payments and principal repayment at maturity. We can thus compute the IRR, which in this case is also called the YTM. In Excel, this can be obtained using "Goal Seek" or the IRR formula.

> # KEY LEARNING POINT
>
> *The yield curve is the graphic representation of the YTM for government bonds of different maturities.*

Historically, the slope of the yield curve has been the primary indicator of economic activity. An *upward sloping yield curve* (long-term rates higher than short-term ones) has often preceded an economic upturn. This is considered "normal" as the market expects more compensation for greater risk. As seen previously, longer-term bonds are exposed to more risks.

A *flat yield curve* typically signals an economic slowdown, and an *inverted yield curve* can signal a recession. When short-term yields are higher than long-term ones, investors expect interest rates to decline in the future, usually as a response to a slowing economy and lower inflation. For instance, the yield curve of July 2000 is represented at the right of **Figure 6.5.** The inverted yield curve correctly forecasted a recession, which would later occur (starting in June 2001). Typically, the yield curve becomes inverted 12 to 18 months before a recession.

FIGURE 6.5:   Yield curve for US bonds in May 2007 (left, flat yield curve), and July 2000 (right, downward sloping yield curve).

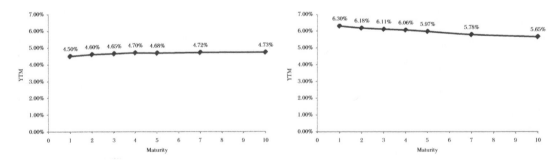

> # KEY LEARNING POINT
>
> *An inverted yield curve typically signals a recession coming in the next 12–18 months.*

6.4   BORROWING THROUGH CORPORATE BONDS

Until now we have been considering risk-free government bonds, where the coupon payments and the principal repayment are guaranteed — hence the name *risk-free bonds*. We now look at corporate bonds or, more generally, bonds with a potential default risk, which have the following features:

- The valuation principles are the same as for risk-free government bonds.
- The bond price is the present value of the bond's cash flows.
- There is a negative relationship between bond prices and the YTM.
- Bonds trade above par if the YTM is lower than the stated coupon rate and below par if the YTM is higher than the stated coupon rate.
- The price of long-term bonds is more sensitive to changes in the YTM than the price of short-term bonds.

The main difference between the two bond types is the YTM. In the case of corporate bonds, the rate required by investors is (for a given maturity) higher than the risk-free rate:

$$r_{corporate} = r_f + Spread \tag{6.2}$$

| $r_{corporate}$ is the corporate bond YTM (also called the *cost of debt*), r_f is the risk-free rate, and the spread is a function of the credit risk of the company.
| The spread is higher for riskier borrowers than for safer ones.
| The spread is higher for illiquid bonds than for liquid ones.

6.4.1   Credit Ratings and Credit Spreads

Credit ratings play an important role in helping investors make better-informed decisions and judge the risk of lending money to a given company. A credit rating is an opinion regarding the creditworthiness of an issuer (or of a specific bond).

The main global rating agencies are Moody's Investor Services (Moody's) and Standard & Poor's (S&P). **Table 6.6** shows their major rating categories.

Within each rating category, there are subcategories — also called *notches*. Moody's uses numbers (1 for the safest tier and 3 for the riskiest one), while S&P uses plus and minus signs. For instance, within the A category there are three different tiers/notches: Moody's has A1, A2, and A3; S&P has A+, A, and A-.

TABLE 6.6:   Rating categories for Moody's and S&P

	Moody's	S&P
Investment grade	Aaa	AAA
	Aa	AA
	A	A
	Baa	BBB
Junk bonds	Ba	BB
	B	B
	Caa	CCC
	Ca	CC
	C	C

Bonds with a rating equal to or above Baa3 (Moody's) or BBB- (S&P) are considered *investment grade*. Bonds with lower ratings are considered *speculative grade* — also called *junk bonds, sub-investment grade,* or *high-yield bonds.*[6]

KEY LEARNING POINT ✓

Junk or high-yield bonds are those with a credit rating below BBB- or Baa3 (by S&P and Moody's, respectively).

Rating agencies use a number of factors to analyze the risk of a company. It is important to remember that rating agencies are concerned about the risk to bondholders; thus, they are mainly concerned about two types of risks:

- The risk that the intermediate coupons will not be paid
- The risk that the final principal will not be paid

Several *financial factors* are used to assess these two risks. **Table 6.7** shows some indicators of companies in the different rating categories:

---

[6] An AAA rating suggests that an issuer has an extremely strong capacity to meet its financial obligations. A BBB rating suggests that the issuer has adequate resources to honor its commitment. However, in an adverse economic environment, such a rating can lead to a weakened capacity to meet the issuer's obligations. A company with a BB rating has some major ongoing uncertainties that could undermine its capacity to meet its financial commitments.

TABLE 6.7: Key financial ratios for global companies across different ratings

	Operating Margin (%)	EBIT/Interest Expense	Debt/ EBITDA	Debt/Book Capitalization (%)
Aaa	20.3	21.6	1.0	24.7
Aa	13.1	9.6	1.7	35.4
A	11.2	6.9	2.2	43.5
Baa	10.9	4.2	2.9	47.0
Ba	11.1	3.0	3.3	51.1
B	8.0	1.4	5.1	72.3
C	2.7	0.4	7.6	98.1

Source: Moody's Financial Metrics Key Ratios for Global Non-financial Corporations, December 2010.

The data in the third and fourth columns (Debt/EBITDA and Debt/Book Capitalization[7]) clearly show how ratings go down as debt increases. For instance, Debt/EBITDA = 2.9 (Baa) means that if the EBITDA stays constant and it is all used to repay debt, it will take 2.9 years on average to repay all the debt. Having a high Debt/EBITDA means that it is more difficult for the company to repay the outstanding debt. Also, as the company's ability to pay the interest costs decreases (EBIT/Interest Expense), the rating tends to be lower, as creditors perceive a higher risk of not being paid their coupons.

Rating agencies use many other *non-financial factors* to determine a company's credit rating — for instance, cyclicality of sales, product differentiation, geographical diversification, and asset tangibility. These business profile and geographic diversity factors are included because they indicate the capability of the company to pay its debts — the coupons and principal — in the future. Also, these factors take into account how differences in the company's operating model affect its ability to maintain its credit standing over the course of the economic cycle. **Table 6.8** shows some examples of important factors used in different sectors.

Different factors are used for different industries. In all cases, the rating agencies define the factors and then apply them consistently to all the companies in a certain sector. For instance, proved reserves, replacement of reserves, and development costs are important factors in rating companies in the oil sector. In the airline sector, the fleet age is a proxy indicator for operating efficiency and future investment needs.

---

[7] Equity of the firm at book value.

TABLE 6.8:   Non-financial factors used by rating agencies across sectors

Oil	Software	Airlines	Retailers	Alcoholic beverages
Proved reserves	Product line diversity	Fleet age	Product range	Brand diversification
Finding and development (F&D) costs[8]	Geographic diversity	Geographic diversity	Market concentration	Innovation and organic growth
Crude distillation capacity	End-market diversity	Business profile	Geographic presence	Market position
Reserve replacement	Market share	Financial policy	Quality of execution	Geographic diversification

KEY LEARNING POINT

Credit ratings depend on a number of company-specific factors, which include financial and non-financial metrics.

Given that ratings assess the potential default risk, lower ratings are associated with a higher cost of debt. **Table 6.9** shows the average spread (above a risk-free bond with similar maturity) required by investors for different investment-grade and speculative-grade bonds.

TABLE 6.9:   Credit spreads for different ratings

Investment grade		Speculative grade	
AAA	0.21%	BB+	2.18%
AA	0.34%	BB	2.41%
A+	0.48%	BB-	2.64%
A	0.56%	B+	3.14%
A-	0.88%	B	3.41%
BBB+	0.94%	B-	4.08%
BBB	1.13%		
BBB-	1.70%		

Source: Bloomberg, January 2014.

---
[8] The cost of doing business for companies in the sector.

The corporate bond YTM thus represents the cost of debt for a company. Suppose the risk-free rate equals 4%. The above credit spread indicates that an AAA borrower pays on average 4.21% (risk-free rate of 4% + spread of 0.21%) for its debt. For a BBB borrower that wants to issue debt as of January 2014, the above data suggest that the total borrowing costs (or YTM) are on average 5.13% (4% + 1.13%).

6.4.2   Credit Spreads Change over Time

Credit spreads are not constant. From an investor's perspective, the prices of corporate bonds fluctuate as credit spreads widen or narrow. In general, corporate bond prices increase when spreads narrow. **Figure 6.6** shows the evolution of the average credit spreads for issuers of different ratings from 2005 to 2013.

FIGURE 6.6:   Corporate bond spreads.

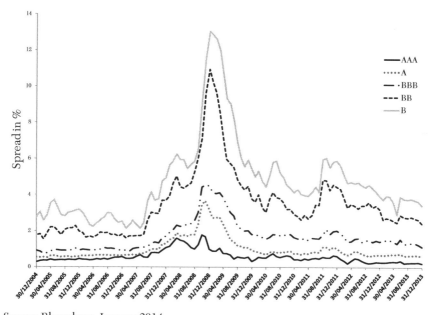

Source: Bloomberg, January 2014.

All spreads increased significantly during the financial crisis of 2008/09. However, **Figure 6.6** also shows that the increase in spreads was not constant across the different rating categories. Indeed, the spreads increased mostly for issuers of lower-quality credit.

The company (and its management) has some control over its own rating, but not over the overall spreads in the market. The above data show how the cost of debt for a certain issuer changes substantially over time, even if its credit rating does not change. This means that if substantial refinancing is required, the company never knows exactly what the cost of debt (or spreads) will be in a certain period. Chapter 2 also shows data on the risk-free rate for different countries over the last two decades.

KEY LEARNING POINT

The cost of financing can change significantly — even if a company's fundamental indicators remain unchanged — because of changes in the credit market.

6.4.3   Who Buys Corporate Bonds?

Buyers of bonds are mainly large institutional investors such as pension funds, insurance companies, mutual funds, and sovereign wealth funds. The bond market has traditionally not been designed for individual investors.[9] This is mainly owing to the high costs involved in trading small quantities of bonds. Indeed, the typical trade is much higher than trades of equities in the stock exchanges. The average size of a bond trade is between €1 million and €2 million. Trades above €100 million are frequent.[10]

In addition, the majority of bonds trade very infrequently, unlike equities, because there is not a constant supply of buyers and sellers looking to trade. This lack of liquidity is also important in determining which investors buy bonds. Most buyers tend to be long-term investors, who simply hold the bonds in their portfolios. For instance, research evidence[11] suggests that approximately 50% of bond issues do not trade at all in a certain year, and only about 20% of the bonds trade more than 10 days in a year.

---

[9] With the exception of municipal bonds in the US.

[10] *Source:* International Capital Market Association.

[11] See Mahanti et al. (2008) for evidence on the buy-and-hold strategies of long-term investors, who typically have a low portfolio turnover.

Apple Bonds

In April 2013, Apple sold bonds worth $17 billion, with maturities of 3, 5, 10, and 30 years. Apple stated that the proceeds would be used to finance part of the previously announced $100 billion cash return to shareholders. The company paid $53 million in fees (0.31% of the funds raised) to underwriters led by Goldman Sachs and Deutsche Bank. Apple's fees were significantly lower than those for deals from other high-grade companies, likely because of the large size of the sale. Investors came from different markets, including foreign investors, pension funds, insurance companies, and hedge funds.

As shown earlier, lower-rated bonds typically offer a higher yield, making them attractive investment vehicles for certain types of investors. However, many pension funds and insurance companies (who are the largest investors in bond markets worldwide) are prohibited by their by-laws from investing in junk bonds. As a result, junk-bond issuers have a different investor base than investment-grade bonds, and the liquidity of this market is lower than for highly rated bonds. Thus, the cost of debt when a company has a junk bond rating is significantly higher than when it has an investment-grade rating.

KEY LEARNING POINT ✓

Many institutional investors cannot invest in high-yield bonds.

6.4.4 Retail Bonds

Recently, retail bonds issues have been growing in importance, and for many companies they are increasingly being seen as an alternative to traditional bond markets and bank loans.

Retail bonds are bonds that are sold mainly to individual private investors looking for an alternative to traditional savings products.

Borealis Retail Bonds

Borealis, a company specialized in chemical and plastics solutions, issued a retail-targeted corporate bond in July 2012. The nominal amount of each bond was €1,000, with a maturity of seven years. After a road show in Vienna and conference calls with analysts and banks, individual investors started placing their orders. Owing to strong investor demand from Austrian savers (in two hours, the orders had already exceeded the planned amount of the issue), the final amount placed by Borealis was €125 million (up from the originally planned €100 million), and the coupon rate was set at the lower end of the expected range at 4%. "The Austrian bond is a significant step in an overall strategy to diversify our funding investor base while extending our maturity profile," said Daniel Shook, Borealis CFO.

KEY LEARNING POINT

Traditionally, bonds were only bought by large institutional investors, but some companies have now placed retail bond issues, in which the bonds are bought by individual private investors.

6.4.5   Selecting the Right Maturity for Debt

Once the amount of debt to issue has been decided, an important consideration is the actual maturity of the bonds (short term: less than 1 year, or long term: more than 1 year).[12] Several factors must be taken into account when determining the maturity. First, what cash flows are going to be generated as a result of this bond financing (in new investments, for instance)? Second, what are the company's expected cash flows over time? Third, is additional refinancing planned?

On average, short-term debt is relatively cheaper, as long-term rates are typically higher than short-term ones (see section 6.3). However, short-term debt requires frequent renegotiation of terms, and possible changes in interest rates. Therefore, companies that have a high proportion of short-term debt can see their interest costs spike up (also called *rollover risk*). This was a frequent problem for many companies (with mostly short-term debt) during the 2008/2009 financial crisis.

On the other hand, long-term debt is relatively more expensive, as long-term rates are on average higher than short-term ones. But it is more stable and less risky (from the company's point of view) than short-term debt.

Empirically speaking, the maturity of debt varies significantly across companies. Some companies have very short-maturity debt, whereas others have longer-maturity debt. Research

---

[12] When a company raises short-term debt using debt capital markets, it issues commercial paper (the term bond is only used for maturities above 1 year). Typically, only companies with high-quality ratings have access to a liquid commercial paper market.

shows that companies that are larger, profitable, and have more tangible assets tend to have more long-term debt.[13] In general, larger companies can more easily raise long-term debt. In smaller companies, the asymmetry of information between shareholders and lenders is particularly high. As a result, lenders typically restrict the length of maturity offered.[14] The tangibility of assets is positively related to debt maturity, which suggests that companies try to match the maturity of assets with that of liabilities. Companies with more long-term assets also tend to have longer-maturity debt.

Ford 30-year bonds

In January 2013, Ford, the second-largest US automaker, issued $2 billion of bonds, maturing in 30 years. The 4.75% coupon bonds are due in January 2043. The proceeds from the sale will be used to refinance debt and to fund the company's pension plan. The bonds were ultimately placed at a yield of 180 basis points above similar-maturity Treasury bonds. Investors included pension funds, municipalities, and insurance companies. Neil Schloss, Ford's treasurer, commented: "There is a desire to lengthen our maturity profile on average … The auto company has a longer duration because we're financing long-lived assets, investments in plants and equipment."[15]

Companies also try to smooth their leverage requirements to match their cash flows over time. Smoothing the leverage means issuing several bonds (or loans) with a range of maturities, so that only part of the debt has to be paid (or renegotiated/renewed) each year. A good practice, used by many companies, is to match the forecasted cash flows from operations with bond payments (coupon and principal repayments) in an effort to avoid significant mismatches in any year. Also, companies with more business risk (for instance, volatility in return on assets — ROA) tend to smooth their leverage requirements over time, so that they are not forced to renegotiate short-term debt frequently[16] and in a period when their ROA is low.

KEY LEARNING POINT

The maturity structure of debt depends on the business the company is in and the company's forecasted capital needs.

---

[13] See Fernandes (2011) for a complete analysis of determinants of the choices between long- and short-term debt for 30,000 companies around the world.
[14] See Barnea, Haugen, and Senbet (1980); Barclay and Smith (1995).
[15] *Source:* Bloomberg News.
[16] See Guedes and Opler (1996).

6.4.6   Bond Spreads and Liquidity

The liquidity of a market reflects how easy or costly it is for buyers and sellers to be matched. A liquid market is a market where traders can buy and sell something, without large transaction costs, and above all, without significantly affecting the market price. As expected, the liquidity of a market depends on how many people actively trade in it. And investors demand a liquidity premium for illiquid securities.[17]

Liquidity is a qualitative measure, and there is no exact way of measuring it. However, it is typically quantified using

- Trading volume — This is the number of trades of a certain asset over a period of time. A higher number of trades is associated with higher liquidity.
- Bid-ask spread — This is the difference between the highest price that a buyer is willing to pay, and the lowest price for which a seller is willing to sell. Higher bid-ask spreads reflect the low liquidity of the asset. If there are no outstanding orders (either buy or sell), the bid-ask spread is not available.
- The percentage of days in a year with zero percent returns — If the price does not move during a certain day, that is an indication of low liquidity.[18]

Corporate bond markets are often illiquid. After a bond is originally sold by the company, many investors (who bought in the primary bond issue) do not trade actively (in the secondary market[19]), and follow a buy-and-hold approach.[20] As a consequence, corporate bond spreads also reflect liquidity (in addition to credit risk). That means that for the same promised cash flows, illiquid bonds have lower prices and higher yield spreads.[21]

KEY LEARNING POINT ✓

Illiquid bonds pay investors higher spreads.

---

[17] See Amihud and Mendelson (1986).

[18] Empirically, this measure has been found to be an effective liquidity measure (see Lesmond, Ogden, and Trzcinka (1999), Lesmond, Schill, and Zhou (2004)) and Bekaert, Harvey, and Lundblad (2007)).

[19] Also called *aftermarket*. A secondary market is the market or exchange in which previously issued financial instruments are bought and sold.

[20] Edwards, Harris, and Piwowar (2007) find that the median bond trades less than 50% of the days. Also, across 20,000 corporate bonds, the average number of trades per day is 2.4 (median 1.1).

[21] Chen, Lesmond, and Wei (2007) investigate over 4,000 corporate bonds (investment and high-yield) and find that more illiquid bonds have higher yield spreads. See also Longstaff, Mithal, and Neis (2005), Edwards, Harris, and Piwowar (2007), Chen, Lesmond, and Wei (2007), Bao, Pan, and Wang (2011), and Lin, Wang, and Wu (2011) for additional evidence on the effects of liquidity on corporate bonds.

Research has revealed that the liquidity of corporate bonds is influenced by the following factors:

- *Issuance size:* Bonds with a larger issuance size are in general more liquid.[22] Smaller-sized issues tend to be held by a small number of investors, which leads to low liquidity in the secondary market.

- *Age:* Recently issued bonds have higher liquidity. As the bond gets "older," fewer investors will actively trade the bond. When a bond is initially issued, it is called "on the run." It has a much higher liquidity than later on (when it starts to be called "off the run").

- *Time to maturity:* Typically, longer-term bonds are less liquid. Bonds close to maturity are more liquid.

- *Rating:* As discussed in section 6.4.3, the majority of long-term investors (pension funds, insurance companies, etc.) are prohibited from investing in high-yield bonds. As a result, high-yield bond issuers have a different investor base compared to investment-grade bonds. In practice, high-yield bonds tend to have higher liquidity.[23]

6.4.7   Credit Default Swaps

Credit ratings provide an assessment of the credit risk of a particular issuer. Credit default swaps (CDSs) are also frequently used as measures of risk.

A CDS is a derivative contract that relates to the credit risk of a particular company or country. In a CDS, there are two counterparties:

- One party sells insurance: It receives a premium, and if a certain event occurs, it must pay the losses.

- The other party buys insurance: It pays a yearly premium for protection against certain events.

This insurance — and thus the payments on a CDS — is tied to the financial health of a particular issuer. The buyer of insurance pays a fee (or premium) in advance and, in exchange, receives compensation if there is a credit event in the company or country of a particular CDS. The CDS market is a very liquid market[24] and allows investors to protect themselves against credit events such as the deferral (or reduction) of the payment of interest or the principal amount.[25]

---

[22] See Bao, Pan, and Wang (2011).
[23] See Mahanti et al. (2008).
[24] As in any other over-the-counter market, counterparty risk is present.
[25] The standards for CDS contracts are defined by the International Swaps and Derivatives Association (ISDA).

Figure 6.7 shows the CDS spreads (in basis points[26]) of the nominal amount covered for different countries as of January 2014.

FIGURE 6.7: CDS SPREADS FOR DIFFERENT COUNTRIES.

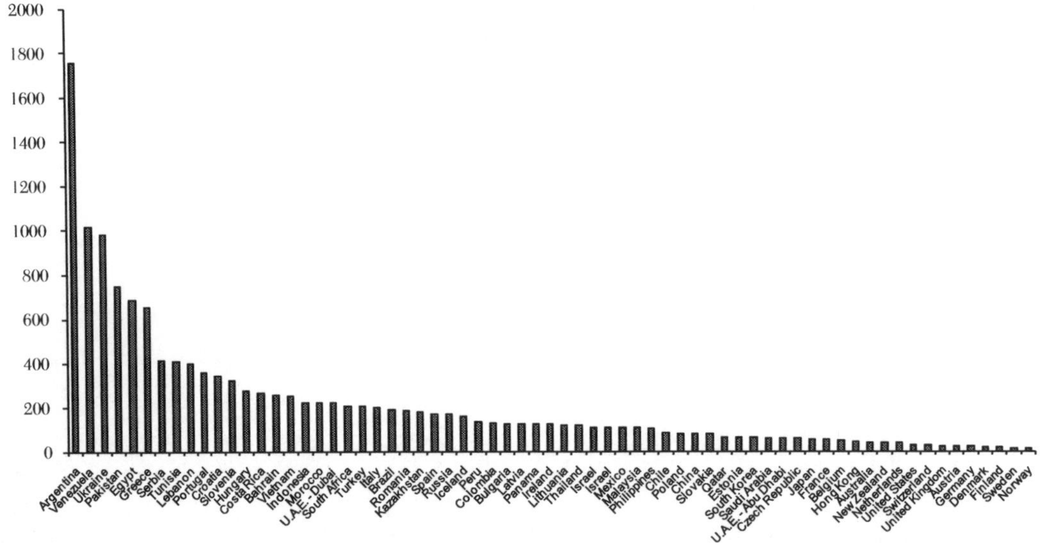

Source: Bloomberg, January 2014.

The CDS spread for Vietnam is 271 b.p. This means that an investor who wants to protect against the default of Vietnamese government bonds must pay 2.71% of the nominal value under protection. Suppose the investor wants to protect a portfolio of $100 million of Vietnamese government bonds. In this case, the annual premium for protection at today's prices would be $2.71 million ($100,000,000 × 0.0271). If there is a subsequent default on the Vietnamese bonds, the investor who bought the CDS would be compensated and receive the promised amount ($100 million) from the CDS seller.

CDSs also exist for companies (see **Table 6.10** for a few examples).

---

[26] 100 basis points (b.p.) equal 1%.

TABLE 6.10: Company CDSs

	CDS spread (in b.p.)
Exxon Mobil	20
Shell	48
BP	64
Microsoft	38
Citigroup	121

Source: Bloomberg, January 2014.

In general, companies that are riskier borrowers have higher CDS spreads. Safer companies, where default is very unlikely, have lower CDS spreads.

A large institutional investor has bought some bonds issued by Microsoft. The investor expects to receive a stream of payments from Microsoft over the years (including coupon payments and the principal repayment at maturity). But the investor is now concerned that Microsoft might go bankrupt. The chances are small, but they are greater than zero. If this happens, the investor will no longer receive any payments. In such a situation, the investor might decide to buy a CDS, which works like an insurance policy. The investor would then pay a periodic premium (a percentage of the total amount covered) to the protection seller (insurer). If Microsoft never goes bankrupt, the investor will have paid the premium and received nothing in return. However, if Microsoft does become bankrupt (and stops paying its bondholders), the investor will receive this money from the CDS seller to compensate for the losses on the bond.

The CDS market provides an alternative way (relative to credit spreads using corporate bonds) to identify the cost of debt for different issuers. Given their high liquidity and the fact that they are priced daily, CDS premiums reflect the current perception of risk that investors see in the debt of a particular issuer.

KEY LEARNING POINT ✓

The CDS market provides evidence about the credit risk of a particular issuer. Higher CDS spreads are associated with a higher probability of a credit event.

6.5   BORROWING THROUGH BANK LOANS

For many companies, taking a bank loan is an alternative to issuing bonds. Most of the principles that apply to bank loans also apply to bonds, but there are some differences between bank loans and bonds (see **Table 6.11**).

TABLE 6.11:   Differences between bank loans and corporate bonds

Bank loans	Corporate bonds
The interest rate is determined by the bank, which uses its internal risk models to assess risk	The interest rate is determined in the market and is typically related to the company's rating
Banks generally demand collateral[27]	Collateral is not generally required
Can be used for smaller sums	Are usually issued in large amounts
Rely on the relationship with a particular bank (or a few banks)	Help to make the company better known in the capital markets
Concentrate the borrowing with a single bank (or a few)	Funds are obtained from a diversified pool of investors

The bank will analyze the company's credit risk and determine what spread to charge the company. And this spread (based on the bank's internal rating system) will be higher for riskier borrowers.

Bank loans usually have several covenants.[28] If these covenants are breached, the bank typically has the right to call in the loan and force the company to pay back the full amount of debt immediately. Covenants are intended to protect the lender, by mitigating risk and ensuring the loan is repaid. But if the bank loan is terminated earlier by the bank, the company will be put in a very difficult position.

Roche and the Genentech Acquisition Financing

In July 2008, Roche announced the purchase of all outstanding Genentech shares,[29] in a deal valued at $43 billion. To finance the deal, a syndicated bank loan was planned, and banks from around the world had offered to finance it. However, after Lehman Brothers collapsed on September 15,

---

[27] Assets that can be sold off if the issuer defaults on loan payments — these can include land, buildings, financial instruments, and any other assets.

[28] Covenants are promises stated within the formal debt agreement that certain activities will not be carried out. These rules are designed to reduce the risk to which the bank is exposed. Typical covenants include limits on the kinds and levels of debt until the bank loan is paid off, restrictions on asset sales, limits on acquisitions, minimum ratios that the company must maintain, and the like.

[29] Roche had owned a majority stake in Genentech since 1990.

2008, banks froze their lending activities, and all the finance for the deal evaporated overnight. Roche then decided to target bond market investors and embarked on a road show, with a compelling story for investors: This is a long-term deal, in real assets, that will pay off regardless of the financial crisis. Ultimately, the bond issue was completed for a total of $42 billion, split between the US ($19 billion), Europe (€11.25 billion and £1.25 billion), and Switzerland (CHF 8 billion). This record amount was possible because Roche had devised many different tranches of bonds, with maturities ranging from 6 months to 30 years, across many different currencies. This strategy suited the needs (and cash flow generation) of the company and, more importantly, the amounts and currencies were tailored to the needs and preferences of different types of bond investors.

Bank loans are an important financing option for many companies around the world. However, using only bank loans can be challenging in some situations and can represents a risky debt choice.

Banks and public debt markets compete to provide capital (either bank loans or bonds) to companies. As expected, companies that use this competition to their advantage gain significant benefits. First, they have lower financing costs: companies with public debt access pay lower spreads, even when they are borrowing money from a bank. Second, what happens if the banks fall into difficulties, as happened during the 2008/2009 financial crisis? Companies that rely exclusively on bank loans will face increasing difficulty in renewing their loans or will have to pay much higher rates to do so.[30] Bank-only companies also suffer substantial losses and reduction in profitability during crisis periods, and have to cut capital expenditure heavily in order to pay bank loans (much more than companies that have access to the public debt market).[31]

Banks are still the dominant supplier of external finance in many economies around the world. For instance, in Europe the role of banks has traditionally been much more important than in the US, where capital markets play a greater role in financing companies. The empirical evidence shows that the more advanced the capital market is, in particular for high-yield smaller-size borrowers, the less dependent the economy is on bank lending.

The access to public debt markets facilitates access to different investors and often allows the company to increase the amount of debt raised, at a lower risk for the company. Therefore, diversifying the sources of funding is a key recommendation for most companies.

---

[30] Brunnermeier (2010), Ivashina and Scharfstein (2010), and Santos (2011) find that loan spreads increased substantially during the 2007–2008 subprime crisis period. Santos (2011) also finds that the increase in loan spreads was higher for firms that borrowed from banks which incurred larger losses. Puri, Rocholl, and Steffen (2011) find that the US financial crisis also induced a contraction in bank lending in Germany. But the contraction is smaller when the company has a strong relation with the bank, for instance, by having also a bank-depositor relationships. See Boot (2000) for a review of the literature on the costs and benefits of relationship banking.
[31] Chava and Purnanandam (2011) find that rated firms, which have access to public debt markets, are likely to be less dependent on banks.

6.6   HYBRID FINANCING INSTRUMENTS

Several types of hybrid instruments exist, which can be seen as normal bonds combined with some additional options. These instruments are useful in different contexts, and allow for a different trade-off between return and risk than normal bonds. The name *hybrid* means that these are not just debt instruments, but also have exposure to the equity of the company.

6.6.1   Callable Bonds

Some bonds are issued with call provisions. This means that the company that issued the bond can call (buy back) the bond before maturity — *callable bond*. The terms under which the bond can be called are defined ex-ante. From the issuing company's point of view, a callable bond is a normal bond combined with a call option (see chapter 13). This call option is useful if interest rates in the market decrease after the bond issue. The company can then use the option to replace existing bonds with new ones at lower interest rates. Given that this call option is valuable for the issuer, callable bonds pay a higher interest rate than normal bonds. Or if we consider the perspective of the investor who buys callable bonds, they are in practice investing in a bond, and selling a call option.

6.6.2   Convertible Bonds

These hybrid convertible bonds are bonds that can be converted into common shares. The number of shares into which each bond can be converted is defined by the conversion ratio. This instrument is a hybrid of debt and equity, as the owner of the bond has the option to convert it into equity at a fixed ratio. Thus, if the stock goes up, the option is exercised, and the investor converts the bond into shares. However, if the stock price goes down, the investor keeps the bond (receiving the promised coupon and principal).

In May 2013, Tesla Motors, a US electrical car maker, announced a $450 million convertible bond issue. The bond has a coupon rate of 1.5, and the conversion premium is 35%. This means investors can convert the bonds into stocks if Tesla shares rise 35% from the stock price in May. The convertible offering was very successful with investors who wanted exposure to the company's growth.

For investors, convertible bonds are a normal bond combined with a call option on the company's stock. Investors have the option to convert the bond into shares, if this is profitable for them. For companies, convertible bonds can be an interesting financing alternative, as they allow for a lower interest rate to be paid in exchange for granting investors the option to convert the bonds into shares.

6.6.3   Contingent Convertibles (CoCos)

Contingent convertibles (also known as CoCo bonds, or CoCos) are slightly different from regular convertible bonds in that the conversion is "contingent" on a specified event, such as the stock price of the company exceeding a particular level for a certain period of time. CoCos are hybrids of debt and equity, as they are designed to convert into shares if a pre-set trigger value is breached. However, if the trigger value is not breached, they continue as normal bonds.

This is an instrument that gained popularity in the aftermath of the financial crisis of 2008. Financial institutions were required to increase their capital buffers in order to weather economic crises without having to be bailed out by the taxpayer. This led to the popularity of this new financial instrument. The typical version of CoCos will be converted into equity if the bank capital ratios drop below a certain threshold. That means that if business conditions worsen, and the bank capital ratios go down, the debt is converted into equity, which immediately raises the bank capital ratio.

In 2009, Lloyds issued £9 billion of *contingent convertible bonds*. These bonds pay a higher than usual coupon rate. They are convertible into equity of Lloyds if the regulator declares that the core tier one capital ratio has fallen below 5%. In that situation, the conversion of its CoCos would push the ratio above 6.5%.

In 2010, the Dutch bank Rabobank issued €1.25 billion of *contingent bonds*. These are contingent, but not convertible. If Rabobank's core capital ratio falls below 7%, the bond amount is written down to 25%. That is, in case the equity ratio of the bank falls, the effective bond debt is reduced to one-fourth. In exchange for this additional risk, these bonds pay a high coupon rate (6.875%).

In 2013 Credit Suisse issued a $2.5 billion *wipeout* bond. This is also called a *sudden death* because investors stand to lose everything. In normal conditions, the bond yields 6.5% per year. However, if the bank breaches a trigger (5% tier one capital ratio) at any time over the life of the bonds, they will immediately lose their value.

The above examples highlight the two types of CoCos to date: those that convert into equity and those that are written off (either entirely or partially). These bonds appeal to different investors, who are typically less risk averse and are looking for higher yields. In order to balance the risk of losing capital, the coupon paid for these hybrid bonds is much higher than for a traditional bond.

From the banks' perspective, CoCos have several advantages. First, they are recognized as core equity capital, and thus improve the solvency ratios of the issuing institutions. Second, they are not treated as debt by the rating agencies, and thus do not affect the rating. Third, they enable the issuer to avoid the immediate dilution of long-standing shareholders' through a capital increase. Finally, they offer funding that will not need repayment in case the business environment turns south (the debt is wiped out completely, or is converted into equity).

SUMMARY

In this chapter, we have discussed debt financing and its costs. We started by identifying the risk-free rate and showing that there is a negative relationship between the interest rates required by the market (YTM) and bond prices. We also showed how long-term bonds are more sensitive to changes in market interest rates than short-term ones. Overall, even if an investor invests in a government bond without credit risk, it is subject to losses if the investment horizon is different from the bond maturity.

Corporate bonds (as well as loans) have a spread above the risk-free rate, and this spread varies according to the riskiness of the company and the liquidity of the bonds. Rating agencies use a number of company-specific factors that include both financial and non-financial metrics to assess the credit risk of companies. Importantly, credit spreads are not constant, which means that the rate at which an issuer can finance itself varies over time, even if its credit rating does not change.

For many companies, issuing bonds opens up a new source of financing. It is important to bear in mind that tapping the bond market for the first time takes a while. The company must meet with potential investors, prepare the necessary filings with regulators and exchanges and, most important, the company must have a rating from an agency.[32] Currently, the main investors in bond markets are large institutional investors such as pension funds, insurance companies, mutual funds, and sovereign wealth funds. But there is a trend in the market toward retail bonds — smaller bonds that are bought by individual investors.

Bank loans are another financing option. We discuss the difference between obtaining debt financing through bank loans and through bonds. One important point is that restricting all credit lines to loans is a dangerous concentration of risk, and can expose the company to problems when banks decide to reduce the amount of loans they grant (which is what

---

[31] In some cases, this is not mandatory, for instance, when the bond is only sold to US QIBs (qualified institutional buyers) under Rule 144A. This rule requires QIBs to have at least $100 million of assets under management.

happened after the financial crisis of 2008/2009). The bond market facilitates access to different investors and often allows the company to increase the amount of debt raised.

REFERENCES

Amihud, Y., and H. Mendelson, 1986, Asset Pricing and the Bid-Ask Spread, *Journal of Financial Economics*, Vol. 17, Iss 2:223–249.

Bao, J., J. Pan, and J. Wang, 2011, The Illiquidity of Corporate Bonds, *The Journal of Finance*, Vol. 66, Iss. 3:911–946.

Barclay, M.J., and C.W. Smith, 1995, The Maturity Structure of Corporate Debt, *Journal of Finance*, Vol. 50, Iss. 2:609–631.

Barnea, A., R. Haugen, and L. Senbet, 1980, A Rationale for Debt Maturity Structure and Call Provisions in the Agency Theory Framework, *Journal of Finance*, Vol. 35, Iss. 5:1223–1234.

Bekaert, G., C. Harvey, and C. Lundblad, 2007, Liquidity and Expected Returns: Lessons from Emerging Markets, *Review of Financial Studies*, Vol. 20, Iss. 6:1783–1831.

Boot, A., 2000, Relationship Banking: What Do We Know?, *Journal of Financial Intermediation*, Vol. 9, Iss. 1:7–25.

Brunnermeier, M., 2010, Deciphering the Liquidity and Credit Crunch 2007–2008, *Journal of Economic Perspectives*, Vol. 23, Iss. 1:77–100.

Chava, S., and A. Purnanandam, 2011, The Effect of Banking Crisis on Bank-Dependent Borrowers, *Journal of Financial Economics*, Vol. 99, Iss. 1:116–35.

Chen, L., D. Lesmond, and J. Wei, 2007, Corporate Yield Spreads and Bond Liquidity, *Journal of Finance*, Vol. 62, Iss. 1:119–149.

Edwards, A.K., L.E. Harris, and M.S. Piwowar, 2007. Corporate Bond Market Transaction Costs and Transparency, *The Journal of Finance*, Vol. 62, Iss. 3:1421–1451.

Fernandes, N., 2011, Global Convergence of Financing Policies: Evidence for Emerging-Market Firms, *Journal of International Business Studies*, Vol. 42, Iss. 9:1043–1059.

Guedes, J., and T. Opler, 1996, The Determinants of the Maturity of Corporate Debt Issues, *Journal of Finance*, Vol. 51, Iss. 5:1809–1833.

Ivashina, V., and D. Scharfstein, 2010, Bank Lending during the Financial Crisis of 2008, *Journal of Financial Economics*, Vol. 97, Iss. 3:319–38.

Lesmond, D., J. Ogden, and C. Trzcinka, 1999, A New Estimate of Transaction Costs, *Review of Financial Studies*, Vol. 12, Iss. 5:1113–1141.

Lesmond, D., M. Schill, and C. Zhou, 2004, The Illusory Nature of Momentum Profits, *Journal of Financial Economics*, Vol. 71, Iss. 3:349–380.

Longstaff, F.A., S. Mithal, and E. Neis, 2005, Corporate Yield Spreads: Default Risk or Liquidity? New Evidence from the Credit Default Swap Market, *The Journal of Finance*, Vol. 60, Iss. 5:2213–2253.

Lin H., J. Wang, and C. Wu, 2011, Liquidity Risk and the Cross-Section of Expected Corporate Bond Returns, *Journal of Financial Economics*, Vol. 99, Iss. 3:628–650.

Mahanti, S., Nashikkar, A., M. Subrahmanyam, G. Chacko, and G. Mallik, 2008, Latent Liquidity: A New Measure of Liquidity, with an Application to Corporate Bonds, *Journal of Financial Economics*, Vol. 88, Iss. 2:272–298.

Puri, M., J. Rocholl, and S. Steffen, 2011, Global Retail Lending in the Aftermath of the U.S. Financial Crisis: Distinguishing Between Supply and Demand Effects, *Journal of Financial Economics*, Vol. 100, Iss. 3:556–78.

Santos, J., 2011, Bank Loan Pricing Following the Subprime Crisis, *Review of Financial Studies*, Vol. 24, Iss. 6:1916–43.

Raising Equity — IPOs and SEOs

Internally generated cash is the major source of funds for most companies. But when internally generated cash is not enough to fund operations or expansion projects, companies must raise additional capital from debt and equity investors.

This chapter covers the main principles behind equity-issuing activities. We describe the various forms of equity capital as well as how companies use equity markets to raise capital.

7.1 WHY SHOULD A COMPANY GO PUBLIC?

Companies decide to go public, i.e., sell their shares on a stock exchange, for a variety of reasons. The most important reason for companies to go public is to raise investment capital.[1] Besides the direct cash aspect (either a new cash injection for the company or cash to its previous shareholders), there are other benefits of going public:

- Companies can use the market value of the stock as a metric for performance evaluation and to compare the company's performance against that of its competitors.[2]

- Companies get an opportunity to reward management and employees with stocks or options, thus linking their rewards to the company's stock price.

- Companies can diversify their sources of funding at a lower cost.

- Companies that are publicly traded can use their stock rather than cash to pay for acquisitions, which facilitates growth.

- Companies' shareholders will benefit from higher liquidity because they can more easily dispose of their shares when necessary.

---

[1] Kim and Weisbach (2010) show that cash savings is the largest use of proceeds from initial public offerings.

[2] In the privatization setting, Megginson, Nash, and van Randenborgh (1994) show that companies that go public increase sales and capital investment, and improve their efficiency and profitability.

However, there are also some disadvantages associated with being a publicly traded company:

- Direct costs (fees) related to the stock exchange and the public issue of stocks, which are relatively small
- Additional disclosure requirements and scrutiny by regulators
- Mandatory reporting of (usually) quarterly results, which may lead to an excessive focus on short-term results
- Potential liability for directors and officers
- Less control over the company's shareholder base

Primary and secondary offerings

In many cases, when companies go public, the issue is intended to raise new capital for the company. This is called a *primary offering*. In this case, the company offers a new block of shares for sale to the public, and the net proceeds of the sale will be available for the company's use, often in growth-related projects. The investors pay for the new shares, and the cash is injected into the company.

But there are also occasions when no new capital enters the company when it goes public. This is called a *secondary offering*. In this case, the shares that were sold on the stock exchange belong to the previous shareholders. In this case, no new cash enters the company, and the new shareholders simply buy shares from the old shareholders.

In addition, companies can also go public with a combination of primary and secondary shares.

7.2   BECOMING A PUBLIC TRADED COMPANY — INITIAL PUBLIC OFFERINGS

An initial public offering (IPO) is the process by which the company sells stock to the public for the first time.[3] It typically follows a standard process:

1. The financial advisor (which can be a single investment bank or a syndicate of several investment banks that manages the IPO) is appointed. The IPO mechanism and thus the arrangement with the bank is set; this includes an agreement on fees and possibly an underwriting[4] agreement.

---

[3] Subsequent sales of shares are done through a seasoned equity offering (SEO).

[4] When an IPO is underwritten, the underwriting firm or syndicate takes the responsibility, and the risk, of selling a specific allotment of shares.

2. The preliminary prospectus is prepared, and the company is registered with the securities regulator (e.g., the US Securities Exchange Commission (SEC)).

3. The company's shares are promoted via a road show[5] with potential investors.

4. Following the road show, the company and financial advisor agree on the issue price.

5. The financial advisor allots the stock to investors (which may include keeping some shares on the books of the investment banks involved).

6. Trading of the stock starts on the stock exchange.

Investment banks prepare the necessary filings, help market the IPO and sell the shares, and actively participate in determining the selling price. In addition, in most cases, the underwriters also commit to undertake market-making activities[6] for the stock during a certain period (and sometimes dedicate a sell-side analyst[7] to cover the new stock). The objective is to guarantee that the stock will be liquid in the post-IPO period.

7.2.1 A Firm Commitment Lowers the Risk to the Company

The contract with the financial advisor may include a guarantee (firm commitment) that the underwriter (the investment bank or the financial advisor working with the company) will sell all the stocks in the IPO issue. Should the underwriter (or the syndicate) not be able to find enough investors, the underwriter will have to hold the leftover stocks on its balance sheet. This, of course, increases the risk to the underwriter, who bears the entire risk of selling the stock. Naturally, the fees the company pays to the investment bank will be higher, as it must compensate the bank for this additional risk.

A firm commitment is not without risks

In October 1987, the British government sold its remaining 31.5% stake in BP. This deal was underwritten right before the stock market plunge that occurred a few days later.[8] The agreed price was 330 pence, and the total issue amounted to 2.1 billion shares. Given the turmoil in the financial markets following the October crash, the underwriters could not place all the shares, so they had to keep them on their balance sheet. As a result, the international group of underwriters lost more than $1 billion.

---

[5] During a road show, a company and its advisors meet with potential investors to promote the sale of the new share issue.

[6] If there are not enough counterparties, the underwriter ensures liquidity in the post-IPO secondary market; i.e., the investment bank commits to buy or sell shares to match the incoming orders from the market — this is called "market-making."

[7] Sell-side analysts issue research reports with recommendations to their clients, who typically are mutual funds, pension funds, and other institutional investors.

[8] The price was agreed to on October 14, 1987.

Alternatively, the contract with the underwriter may be on a best-efforts basis. In this case, the underwriter is not responsible for any portion of the offering if it fails to sell.

7.2.2 How the IPO Price Is Set

Setting the correct price in an IPO is not an easy task. If the price is set too low, the company's existing shareholders will lose because their stake will sell for a low value. If the price is set too high, new investors may fear that the future returns (given the high price) will not be high, and may not buy the securities being offered, thus endangering the IPO.

There are different methods for setting the price:

Fixed price public offer: The price is set before any information is received (demand forecasts) from the market. Investors then state how many shares they want to buy at that fixed price, and the transactions are performed.

Book building: During the road show, the underwriter collects an indication of interest (which is non-binding). The aggregation of all these orders (called order book) is used to set the final offering price. The underwriter has discretion over the allocation of shares in case of oversubscription (when demand exceeds the available shares for sale).

Auction: Pricing and allocations are based on closed bids, indicating the number of shares and the price that investors are willing to pay. The underwriters will then gather all the bids and calculate the cutoff point at which all the shares available can be sold.[9]

Book building is the dominant method used in the US and Canada, and since the early 1990s its use has spread widely in Asia and Europe.

KEY LEARNING POINT ✓

The majority of IPOs nowadays use the book-building method.

---

[9] Significant variations in the number of bidders, as well as the presence of unsophisticated investors, make auction outcomes unstable. Also, a significant free-rider problem exists in the auction, as investors have an incentive to rely on others to collect information on the IPO. In particular, uninformed investors bid high, hoping that the final auction price will be cleared using the information of the investors who do their homework. As a result, many institutional investors do not like to participate in auction IPOs, which explains why they are almost non-existent.

If a book-building procedure is used, the underwriter sets an indicative price range[10] before setting the final issue price for the equity offering. Then the underwriter initiates the book-building period by trying to evaluate investor demand. At this stage, investors indicate their intention of participating in the offering and specify the number of shares they wish to buy. They may include a price limit or place a market order.[11] At this stage, these are non-binding interests. However, for reputational reasons, institutional investors infrequently back off from their expressed intentions at the book-building stage. Once the book-building period is over, the underwriter aggregates the bids into a demand curve — called *the book* — and together with the company, sets the final offer price (which will be the same for all successful investors, so as not to discriminate among them).

The Microsoft IPO in 1986

Microsoft's IPO in 1986 followed these steps:

1. The lead underwriters were selected: Goldman Sachs and a technology boutique, Alex. Brown & Sons.
2. The base amount of shares to be sold was decided: 2 million new shares to be issued by Microsoft (primary offering) and about 600,000 shares to be sold by existing shareholders (secondary offering, which included 80,000 shares from Bill Gates). In addition, there was a 15% overallotment option[12] (300,000 additional shares).
3. A preliminary valuation range of $16–$19 was announced to the market by the underwriters.
4. A preliminary prospectus was registered with the SEC.
5. A road show, which included Microsoft's top management, was organized by the underwriters to showcase Microsoft to potential investors.
6. Microsoft and the banks came to an agreement on the final price of $21 per share.
7. Microsoft and the banks came to an agreement on final fees of $1.31 per share.
8. Shares were distributed to investors that had expressed interest (with prices equal to or above $21) during the road show, at the fixed price of $21 for all investors.
9. Trading started on the stock exchange — Microsoft closed the first day of trading at $27.75 (32% above the offer price).

Book building is designed to extract information from investors to price an issue more accurately. However, at the start of the IPO process, the company's owners do not know what the final price of the IPO will be. In the Microsoft example, the final price was above the initial price range. But there are many other situations where the final IPO price is below the indicated range.

---

[10] The underwriters work with the company to provide a reasonable valuation for the firm's shares, based on discounted cash flows, and also comparable companies' multiples. These methods of valuation are not covered in this chapter.

[11] A market order means the investor is willing to buy the defined amount of shares at the final IPO price.

[12] Overallotment and greenshoe options are explained later in this chapter.

7.2.3 Underpricing

On average, offering prices are less than the value of the issued stocks on the stock exchange in the post-IPO period — this is called *underpricing*. Investors who bought shares during the IPO are naturally happy, as their investment generated an immediate return. However, the pre-IPO shareholders of the issuing companies sold their shares for less than what they are worth in the post-IPO period.

In Microsoft's case, it closed the first day of trading at $27.75, which was 32% above the offer price of $21. Because Microsoft and its existing shareholders sold 2.9 million shares, this meant that the value of the shares sold at the end of the first day was $80.5 million (2.9 million shares × $27.75), whereas the company sold them early that morning for $60.9 million (2.9 million shares × $21). This meant that investors who bought Microsoft stocks during the IPO gained $19.5 million. Conversely, one could say that the existing shareholders "left money on the table."

Underpricing is a widespread phenomenon worldwide. **Figure 7.1** reports average underpricing in different countries. Across a sample of more than 4,462 IPOs in 29 countries from 2000 to 2004, the mean first-day return is close to 28%, but it varies across countries.

FIGURE 7.1:   Underpricing around the world.

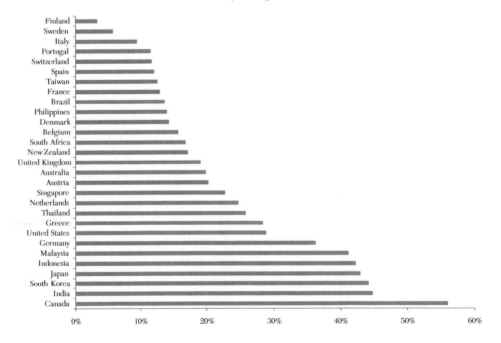

Source: Boulton, Smart, and Zutter (2010).

KEY LEARNING POINT ✓

On average, the first-day return after an IPO is positive.

Underpricing is not a recent phenomenon; studies have documented it for more than 20 years. So, why do investors (pre-IPO) keep leaving money on the table? The main answer is that it may indeed be necessary for the underwriter and the company selling stock in an IPO underpricing to reward new investors for participating in the IPO. Underwriters typically try to set the issue price so that the first-day return is positive. In this way, they compensate their loyal clients for buying shares during the IPO. Also, by treating the investors fairly (or favorably), the underwriters increase their credibility (as obviously the underwriters have much more information about the company than what is disclosed to the market). In addition, the underwriters benefit from underpricing as it controls their risk of having to keep the shares on their own balance sheets (in case the price is set too high and not all the shares are sold). It is also important to remember that the numbers in **Figure 7.1** are averages. Some IPOs will not perform well on the first day.

The Facebook IPO

Facebook went public in May 18, 2012. The company initially set an IPO price of $28 to $35 a share, but it amended the filing during the road show, raising the range to $34 to $38 a share. The final price at which the 421 million shares were sold was $38. The day after the IPO, Facebook stock closed at $34.03, which was 10% below the offer price of $38.

Indeed, ex-ante, investors in an IPO do not know whether the stock will perform well in the post-IPO period. Also, when they submit their bid for a certain number of shares, they do not know exactly how many shares they will ultimately be awarded. Rationing of shares occurs when the overall demand exceeds the available stocks for sale. Thus, if a certain IPO generates a weak demand (cold IPO) and is priced too high (with the result that the first-day return is negative, as in the Facebook example), investors will be allocated a higher number of shares and face substantial losses. Conversely, during a hot IPO with high demand, investors will be allocated a lower number of shares, as the rationing will be severe.

The "winner's curse"

Consider two IPOs — one successful, the other unsuccessful. An investor orders the same amount of shares, and each IPO was priced at $10. However, given rationing (due to oversubscription), when the IPO is very successful (and prices increase substantially on the first day of trading), the absolute gain is not that high (as rationing of the number of shares is severe) as the table below shows. But when demand is weak, the losses are high. This is the so-called "winner's curse." Given this and the asymmetry in information, underpricing may be necessary to attract less well-informed investors to participate in the IPO.

	Hot IPO	Cold IPO
Shares demanded	1,000	1,000
Rationing[13]	10 to 1	2 to 1
Actual shares bought	100	500
IPO price ($)	10.00	10.00
Closing price day 1 ($)	11.50	8.50
Daily stock return	15%	−15%
Invested capital ($)	1,000	5,000
Total gain/loss ($)	**150**	**−750**

More importantly, even though the offering price is frequently underpriced, it is inconsequential compared to the post-IPO wealth of some investors. Indeed, in the Microsoft example, Bill Gates sold only 80,000 shares. Given the underpricing of that IPO, one could say he "lost" $500,000.[14] However, the more important number is his total wealth in the post-IPO period. Given the strong valuation of Microsoft in the aftermarket, his net wealth was valued at $350 million, which makes the underpricing insignificant in relative terms.

7.2.4   The Costs of a New Issue — Investment Banking Fees

The company must agree with the underwriters on the underwriting discount or "spread"[15]: the percentage of the price that goes to the underwriters to cover sales commissions, underwriting expenses, and management fees. Importantly, if there is an agreed-upon firm commitment, any unsold shares will be held by the underwriter. The fees compensate the underwriters for the risk they assume when they agree to keep the unsold shares on their balance sheets, and thus take a loss (as in the BP example).

---

[13] For instance, a 10 to 1 rationing occurs when demand is 10 times greater than the amount available for sale. This implies that investors will get one share for each 10 demanded.

[14] 80,000 shares times the difference of the first day closing price ($27.75) and the IPO price ($21).

[15] The fee or compensation to the underwriter is called a "spread," as it is based on the difference between the price for which the underwriter buys the stock from the issuer and the price for which it is sold to the public.

KEY LEARNING POINT ✓

Fees are higher when there is an agreed-upon firm commitment.

Many of these costs are fixed, so one would expect the spread to decline with issue size. Though the percentage of the spread declines for larger deals, it is relatively flat up to a certain issue size. Research has found that in the US more than 90% of deals raising $20 million to $80 million[16] have spreads of exactly 7%.[17]

TABLE 7.1: Average spreads (%) in the US and Europe

	US	Europe
≥ $25 < 100 million	6.98	4.23
≥ $100 < 500 million	6.63	3.57
≥ $500 million	4.42	2.34
All IPOs	5.64	2.68

Source: Abrahamson, Jenkinson, and Jones (2011).

Spreads received by underwriters in the US are higher than in other countries. And US investment banks typically do not compete on fees to avoid turning the business into a commodity business. Also, investment banks avoid undercutting rivals because it may result in their being perceived as lower-quality institutions. In contrast, European IPO spreads are consistently lower by about 3%, which suggests a more competitive environment for investment banking in Europe (Table 7.1).

7.2.5 Overallotment Options — Greenshoe

An overallotment or greenshoe option allows the underwriter to expand the initial offering through an additional batch of shares. If demand is high, the underwriters can then sell up to 115% of the offer size. But they have a specific period in which to close their position.[18]

---

[16] In recent years, the "7% solution" has become the norm for IPOs raising up to $250 million.

[17] See Chen and Ritter (2000).

[18] The usual terms grant the underwriters an option to purchase additional shares (up to 15% of the offer size) for a period of 30 days after the offer, at the original offer price.

By selling 15% more shares, the underwriter gets higher fees (fees are a percentage of the amount sold). But the indirect impacts of a greenshoe option are even more important. Indeed, the usage of a greenshoe option can stabilize prices in the aftermath of the IPO.

Consider an IPO, with an offer size of 1,000,000 shares, in which the investment bank chooses to sell 1,150,000 shares to investors (15% more than the offer size). The offering price equals $10. There are two possible scenarios during that month: the stock price goes either up or down after the IPO.

	Stock goes up after the IPO	Stock goes down after the IPO
Stock price after one month	$15	$7
Action of the bank	Exercises the greenshoe option, and buys shares from the company at the original $10	Bank buys shares in the stock market at the going price

The greenshoe option provides price stabilization in the post-IPO market. After selling 15% more than the offer size, the bank must cover its short position over the coming month. The bank can choose to buy those 150,000 shares on the stock exchange or from the company (by exercising its option). If the stock proves unpopular and its price drops after the IPO, the bank simply buys 150,000 shares on the market. Because the bank is buying shares below the initial IPO price, it generates gains from the additional 15% of shares sold.[19] Importantly, in this case, the bank is effectively performing price-stabilizing transactions with its additional buy orders.

Alternatively, if the stock went up, the bank would be forced to buy the shares at the higher price, and thus incur heavy losses. But here is where the greenshoe option becomes important. The bank has the right to buy shares at the original offer price ($10 in this example) from the company and thus close its position without any loss.

Greenshoe options ensure that the underwriters are able to sell extra shares to investors when there is strong demand, without the fear of losing money in the aftermarket. In addition, it guarantees some price stabilization for the company should the price drop following the IPO.

KEY LEARNING POINT ✓

Greenshoe options provide stabilization of the stock price in the period following the IPO.

---

[19] The IPO contract often specifies that this gain has to be split with the company according to some ratio.

7.2.6 Market Timing — The Long-Run Performance Following IPOs

IPOs are cyclical. The number of IPOs in the US each year is presented in **Figure 7.2.**

FIGURE 7.2: Number of IPOs per year in the US.

Source: SDC, Jay Ritter.

From 1980 to 2012, an average of 233 companies went public every year. However, this average hides more than it reveals. The minimum number of IPOs was 21 (in 2008), and the maximum was 675 (in 1997).

On average, IPO shares perform very well on the day following the IPO. However, the long-term results are very different. The average IPO underperforms the market (or a size–industry-matched benchmark) by about 25% to 40% over a five-year period.[20] That is, if you buy stocks during the IPO and hold them for periods of three to five years, you will underperform the market as well as comparable companies (based on industry/size/risk categories).

---

[20] See Ritter (1991), Loughran and Ritter (1995), Baker and Wurgler (2000), and Gompers and Lerner (2003) for US evidence, and Henderson, Jegadeesh, and Weisbach (2006) for international results.

```
                                                            ✓
              KEY LEARNING POINT ✓
--------------------------------------------------------------
 There is generally long-term underperformance following IPOs.
```

This suggests that companies tend to time the market for their IPOs, and only raise equity when they may be overvalued. Indeed, equity issuance has been frequently associated with indicators of overvaluation. A survey of about 400 CFOs reveals that almost two-thirds state that when issuing equity, "the amount by which our stock is undervalued or overvalued was an important or very important consideration."[21]

If companies only issue equity when their managers and owners believe they are overvalued, then ex-post returns to investors who buy at the IPO (or SEO) are low. That also explains why the number of IPOs fluctuates so much from year to year. When the market is depressed, owners of private companies do not want to sell; instead, they wait until the stock market is hot and potentially overvalued.[22]

7.3   NEW EQUITY FINANCING — SEASONED EQUITY OFFERINGS

An IPO is the process by which a company sells stock to the public for the first time. Subsequent sales of shares are done through a seasoned equity offering (SEO), also called a follow-on offering.

These usually occur when a company needs to finance additional growth opportunities, for which debt and current earnings are insufficient. Also, a company may be buying another company and may need cash to pay for the purchase. In these, and other related cases, the company issues new shares to investors and retains the proceeds from those issues — a primary issue. Alternatively, SEOs can use the shares sold by existing shareholders — a secondary issue.

As with IPOs, SEOs can be underwritten or not. If they are underwritten, there is a guarantee of a successful transaction for the company. And the investment bank incurs the risk of having to itself buy all the shares not demanded by investors.[23] However, if they are not

---

[21] *Source:* Graham and Harvey (2001).

[22] For instance, privately held companies in the biotech sector do not launch any IPOs when the biotech indices are depressed. But the IPO volume rises significantly after stock prices of publicly traded biotech firms go up (*Source:* Lerner (1994)).

[23] Naturally, fees are higher when it is underwritten.

underwritten, the company incurs the risk of not being able to place all the shares, and thus may compromise its expansion plans.

The SEO can be executed as a cash offer or as a rights offer. This choice has significant implications for the post-SEO ownership structure, as well as for the risk of the transaction.

7.3.1   Cash Offer SEO

In a cash offer, the shares are offered to all possible investors. In this case, the company announces that it will sell a certain number of shares. After the registration documents are filed with the securities regulator, there is usually a road show and a book-building period. In this period, financial advisors receive indications of demand from prospective investors.

An important difference from IPOs is that the SEO company's stock is already traded on the market. Thus, an indication of its value is available. For instance, if the stock price (on the stock exchange, pre-SEO) is $100, and a company announces that it will sell new shares for $200, no rational investor will buy the shares. On the other hand, if the company announces the sale of new shares for $50, it will be inflicting severe losses on current shareholders, as new shareholders can buy shares for 50% of their value. That is why, after the book building is completed, the final price is typically set close to the last known market price (usually with a small 1% to 3% discount).

The Petrobras SEO

In 2010, Petrobras, the biggest company in Brazil, raised more than $60 billion in an SEO. Petrobras was the third largest energy company in the world in terms of market value, with a market capitalization of $199.2 billion as of 2009. Until 2007, operating cash flows were always enough to pay for all the capital expenditures. As a result, the company had never needed to raise new equity capital during the previous 30 years. However, the company was now facing a huge investment program (more than $200 billion, related to exploration and production of new pre-salt fields) and had to raise money to capitalize the company.

Petrobras chose both international and Brazilian banks to underwrite the international and Brazilian issues. The American banks — Merrill Lynch, Citigroup, and Morgan Stanley — and the Brazilian banks — Banco Bradesco BBI, Santander, and Itaú BBA — would act as global coordinators and joint book runners for the deal.

On September 3, 2010, Petrobras issued a preliminary prospectus to the market: The total offering was to raise more than $60 billion. Existing Petrobras shareholders would be offered up to 80% of the shares, based on the number of shares each shareholder owned as of September 17, 2010. The Brazilian government was the main stakeholder of Petrobras, controlling close to 42% of the total shares.

The road show took place from September 7 to 17. It went to New York first, then Europe and Asia. The book-building procedure would end on September 23, 2010. During the book building, investors would show their intention of participating in the offering, including the amount in financial volume ($) and whether they had a price limit, or they would place a market order. Petrobras and the underwriters would then agree on the final offer price, taking into consideration the closing prices over the period as well as the book-building results.

This SEO registered strong demand from existing shareholders and new investors. Thus, at the last minute, Petrobras expanded the size of the offering through a hot issue, which equaled 322.5 million shares (8.6% more shares). Also, underwriters used the greenshoe option to issue additional shares. The deal was priced at a 2% discount to the issue day's closing price.

With both the hot issue and the greenshoe options, the offering raised $71.6 billion, setting a new record. The total capitalization surpassed the previous biggest share issue on record (Japan's Nippon Telephone and Telegraph Corp. raised $36.8 billion in 1987).[24]

7.3.2   Rights Offer SEO

In a rights offer, the company offers existing shareholders the right to buy new shares at a pre-specified price. The underlying principle is that the original shareholders are offered the right to buy new shares in proportion to their current holdings. They can then exercise their right to buy the new shares (thus maintaining their percentage ownership in the company). If they do not want to buy the new shares, they can sell the rights in the market, thus allowing other investors to buy into the company.

The overall value of the equity of a company after issuance is

$$Value\ After = Value\ Before + Amount\ Raised \qquad (7.1)$$

The value before is equal to the prior number of shares multiplied by the share price. The amount raised is the pre-specified price of the rights issue multiplied by the number of rights. Thus, if the underlying value of the company does not change, the theoretical value of the shares after the SEO is completed is

$$TER = \frac{Prior\ number\ of\ shares \times Prior\ share\ price\ +\ Number\ of\ rights \times Offer\ price}{Prior\ number\ of\ shares\ +\ Number\ of\ rights} \qquad (7.2)$$

| TER is the theoretical ex-rights price-per-share post SEO.

In essence, the new share price (TER) will be a weighted average of the share price pre-offer and the new share offer price. Provided the rights exercise price (offer price) is below

---

[24] "Brazil's Petrobras Expands Capitalization to 71.6 bln Dollars," *AFP,* October 2, 2010.

the TER, the rights owner will always benefit from exercising them. And the risk is low for the company that the SEO will not succeed in raising the targeted cash amount.

The UniCredit rights issue

On January 27, 2012, the Italian bank UniCredit raised €7.5 billion in new equity through a rights issue. The rights issue from Italy's largest bank was triggered by the need to meet regulatory requirements set by the European Banking Authority, and thus be better capitalized against possible losses on their portfolios.

UniCredit announced its SEO on January 4, 2012, which would total €7.5 billion in new equity. This would be done through a rights issue, priced at €1.94, which represented a 70% discount to the prior day's stock price (€6.33). The total number of rights was 3.86 billion,[25] which were allocated to the previous 1.93 billion shares, such that each existing shareholder would receive two rights to acquire new shares. It was underwritten by 27 investment banks.[26] The rights could be exercised from January 9 to January 27 and were traded from January 9 to January 20.

The rights price represented a 43% discount on the bank's price on a fully diluted basis (the theoretical ex-rights market price of UniCredit's shares):

Before rights issue	
Number of shares	1.93 billion
Price per share	€6.33
Market value of UniCredit	**€12.217 billion**

After rights issue	
Prior market value	€12.217 billion
Cash infusion (3860 million rights × €1.94 per share)	€7.488 billion
Theoretical value of UniCredit after SEO	**€19.705 billion**

After the issue is complete, and in the absence of any signaling aspects (discussed next), the market value of UniCredit should be equal to €19.7 billion. This is the sum of the prior market value (€12.2 billion) plus the new cash raised with the rights SEO (€7.5 billion). Thus, using formula (7.2), the TER is

$$TER = \frac{Prior\ number\ of\ shares \times Prior\ share\ price\ +\ Number\ of\ rights \times Offer\ price}{Prior\ number\ of\ shares\ +\ Number\ of\ rights}$$

$$= \frac{1930\ million\ shares \times €6.33\ +\ 3860\ million\ rights \times €1.94}{1930\ million\ "old"\ shares + 3860\ million\ "new"\ shares}$$

$$= €3.40$$

---

[25] Which multiplied by the issue price of €1.94 achieves the targeted €7.5 billion of new capital.

[26] Most likely to spread the risk of the offer not being taken up by the market.

Because the total number of shares will be higher after all the rights are exercised (a total of 5.79 billion shares), the theoretical price per share, post-SEO, should be €3.40. Because the rights entitle the holder to buy shares for €1.94, they are issued at a substantial discount, and will likely be exercised.

$$Discount = \frac{Offer\ price}{TER} - 1 = \frac{€1.43}{€3.40} - 1 = -43\%$$

It is clear that UniCredit could have raised the same amount of money using different terms for its rights. In order to raise €7.488 billion, they could have chosen to issue 5.79 billion rights (granting each prior share three rights to acquire a new share) to buy shares at €1.30. The total amount of cash raised would have been the same. This means that the issue price is somewhat irrelevant (provided it is below the TER) when using rights. And previous shareholders do not lose if the rights are issued at a very steep discount — the rights are attributed to the previous shareholders. However, risk aversion justifies higher discounts. Indeed, large discounts such as this are typical, and they aim to ensure that the rights are exercised and the SEO is successful.[27] That is, if during the SEO period the stock price of UniCredit falls, a high rights issue price could jeopardize the offer. With a substantial discount, the probability of failure is much reduced. [28]

In the end, the UniCredit rights issue was very successful. It sold 99.8% of the shares offered, and the banks only had to buy the 0.2% unsold shares.[29] Given the uncertainty in the market regarding this huge recapitalization and the underwriting role of the banks, UniCredit's fees were significantly higher (2.5% to 3%) than in previous equity issues (1% to 1.75%).

Not all rights issues go well — The HBOS case

UK's biggest mortgage lender, HBOS, needed to strengthen its capital base[30] in 2008. HBOS announced on April 29, 2008, its £4 billion rights issue offering investors two new shares for every five held, at a price of 275 pence. The previous day, the HBOS share price had closed at 495.75 pence. The issue was fully underwritten by Morgan Stanley and Dresdner Kleinwort. Overall, the rights issue cost HBOS £160 million, including underwriting fees (4% of the amount issued).

Given the number of old and new shares, the theoretical ex-rights share price was 436 pence, and thus the rights were issued at a 37% discount:

$$Discount = \frac{275p}{436p} - 1 = -37\%$$

---

[27] And the larger the discount, the less likely the investment banks will actually have to be called upon to buy part of it (if they had underwritten it with a firm commitment).

[28] If during the trading period of the rights and prior to the conclusion of the SEO, the UniCredit stock price had gone below €1.94, the rights would not have been exercised, and thus, the capital raising would not have been complete.

[29] There are always a small number of shareholders, usually small individual shareholders, who do not notice that they have rights and so do not exercise them.

[30] After several billion pounds of write-downs due to the international credit crunch and severe losses in its mortgage portfolio.

But given new information on the company, as well as the evolving credit crisis in 2008, the stock price continued its downward trend until late June, the date on which the shareholders had to decide whether to exercise their rights to buy new stocks at 275 pence.

FIGURE 7.3:   HBOS share price from February to July 2008.

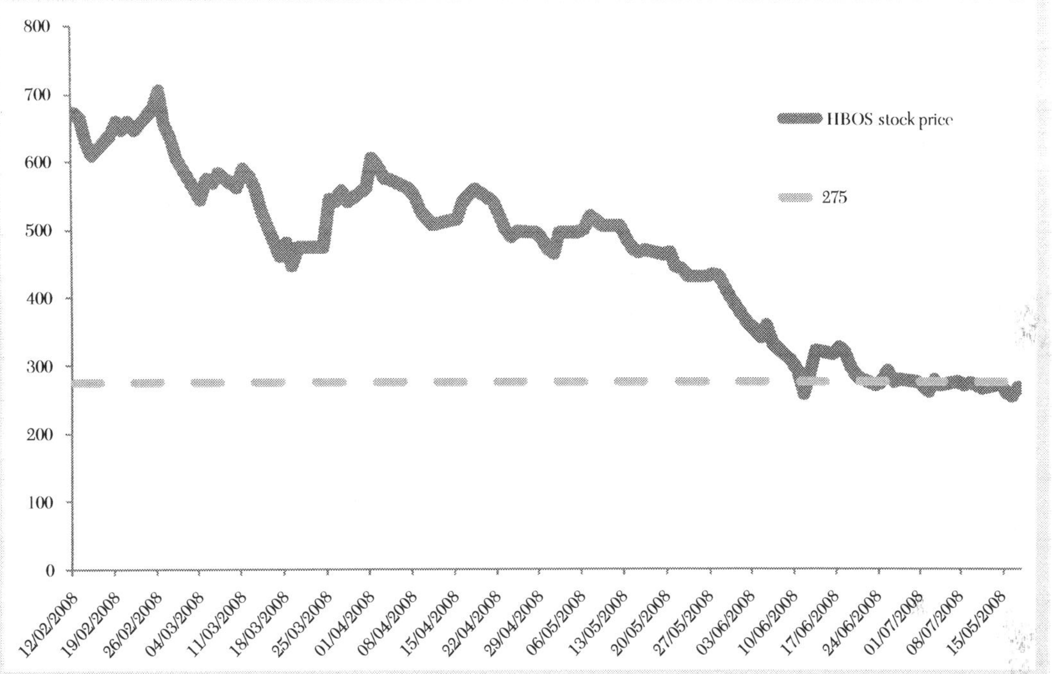

Source: Datastream and IMD research.

The HBOS share price fell below 275 pence in June (see **Figure 7.3**) and was trading close to that value (most often below it) during the days just before the deadline (July 18). As a result, very few investors took up shares (just 8.3%). This left the underwriters, Morgan Stanley and Dresdner Kleinwort, holding £3.8 billion of unwanted stock and facing substantial losses.

KEY LEARNING POINT ✓

A higher discount on a rights issue reduces the risk that the issue is not successful, but it does not fully eliminate it.

7.3.3 Market Timing and SEOs

Research has found that following an announcement of an SEO, the stock price of the company falls by about 2% to 3% on average.[31] The main reason offered for the price decline is that SEOs reveal negative information about the existing value of the company. Indeed, as the company is usually concerned about its current shareholders, it will tend not to issue equity when it feels it is undervalued. Similarly, surveys reveal that most CFOs state that the amount by which their stock is undervalued or overvalued is the key consideration when issuing new equity. Thus, when a company issues equity, the market thinks there is some missing information, and likely, the company is overvalued; thus, the price drops owing to the signaling effect.

When issuers time the market, they tend to issue equity at the top of the valuation curve, which leads to long-term underperformance. Over different sample periods, the results are consistent: SEOs underperform the market by 20% to 30% over a five-year period.[32]

Overall, this evidence suggests that companies tend to raise equity when they are overvalued, and the stock price reacts negatively. However, there are significant cases in which the stock price actually rises. This is particularly true when the company can demonstrate that the capital raised is needed to pursue valuable (or positive NPV – net present value) investment opportunities. In these cases, shareholders are less afraid that the capital issue is being used for empire building by the company's managers, and it may even lead to an appreciation in the stock price.

KEY LEARNING POINT ✓

There is long-term underperformance following SEOs, and the stock price reacts negatively to the announcement of an SEO.

7.4 WHY DO COMPANIES HAVE STOCK SPLITS?

A stock split is not an equity issue. A stock split just alters the number of shares in circulation, with a corresponding adjustment to their price.

---

[31] After the HBOS announcement, the company's stock price fell by 6% over the next three days.

[32] The results have been shown relative to size–industry-matched peers as well (Loughran and Ritter (1995)).

A 10-for-1 split means that 9 new shares of stock are issued for each share in existence prior to the split:

- The number of shares outstanding increases 10 times.
- Earnings per share will be 10 times lower, as the same net earnings are divided into 10 times as many shares.
- After the split, each share is worth one-tenth of what it was worth immediately prior to the split.

An investor holds 1,000 shares of Coca-Cola, which has a price per share of $80. This means the total investment in Coca-Cola is worth $80,000. On August 12, 2012, Coca-Cola split its shares 2-for-1. The stock price of the company halved. Immediately after the split, the investor would own 2,000 shares, but the market price would be $40 per share. The investor's total investment value would remain the same at $80,000. The split increased the number of Coca-Cola shares to 11.2 billion from 5.6 billion.

In reality, a stock split changes nothing about a company. And when a company splits, a 2-for-1 split reduces the share price by one-half; a 3-for-1 split reduces the price by two-thirds; and a 1-for-10 reduces it 10 times.

Cutting a pizza into smaller slices does not change the total amount of calories the pizza has. Similarly, after a stock split, the owner of the stock has more shares, but each with less value, so that the total value of the shares is unchanged.

KEY LEARNING POINT

A stock split does not change the fundamental value of the company.

Even though the value of the company is unchanged, companies claim that there are a number of reasons for a stock split:

- A stock split reduces the share price, which makes it easier for small investors to buy 100 shares. This used to be the standard lot that retail investors needed to buy. Nowadays, with the growth of discount brokers, this reason no longer applies.
- A stock split generates publicity for the company, which is good from the marketing point of view.

- A stock split can make the share price psychologically appealing. A stock split can attract some less sophisticated investors who think low-price shares are a bargain. Some investors also feel better about owning a larger number of shares.

- A stock split may be motivated by market preferences for a certain share price range. A stock split is sometimes done by companies that have seen their share price increase to levels that are too high relative to that of similar companies in their sector.

- A stock split may be done to comply with certain market indices' inclusion criteria.

Companies can also do a reverse split. This is used by companies with low share prices that would like to increase these prices. One reason for this is that some stock exchanges delist stocks if they fall below a certain price per share. For example, in a reverse 5-for-1 split, 5 million outstanding shares at 30 cents each would become 1 million shares outstanding at $1.50 per share. However, the company's value is unchanged at $1.5 million.

TABLE 7.2: History of stock splits for Coca-Cola

Year	Stock Split	Cumulative Shares
2012	2-for-1	9,216
1996	2-for-1	4,608
1992	2-for-1	2,304
1990	2-for-1	1,152
1986	3-for-1	576
1977	2-for-1	192
1968	2-for-1	96
1965	2-for-1	48
1960	3-for-1	24
1935	4-for-1	8
1927	1-for-1	2
1919		1

Source: Coca-Cola.

These splits in **Table 7.2** mean that if an investor had one share of Coca-Cola in 1919 (the year Coca-Cola went public), she would now have 9,216 shares. At the end of 2012, Coca-Cola's share price was approximately $35. This means that if Coca-Cola had never split a single share, the value of a single share today would be $322,560 ($35 multiplied by 9,216). In this case, not many people could afford even a single share.

On the other hand, Warren Buffett's Berkshire Hathaway has never split its stock. Accordingly, an original share of Berkshire (BRK.A ticker) was trading for around $140,000 at the end of 2012. Given the low liquidity of the share, and despite being one of the US's largest companies, Berkshire was not included in any of the major indices (Dow Jones, S&P 500, etc.).

Since 2010, Berkshire Hathaway has had two classes of stocks: Class A and Class B. It created a Class B stock (BRK.B ticker), with a per-share value that is significantly lower than the Class A shares, but that carries substantially less cash flow and voting rights (1/10,000 of the voting rights and 1/1,500 of the dividends of the Class A shares). As of February 5, 2013, Class A shares were priced at $146,600, while Class B shares traded at $97.46 (1,500 times less, as expected given the 1,500 times lower cash flow rights). This helped many investors to buy Berkshire Hathaway stock, and given the added liquidity, its shares met the S&P 500 index standards, and they were added to this benchmark index on January 26, 2010.

KEY LEARNING POINT ✓

A stock split does not change the fundamental value of the company, but it may attract a different set of investors.

Some companies perform the opposite operation, a *reverse stock split*. In this case, a 1-for-10 reverse split means that the shares of a company are merged to form a smaller number of more valuable shares. One reason why companies go in for a reverse split is their prior low share price. Indeed, many institutional investors have rules against purchasing stock below $5. And some stock exchanges and indices also have a required minimum share price.

Citigroup Reverse Stock Split

In May 2011, Citigroup stock went from $4 to $40. Yet investors did not gain a dime. The reason is the 1-for-10 reverse stock split. The split reduced the number of outstanding shares from 29 billion to 2.9 billion.

7.5   CONTROL AND OWNERSHIP DILUTION

When a company decides to sell equity to outside shareholders, it will obviously weaken the position of existing shareholders. In order to maintain control, some companies have different classes of shares:

- *Common stocks:* These are securities that represent part of the equity of a company. Common stock usually carries with it the right to vote on significant corporate matters, such as the board of directors, mergers and acquisitions, changes in payout policy, etc.

- *Preferred stocks:* These are a form of equity that share some of the attributes of debt instruments. They are considered a hybrid form of capital. They entitle the owner to a preferential dividend, and they usually do not carry with them voting rights. Preferred stocks are senior to common stock (that is, in the event of bankruptcy, preferred stockholders would be paid before common stockholders), but they are junior to corporate debt.

- *Non-voting stocks:* These stocks, which are sometimes issued by companies, do not entitle the shareholders to vote on corporate matters.

- *Dual-class shares:* Such shares are restricted to different investors. For instance, Chinese companies have A-class shares traded on the Shanghai stock exchange that are only available to Chinese nationals. Several of these companies also have H-class shares traded on the Hong Kong stock exchange that are only available to foreigners.

Sinopec dual-class structure

Sinopec, the large Chinese oil company, has two classes of shares: A and H. A-shares are traded in yuan on the Shanghai and Shenzhen stock exchanges, and only available to Chinese nationals. H-shares of Sinopec trade in Hong Kong, in HK dollars. These are open only to foreign investors. There are significant differences between the prices at which mainland companies trade on both exchanges. Because the A- and H-shares are not convertible, and are only available to different groups of investors, there is no available channel to arbitrage away these price differentials. Indeed, the imbalances between supply and demand of shares in each market will determine the final price at which they trade.[33]

Most institutional investors oppose the use of dual-class shares, arguing that they allow controlling shareholders (insiders) to enjoy private benefits of control at the expense of minority shareholders. Several studies examined alternative ownership schemes, including different classes of shares, as well as pyramidal structures and cross-holdings, which also allow for a significant divergence between the controlling shareholders' voting rights and cash flow

---

[33] There is an index (Hang Seng China AH Premium Index) that tracks the price difference of A-shares over H-shares for the Chinese companies with both A-share and H-share listings (see www.hsi.com.hk/HSI-Net/HSI-Net for more information).

rights. In practice, when insiders disproportionally control more voting rights than cash flow rights, firm value is lower than the optimal value.[34]

The empirical evidence also indicates that voting shares usually sell at a premium — voting premium — relative to their counterpart non-voting shares. However, shares with superior voting rights are less liquid, as they tend to be held by people who do not want to dispose of them; these shares are used to acquire and maintain control.

KEY LEARNING POINT ✓

Voting shares typically trade at a premium relative to non-voting shares.

The size of the valuation discount (on non-voting shares) depends on company- and economy-specific circumstances. For instance, in countries where the legal and judicial protection of individual shareholders is strong, the discount is smaller. In countries with weak institutions, the difference in value between voting and non-voting shares is larger.

Researchers have looked at the value of controlling shares (relative to non-voting shares) and found significant differences around the world. For instance, in Anglo-Saxon and Scandinavian countries, the value is close to zero (as the example of Berkshire Hathaway shows).[35] However, in other countries like Brazil, Chile, Italy, Mexico, and South Korea, the voting shares are valued at about a 25% premium relative to non-voting shares. Therefore, institutional differences across economies affect the valuation discount/premium significantly.

Conversely, some companies take steps to eliminate the distinction between voting and non-voting shares. These steps are appreciated by the investors, and they are usually associated with a positive stock-price reaction.

Ultrapar announces the end of non-voting shares

In August 2011, Ultrapar, a large Brazilian company, took an unusual step. It announced the conversion of its preferred shares into common shares, in a 1-to-1 ratio. Until then, the company had a dual-class structure that allowed the controlling shareholders to have 66% of the votes, with only 24% of the cash flow rights. They managed to do this through a significant holding of the voting (common) shares, whereas other investors invested mainly in preferred shares (no voting).

---

[34] Claessens et al. (2002), Lins (2003), Harvey, Lins, and Roper (2004), and Gompers, Ishii, and Metrick (2010) all document that firm value and stock returns are lower when the controlling shareholders voting rights exceed their cash-flow ownership share.

[35] See Nenova (2003).

This conversion turned Ultrapar into Brazil's largest company without a defined controlling shareholder. From then on, all shares had the same economic and political rights. Upon this announcement, the stock price of Ultrapar increased by more than 6%, as shareholders appreciated this step, which transformed Ultrapar into a real corporation and increased the voting rights of minority shareholders.

KEY LEARNING POINT ✓

Companies without dual-class shares typically have higher value than companies that use mechanisms to create a divergence between cash flow and voting rights.

7.6   CROSS-LISTING IN FOREIGN EXCHANGES

Cross-listing (also called dual listing, or foreign listing) of shares occurs when a company lists its shares in a foreign exchange (in addition to its domestic market). Most stock exchanges trade and list mainly their domestic companies. London and New York, the leading financial centers of the world, have managed to attract a substantial number of foreign listings.

The number of cross-listed companies grew quickly in the 1990s, especially in the US.[36] More recently, Hong Kong and Singapore have become destinations of choice for a number of companies.

7.6.1   Reasons for a Company to List in a Foreign Exchange

Companies choose to list for many reasons, but in general cross-listing

- Improves the liquidity of the company's shares
- Gives the company a currency to use in future acquisitions
- Allows the company to implement share option plans for its employees
- Provides access to additional funding opportunities
- Enhances the status and visibility of the company
- Increases public awareness of the company and its products
- Expands its investor base and raises additional capital

---

[36] Fernandes and Giannetti (2008) document a strong increase in the number of cross-listed firms around the world. For instance, in 1988, foreign listed firms represented 5.6% of firms listed in the UK and US, whereas in 2006 they accounted for more than 17% of the number of firms traded in these two countries.

- Allows shares to be traded in multiple time zones and currencies
- Gives investors access to global companies that trade across a range of home markets
- Enables investors to buy shares in US dollars and receive dividends in US dollars (if it is a US cross-listing)

Cross-listed stocks are usually traded in the form of a depositary receipt (DR). A DR represents a number of original shares held in custody by a financial institution, which acts as an intermediary, owning shares traded in the company's home market and issuing DRs to investors in the cross-listing market. When these receipts are issued in the US (which is what usually happens), they are called American depositary receipts (ADRs). These ADRs then trade on the New York Stock Exchange (NYSE) or the National Association of Securities Dealers Automated Quotations (NASDAQ). Global depositary receipts (GDRs) refer to cross-listings that trade across many foreign markets, for instance, in London or Luxembourg.

The ABB American depositary receipts

ABB, a Swiss multinational, has been cross-listed on the NYSE since 2001. The ratio is 1:1, such that one ADR represents one ordinary share in the Swiss market.

FIGURE 7.4: The value of an ABB share in Switzerland and in the US.

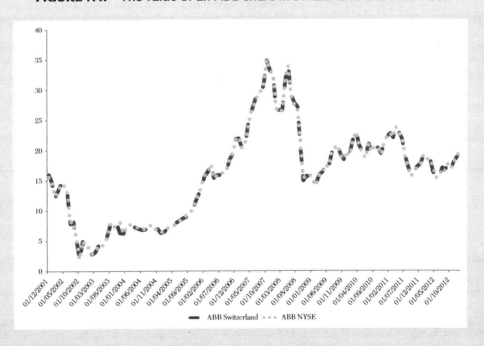

Source: Datastream and IMD Research.

Indeed, once we multiply the US price by the exchange rate (USD/Swiss Franc), the prices in Switzerland and New York (Figure 7.4) are almost indistinguishable, which shows how the price of an ABB share, at the same moment in time, is the same across both sides of the Atlantic.

The ADR represents the same claim to the company as an ordinary share in its home market; thus, the prices should be the same (adjusted, of course, for exchange rate fluctuations).

KEY LEARNING POINT ✓

Cross-listed stocks tend to trade at the same price in different exchanges (adjusted for currency differences), in order to avoid arbitrage opportunities.

7.6.2 Is There Value in Being Cross-Listed?

Research has concluded that cross-listing can be an effective tool to reduce the cost of capital, which in turn increases the stock price.[37] Related to listing on foreign markets is the issue of corporate governance. Weak investor protection make shares riskier, so investors demand higher returns, as a result of which the cost of capital increases. By choosing to cross-list in a stricter environment, where monitoring and compliance are tighter, the company is effectively opting into the foreign regulatory environment.[38] This can mean that the management of the company is ready to comply with the highest governance standards of that market relative to its home market. On average, being cross-listed in a strict corporate governance environment results in higher company valuation. This can be viewed as a governance benefit of cross-listing.[39]

---

[37] See Miller (1999), Foerster and Karolyi (1999), Doidge, Karolyi, and Stulz (2004), and Hail and Leuz (2009) for empirical tests on the stock price and cost-of-capital implications of cross-listings.

[38] By listing in markets with more rigorous corporate governance standards and more sophisticated market participants, owing to enforcement by the legal authorities and also to reputational mechanisms, firms can commit to limit corporate insiders' extraction of private benefits of control. This is known as the "bonding theory of cross-listings." Some authors have questioned the relevance of the mechanism based on direct bonding even in the US. For instance, Siegel (2005) shows that even in the US, where the SEC has the power to enforce minority-shareholder rights in court, legal enforcement has been ineffective. Also, some evidence suggests that the valuation effects of cross-listings may be short-lived (Sarkissian and Schill, 2009).

[39] Fernandes, Lel, and Miller (2010) find that shareholders of non-US firms place a significant value on US securities regulations, especially when the home country investor protection is weak.

KEY LEARNING POINT

Cross-listing requirements vary around the world. Companies that list on stricter exchanges tend to be valued higher than their peers, as this is interpreted as a strong signal of quality and governance.

But alongside the advantages, there are also some disadvantages. There are initial costs, such as registration, exchange fees, and road-show costs, followed by permanent annual reports and disclosure requirements, which impose a level of continuous scrutiny on the company's managers. In addition, because of the increased scrutiny, the companies' management may lose some discretion on how to use the company's money. The Sarbanes–Oxley (SOX) Act adopted in 2002 made cross-listing on US exchanges more costly than in the past. The new requirements create a heavy emphasis on corporate governance and accountability. Together with having to comply with the US's generally accepted accounting principles (GAAP), this makes it a challenge for many companies whose home market may have less stringent standards.

7.6.3 Different Types of ADRs and GDRs

ADRs can be traded and settled on one of the US exchanges (NYSE, NASDAQ, or AMEX — American Stock Exchange) or in the over-the-counter (OTC) market. Another important distinction between the types of ADRs is whether the ADR is associated with raising capital in the US (see **Table 7.3**). If only existing shares are being traded, it is a Level I or Level II ADR. When new capital is being raised in the US, it can be through a Level III ADR or an OTC issue.

Companies that list using Level I or Rule 144a ADRs are exempt from SEC registration and from many disclosure requirements, namely, having to present financial statements according to US GAAP. When companies decide to issue Level II or III ADRs, they become subject to SEC oversight and are therefore exposed to class action lawsuits.[40] In addition, they will also face additional monitoring by important market participants, such as analysts and institutional investors.[41]

---

[40] Fernandes, Lel, and Miller (2010) identify 115 foreign firms that were subject to private class action securities lawsuits in US courts.

[41] Lang, Lins, and Miller [2003] document strong increases in analyst coverage of firms following a cross-listing. Fernandes and Ferreira (2008) show that cross-listing is associated with significant changes in analyst coverage, liquidity, ownership, and accounting quality.

TABLE 7.3: Different types of cross-listings

	US Listing Level I ADR	US Listing Level II ADR	US Listing Level III ADR	US Listing Rule 144a	UK Listing
Trading venue	OTC	NYSE, NASDAQ, AMEX	NYSE, NASDAQ, AMEX	PORTAL (private placement market)	London Stock Exchange
Reporting/ accounting standards	Home country	US GAAP	US GAAP	Home country	US GAAP, UK GAAP, IAS
Compliance standards	Exempt	SEC registration	SEC registration	Exempt	Home country
Share issuance	No	No	Yes	Yes	Yes

For London listings, different requirements exist. Companies must be admitted by the UK Listing Authority, part of the Financial Services Authority (FSA). Only then can they be allowed to trading on the London Stock Exchange. The main requirement for companies with ordinary listings on the London Stock Exchange Main Market is to report financial statements in accordance with UK GAAP, US GAAP, or International Accounting Standards (IAS). However, most of the provisions of the UK listing rules that protect minority investors do not apply to foreign companies. For instance, the Combined Code on Corporate Governance does not oblige foreign listings to comply with the code.[42] The only requirement is that companies must comply with the governance rules of their origin country.

SUMMARY

Issuing new capital is a very important step in the life of a company. Companies can go public through their IPO by issuing new shares, called the *primary offering*. Companies can also go public by selling shares from current shareholders to the public, which is called the

---

[42] Doidge, Karolyi, and Stulz (2009) examine in detail the differences between London and New York listings and conclude that there is a distinct governance benefit for firms that list on the US exchanges, which may derive from the stronger disclosure and governance requirements (compared to the UK requirements).

secondary offering. Different decisions need to be made when a company decides to issue an IPO. One of these relates to whether or not a firm commitment (also called *underwriting*) is included by the financial advisors. When there is a firm commitment, the company's risk is lower, but it is at the expense of higher fees.

Setting the correct price of an IPO is not easy. Book building is currently the dominant method around the world. In a book-building procedure, the company and its advisors try to evaluate investor demand before setting the final price. Once all of the investors' intentions are aggregated, the company sets the final offer price and ultimately distributes the shares to the buyers.

On average, IPOs are underpriced. This means that the first-day return after being traded on a stock exchange is positive. Many IPOs include a greenshoe option. In this case, the underwriter can expand the initial offering of shares by up to 15%. But then, they have one month to close their positions. If the demand is high, more shares can be sold to the public. More importantly, greenshoe, or *overallotment options* as they are legally called, allow for price stabilization in the period following the IPO.

SEOs are the subsequent sales of equity to investors after an IPO. They can be implemented as a cash offer or as a rights offer. If implemented through a rights offer, the company issues rights to current shareholders to buy new shares at a pre-specified price, which often includes a significant discount. As with IPOs, SEOs can be either fully underwritten or not. If not underwritten, the company incurs all the risk if the issue is eventually unsuccessful and the targeted capital amount is not raised. The research evidence is clear on the long-term underperformance of companies following equity issues, whether they are IPOs or SEOs. This suggests that issuers time the market and tend to issue equities only when they believe their company is at the top of the valuation range. As a result, following equity issues, companies will underperform the market and peer groups.

Many companies cross-list on foreign exchanges. Cross-listing has a number of implications that are discussed in this chapter. On average, being cross-listed on an exchange with strict and rigorous corporate governance requirements results in positive stock price returns and higher company valuation.

In this chapter, we also discussed special means through which companies can create differences between cash flow rights and voting rights, effectively allowing some shareholders to control the company without owning a majority of its capital. But the empirical evidence is clear: Companies with dual-class shares typically have lower value than their peers, as investors fear being expropriated by the controlling shareholders. When companies eliminate the distinction between voting and non-voting shares, their stock price usually goes up.

REFERENCES

Abrahamson, M., T. Jenkinson, and H. Jones, 2011, Why Don't U.S. Issuers Demand European Fees for IPOs?, *The Journal of Finance*, Vol. 66, Iss. 6:2055–2082.

Baker, M., and Wurgler, J., 2000, The Equity Shares in New Issues and Aggregate Stock Returns, *The Journal of Finance*, Vol. 55, Iss. 5:2219–2257.

Boulton, T.J., S.B. Smart, and C.J. Zutter, 2010, IPO Underpricing and International Corporate Governance, *Journal of International Business Studies*, Vol. 41, Iss. 2:206–222.

Chen, H.-C., and J.R. Ritter, 2000, The Seven Percent Solution, *The Journal of Finance*, Vol. 55, Iss. 3: 1105–1131. DOI: 10.1111/0022-1082.00242.

Claessens, S., S. Djankov, J.P. H. Fan, and L H.P. Lang, 2002, Disentangling the Incentive and Entrenchment Effects of Large Shareholdings, *Journal of Finance*, Vol. 57, Iss. 6:81–112.

Doidge, C., A.G. Karolyi, and R.M. Stulz, 2004, Why Are Foreign Firms Listed in the U.S. Worth More?, *Journal of Financial Economics*, Vol. 71: Iss. 2:205–238.

Doidge, C., A.G. Karolyi, and R.M. Stulz, 2009, Has New York Become Less Competitive in Global Markets? Evaluating Foreign Listing Choices over Time, *Journal of Financial Economics*, Vol. 91, Iss. 3:253–277.

Fernandes, N., and M. Ferreira, 2008, Does International Cross-listing Improve the Information Environment?, *Journal of Financial Economics*, Vol. 88, Iss. 2:216–244.

Fernandes, N., and M. Giannetti, 2013, On the Fortunes of Stock Exchanges and Their Reversals: Evidence from Foreign Listing Waves, *Journal of Financial Intermediation*, forthcoming.

Fernandes, N., U. Lel, and D.P. Miller, 2010, Escape from New York: The Market Impact of Loosening Disclosure Requirements, *Journal of Financial Economics*, Vol. 95, Iss. 2:129–274.

Foerster, S.R., and A.G. Karolyi, 1999, The Effects of Market Segmentation and Investor Recognition on Asset Prices: Evidence from Foreign Stocks Listing in the United States, *Journal of Finance*, Vol. 54, Iss. 3:981–1013.

Gompers, P.A., and J. Lerner, 2003, The Really Long-Run Performance of Initial Public Offerings: The Pre-Nasdaq Evidence, *Journal of Finance*, Vol. 58, Iss. 4:1355–1392.

Gompers, P.A., J. Ishii, and A. Metrick, 2010, Extreme Governance: An Analysis of Dual-Class Firms in the United States, *Review of Financial Studies*. Vol. 23, Iss. 3:1051–1088.

Hail, L., and C. Leuz 2009 Cost of Capital Effects and Changes in Growth Expectations around U.S. Cross-Listings *Journal of Financial Economics*, Vol. 93, Iss. 3:428–454.

Graham, J.R., and C.R. Harvey, 2001, The Theory and Practice of Corporate Finance: Evidence from the Field, *Journal of Financial Economics*, Vol. 60, Iss. 2:187–243.

Harvey, C.R., K.V. Lins, and A.H. Roper, 2004, The Effect of Capital Structure When Expected Agency Costs Are Extreme, *Journal of Finance Economics*, Vol. 74, Iss. 1:3–30.

Henderson, B., N. Jegadeesh, and M. Weisbach, 2006, World Markets for Raising New Capital, *Journal of Financial Economics,* Vol. 82, Iss. 1:63–101.

Kim, W., and M.S. Weisbach, 2008, Motivations for Public Equity Offers: An International Perspective, *Journal of Financial Economics*, Vol. 87:281–301.

Lang, M., K. Lins, and D. Miller, 2003, ADRs, Analysts, and Accuracy: Does Cross Listing in the United States Improve a Firm's Information Environment and Increase Market Value?, *Journal of Accounting Research*, Vol. 41, Iss. 2:317–345.

Lerner, J., 1994, Venture Capitalists and the Decision To Go Public, *Journal of Financial Economics*, Vol. 35, Iss. 3:293–316.

Lins, K.V., 2003, Equity Ownership and Firm Value in Emerging Markets, *Journal of Financial and Quantitative Analysis,* Vol. 38, Iss. 1:159–184.

Loughran, T., and J.R. Ritter, 1995, The New Issues Puzzle, *The Journal of Finance*, Vol. 50, Iss. 1:23–51.

Megginson, W., R. Nash, and M. van Randenborgh, 1994, The Financial and Operating Performance of Newly Privatized Firms: An International Empirical Analysis, *Journal of Finance*, Vol. 49, Iss. 2:403-452.

Miller, D.P., 1999, The Market Reaction to International Cross-Listings: Evidence from Depository Receipts, *Journal of Financial Economics*, Vol. 51, Iss. 1:103–123.

Nenova, T., 2003, The Value of Corporate Voting Rights and Control: A Cross-Country Analysis, *Journal of Financial Economics*, Vol. 68, Iss. 3:325–351.

Ritter, J.R., 1991, The Long-Run Performance of Initial Public Offerings, *Journal of Finance*, Vol. 46, Iss. 1:3–27.

Sarkissian, S., and M.J. Schill, 2009, Are There Permanent Valuation Gains to Overseas Listing?, *Review of Financial Studies*. Vol. 22, Iss. 1:371–412.

Siegel, J., 2005, Can Foreign Firms Bond Themselves Effectively by Renting U.S. Securities Laws?, *Journal of Financial Economics*, Vol. 75, Iss. 2:319–359.

Returning Money to Shareholders — Dividends, Buybacks, and the Payout Policy

Do you know the only thing that gives me pleasure? It's to see my dividends coming in.

John D. Rockefeller

Why does Vodafone or Eon (a German utility company) pay more than 70% of their earnings as dividends to shareholders, whereas Oracle pays 0%? Why does Apple hold such a large cash reserve, and how does the market view it?

What is the impact on a company when it starts paying dividends? What happens if it has to reduce or cancel them? This chapter addresses these and other questions and discusses the main principles behind payout policies (including dividends and buybacks), the different types of shareholders and their needs, and the market's reaction to different payout announcements.

Payout policies are essentially the financial strategies by which companies remunerate their shareholders. These policies determine not only the flow of funds to investors, but also what funds are available for company reinvestment.

Companies can either return money to the shareholders through dividends or they can repurchase shares (buybacks). These alternative ways of returning money to shareholders have different consequences, and are recommended in different situations. Evidence on how financial markets view payout decisions is presented, as well as empirical evidence based on research and actual payout policies across many different industries and countries.

8.1   DIVIDEND METRICS

Dividends are the regular payouts that the company makes to its equity holders. A company pays dividends when it generates enough cash and profits to not only sustain its future operations but also to distribute some of its current cash among shareholders. Payout ratios and dividend yields are the most common ways to compare dividend levels across companies.

Payout Ratio

$$Payout\ Ratio = \frac{Total\ Dividends}{Total\ Earnings}$$

or

$$Payout\ Ratio = \frac{Dividends/Share\ (DPS)}{Earnings/Share\ (EPS)}$$

Dividend Yield

$$Dividend\ Yield = \frac{Total\ Dividends}{Market\ Capitalization}$$

or

$$Dividend\ Yield = \frac{Dividends/Share\ (DPS)}{Stock\ Price/Share}$$

The payout ratio represents the percentage of the company's earnings that is distributed to shareholders in a given year. The dividend yield shows how much the dividends represent as a percentage of the company's stock price. Dividend yields and payout ratios are highly correlated across companies.

8.2   THE IMPORTANCE OF DIVIDENDS FOR SHAREHOLDER RETURNS

Shareholder returns are a combination of two factors: share price appreciation and dividend payments.

In **Figure 8.1**, we present the stock returns investors have obtained in different markets from 1973 to 2012. For each market, two values are presented. The first column (returns with dividends) shows the total returns, which includes capital gains (share price appreciation) and the dividends. The second column shows just the stock market returns (return without dividends). This allows us to compare how much returns an investor received with and without dividends. Dividends account for over 30% of long-term shareholder returns in most countries, and are thus a very important component of the returns obtained by shareholders.

FIGURE 8.1:   Stock market returns with and without dividends.

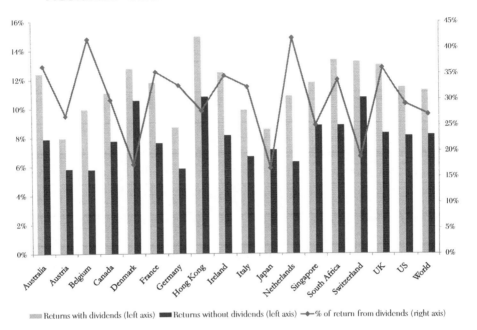

Returns with dividends (left axis)   ▬Returns without dividends (left axis)   ◆% of return from dividends (right axis)

Source: Datastream and IMD research.

8.3   WHEN SHOULD A COMPANY PAY DIVIDENDS?

The payout decision is intimately related to the growth of the company. When there are not enough profitable investment opportunities (low growth) within the company, the optimal choice to create shareholder value is to distribute the extra money to shareholders. On the other hand, for growing companies that require more funds for internal reinvestment, the amount of profit available for distribution to shareholders is lower.

8.3.1   Reinvest in the Company or Pay Dividends?

We can define the company's sustainable growth rate as

$$Sustainable\ growth = (1 - Payout\ Ratio) \times ROIC \qquad (8.1)$$

The ROIC is the return on invested capital,[1] and the Payout Ratio is the percentage of profits distributed as dividends. Thus, (1 – Payout Ratio) represents the fraction of the earnings retained for reinvestment in the business (also called the *retention ratio*).

---

[1] See chapter 3 for a description of the ROIC and its drivers.

The sustainable growth rate represents only the growth rate in sales (or profits) that is consistent for a company that

- Maintains a constant capital structure
- Has a constant operating performance; i.e., profit margins and efficiency ratios are constant (and thus the ROIC is stable)
- Is unable to issue new equity (or the management and shareholders do not want to issue additional shares)

For a company in the above circumstances, growth from one period to the next must be generated by reinvestment in new assets (that will later contribute positively to profits).

Consider a company that has an ROIC of 20% and a payout ratio of 80%. The sustainable growth for this company will be

$$\text{Sustainable Growth} = 20\% \times (1 - 80\%) = 4\%.$$

Of course, it is possible for this company to grow at higher rates than 4%, but that will require one of the following actions:

1. Issue new equity, and invest it in new assets.
2. This, however, will change the capital structure, and there are limits to how much debt a company can have.
3. Improve operating efficiency; i.e., improve the ROIC.

Rapid growth requires more cash for investment. By choosing option 1 above, companies can raise cash and invest it in the business. However, there is usually a limit to how much new equity the company can raise from shareholders, and it is not sustainable for a company to go back to its shareholders every year to ask for new capital injections.[2]

Similarly, choosing option 2 above means that the company will go back to its creditors each year and ask for additional loans. But eventually the company will reach its debt capacity, and new debt capital will be unavailable.[3]

Option 3 above requires improvements in the ROIC. This can be achieved by a higher profit margin or by utilizing the company's assets more efficiently. However, increasing the operating efficiency is not always possible, and profit margin increases have their limits.

There is an alternative way of achieving higher than 4% growth rates in the above example. The company can reduce its dividend payments and thus reinvest more within the business.

---

[2] See chapter 7 for a description of the different equity issue types and their implications.

[3] See chapter 5 for a complete analysis of the company's optimal capital structure and its drivers.

But if the management and shareholders decide to keep a steady-state payout ratio rather than change it, the sustainable growth rate will continue to be 4%.

Empirical evidence

On average, internally generated capital (retained earnings) is the most important source of capital available for new projects. New equity issues are extremely rare, and are a very small percentage of the overall stock market size.[4]

Overall, companies should not maximize growth at all costs. This will force them to reduce dividend payments and leverage the company too much. Indeed, as was seen in chapter 3, there is good growth and bad growth. Good growth occurs when the company invests in new projects that have returns higher than the cost of capital (ROIC > WACC). Bad growth occurs when the company invests in activities with limited profitability (below the cost of capital). Limiting growth is sometimes a way to create more value. Put differently, deploying a company's assets to projects that do not earn the cost of capital is a guaranteed way of destroying value.

Value creation is the responsibility of every manager. This means that managers should invest in projects with higher returns than the minimum rate required by shareholders.[5] Therefore, if the company has positive-NPV investment opportunities, it should invest in those. Otherwise, the company should pay out its free cash flows. If managers ignore these principles, they may continue to invest in businesses that do not generate attractive returns, leading to low returns on invested capital.

In reality, there are limits to a manager's capability to continue on a value-destroying path. In well-governed companies, the board of directors and the shareholders will eventually replace the underperforming manager. More importantly, these underutilized resources eventually attract the attention of corporate raiders. Investors can then target the company, buy it, and redeploy the assets toward more productive uses. This will guarantee a good return on the investment, and lead the company toward a more efficient path in terms of returns on shareholders capital.

8.3.2 Types of Shareholders and Dividends

Companies have various types of shareholders. Some are short-term oriented, and some have a longer-term approach. The types of shareholders include mutual funds, pension

---

[4] Indeed, in the US from 1965 to 2010, new equity has not been a source of capital at all. The average American corporation has actually reduced equity during this period (that is, buybacks of stocks were larger than all the new stock issues combined).

[5] See chapter 4 for a detailed analysis of capital budgeting and project evaluation methods.

funds, insurance companies, other companies, private equity companies, individual investors, governments (such as sovereign wealth funds), family members, employees, and others.

The importance of dividends differs for each type of shareholder. Empirically, it has been found that the stability of dividends is most important for pension funds and insurance companies. Indeed, these two types of shareholders have a long-term orientation and long-term liabilities.[6] Dividends are an important way for shareholders like pension funds to meet their obligations, i.e., pay pensions to pensioners.[7] Therefore, when a company has a large base of pension funds and insurance company investors, it should avoid substantial dividend decreases.

Other types of investors, such as mutual funds, do not rely on dividends as much, but they still appreciate stability, as it is equivalent to more predictability and lower risk on their cash flows.

There are implications related to these so-called clientele effects.[8] Investors self-select into different companies according to the payout policies they follow. Investors who want their value to grow through capital gains tend not to invest too much in high-dividend paying shares. Conversely, investors who need a stream of income from dividends tend to seek out companies that will provide this.

8.3.3 What Are Scrip (or Stock) Dividends?

A scrip dividend (or *stock dividends* as it is commonly called in the US) is the process by which, depending on shareholder choice, dividends can be paid in cash or in stocks. Scrip dividends are useful to investors as a low-cost way of accumulating further shares. And from the company's point of view, it conserves cash (if shareholders choose that option of getting their dividends in shares). The direct effect of a scrip dividend is an increase in the number of shares outstanding. This is the negative side of scrip issuance, as it will be earnings dilutive[9] for the company (and for any shareholders who do not take it up). In order to avoid dilution, most scrip dividend programs are associated with share buyback programs in order to maintain a stable number of shares outstanding.

---

[6] Obligations that fall due more than one year in the future. For instance, a pension fund's long-term liabilities are its future pension obligations. For insurance companies, the long-term liabilities include, for instance, their life insurance policies that have to be paid in the future.

[7] Similarly, an insurance company's long-term liabilities are its future insurance obligations, which rely heavily on dividends to be received. Of course, one could argue that if dividends are not there, these institutional investors can sell a small number of shares in order to fulfill their commitments. However, if they want to keep a balanced portfolio, they can incur high transaction costs by selling a small number of shares from each of the companies in their portfolio.

[8] See Baker and Wurgler (2004).

[9] Reduces the earnings per share, as more shares become available.

Shell's scrip dividend

In September 2010, Shell announced changes to its dividend policy to "provide eligible shareholders with a choice to receive dividends in cash or in shares via a Scrip Dividend Programme."[10] Under the program, shareholders could choose how they wanted to receive their dividends — in cash or in an equivalent amount of new shares of Shell. This scrip dividend effectively allowed investors to increase the number of shares they held in Shell without having to buy them in the market (saving taxes[11] and transaction costs). And, as in a usual dividend, it offered those investors that wanted cash the possibility of getting it. The program had the added benefit, from the company's point of view, of keeping significant amounts of cash within the company. It was very successful, and over the first two years of existence, more than 30% of Shell shareholders have opted for the scrip dividend.

8.4   THE IMPACT OF DIVIDENDS ON STOCK PRICES

8.4.1   What Happens after the Dividend Has Been Paid?

The day the company pays dividends to shareholders, it suffers an adjustment in the share price proportional to the dividends paid. The following are the important dates:

- Announcement date: The date the board of directors of the company announces a dividend payment.

- Ex-dividend date: The date the stock becomes ex-dividend; that is, whoever buys the stock that day is no longer entitled to receive the dividend.

- Payment date: The date the actual dividend is paid to those shareholders that held the stock the day prior to the ex-dividend date.

The day the company pays dividends to shareholders, it suffers an adjustment in the share price proportional to the dividends paid.[12]

Suppose a certain share price equals €100, and this company pays a dividend of €5 per share. After the dividend is paid, the stock price is adjusted to €95. This is called the ex-dividend stock price. In terms of shareholder wealth, nothing changes. Shareholders now have €5 in cash in their hands, plus a stock trading at €95.

---

[10] www.shell.com/global/aboutshell/investor/dividend-information/scrip.html.

[11] In some countries, there are significant tax advantages for the scrip dividend (compared with receiving cash dividends). For instance, in the Netherlands, dividends paid out as shares will not be subject to Dutch dividend withholding tax (15%). But this is subject to individual tax circumstances.

[12] The adjustment may be slightly different owing to taxes.

8.4.2   Signaling New Information through Dividends

Besides the above-mentioned technical adjustment in the stock price, dividends provide information to the market. The first thing to keep in mind is that when dividends are increased, investors become confident that the company will maintain them at that level, which in turn increases the stock price. As a rule, companies and investors prefer stable dividends.

Dividend stability represents predictability for the company in terms of its cash flow usage and thus allows for better forecasting. From the investor side, dividend stability is important as it represents a lower risk of payments back to shareholders.

KEY LEARNING POINT ✓

Most companies have a long-run target dividend policy ratio and try to reduce fluctuations in the dividend level.

Most companies, particularly those in cyclical industries, increase dividends, but not exactly in line with increases in profits. If companies keep the payout ratio constant, then, as profits grow by 50%, the absolute dividend level grows by the same percentage. But then, if the profits are reduced by 30% the next year, so are the dividends. In that case, keeping the payout ratio constant leads to excessive dividend volatility, which is generally not appreciated by investors. That is why rather than having a fixed payout ratio, most companies have a target long-run payout ratio, and then they follow a partial adjustment process.

There is extensive research testing the impact of dividend policy changes.[13] On average, these lead to statistically significant immediate share price reactions:

- Dividend increases: a positive return of 1%
- Dividend initiations: a positive return of 3%
- Dividend cuts or omissions: a negative return of 5% to 10%

Dividend increases, which signal positive news on the future prospects of the company, usually trigger an increase in the stock price of the company. The reason is that when a company announces an increase in dividends, it is actually signaling to the market its confidence

---

[13] Increases in dividends are much more frequent than decreases (by a 20:1 ratio).

that it will maintain them at that higher plateau. Dividend initiations have been associated with even greater stock price increases.

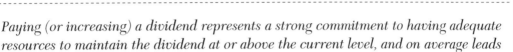

KEY LEARNING POINT ✓

Paying (or increasing) a dividend represents a strong commitment to having adequate resources to maintain the dividend at or above the current level, and on average leads to stock price increases.

Conversely, the market reacts very negatively to cuts in dividends. A company's stock can fall significantly when dividends are cut. And this frequently has implications for management. Indeed, as one CFO of a large multinational company once said, "Cutting dividends is the most threatening career move that a CFO can make."

TABLE 8.1:   The pros and cons of dividends

Pros	Cons
Dividends signal good results and support the share price.	After establishing a dividend program, it is difficult to cut it; investors prefer stable dividends.
Dividends attract long-term investors such as pension funds. This may allow the company to raise capital at a lower cost by reaching a wider range of investors.	Dividends are usually taxed at a higher rate than capital gains.
Dividend increases (or initiations) are usually associated with stock price increases.	Dividend cuts (or omissions) are associated with significant stock price drops.
Dividends use excess cash flow and minimize the conflicts between management and shareholders due to improper use of the company's cash.	Dividends reduce the internal cash available for investments, which may force the company to forgo some positive NPV (net present value) projects.

8.5   IS IT POSSIBLE TO HAVE TOO MUCH CASH?

One of the key motives for holding large cash balances is to have a precautionary cushion for bad times. For example, Microsoft has long held a policy of holding enough cash to survive a year without any sales, and even support suppliers and vendors during that period.

However, many companies have ample resources to fulfill all of their funding requirements due to capital expenditures, as well as to maintain prudent capital structure ratios and working capital levels. In this case, carrying excess cash inside the company is costly for outside shareholders. Having excess cash

- Lowers a company's return on assets (ROA) and return on invested capital (ROIC)
- Increases the cost of capital
- Increases the overall risk of destroying business value

The first two points are technical and should be obvious. High cash reserves are a reflection of the company's past successes. But by having excess cash, the company has more assets than needed (cash is an asset). Because the interest earned on cash is low, a low return on assets and invested capital will follow. Also, because the cost of capital is the weighted average of the debt and equity costs, having excess cash means that the company is using too much equity. This increases the overall cost of capital.

The third point is key for managers. Having excess cash can create an overly confident management team. This can have very damaging consequences for shareholders. For instance, the management of companies with excess cash frequently overpays for acquisitions, which destroys the company's market value. Also, companies with excess cash frequently engage in empire-building quests, which include acquiring companies in unrelated lines of business. There are significant problems with this conglomerate diversification policy: First, it adds no value for shareholders (unless there are significant synergies across the businesses). If shareholders want to achieve a diversified portfolio, they can do it on their own, by acquiring shares of pure players in different industries. Second, conglomerates are well known for having a series of inefficiencies, namely, in the internal allocation of capital. Indeed, it is common for a conglomerate's profitable business units to systematically save and subsidize underperforming business units. This means that the allocation of capital is not efficient, and capital does not flow to the most productive investment alternatives.[14]

Overall, on the negative side, extra cash often leads to wasteful investment decisions. The "we need to do something" syndrome affects many managers with excess available cash. This eventually leads to less profitable investment decisions, including overpayment for mergers and acquisitions (M&As) and diversification into unrelated businesses (remember that shareholders can diversify on their own). Diversification per se does not add value.

---

[14] There is abundant literature on the *diversification discount*, which is the term used to reflect the loss in firm value that occurs in diversified conglomerates. On average, the diversification discount is 15% to 20% of firm value.

TABLE 8.2: The pros and cons of excess cash

Advantages	Costs
Increased ability to sustain liquidity crunches	Wasteful investments
Greater flexibility to invest in new profitable projects	"We need to do something" syndrome
Strong signal to competition: deep pockets	Diversification into unrelated businesses
Faster investment decisions	Overpayment for M&As
Increased ability to attract talent	Overly confident management team

On the positive side, companies with lots of cash are better able to deal with liquidity crises (such as the 2008–2009 financial crisis), as the financing conditions in capital markets have less effect on them. Also, the surplus cash reduces the probability of bankruptcy and financial distress. Extra cash brings flexibility, and the added flexibility has value (for instance, there is value in having a fast decision-making process, and investing in projects that have good returns). Also, having deep pockets can send a signal to the competition that the company has the resources to sustain a price war, which will eventually lead to higher prices in the market (if the market is not very competitive). Finally, a possible added benefit of extra cash relates to talent acquisition, as job applicants typically value the stable financial health of a company. **Figure 8.2** displays the average cash-to-assets ratio for different industries.

FIGURE 8.2: Average cash-to-assets ratio in different industries.

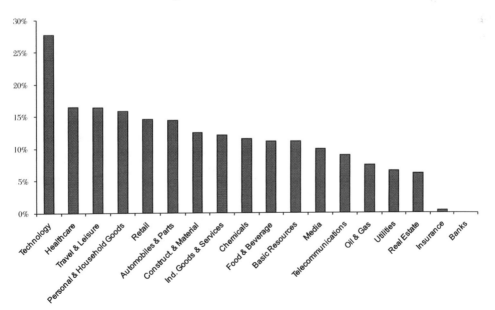

Source: Datastream and IMD research. Ratio of cash and short-term investments to total assets. Data for December 2012, for a sample of the world's 1,500 largest companies.

Higher cash holdings (as a percentage of assets) are common in technology industries and in cyclical sectors. This is expected, as companies in these volatile sectors need to have cash available in order to sustain liquidity crunches and invest in growth projects.[15] Utilities, telecommunications, and oil and gas tend to have lower cash holdings.

Companies viewed as having excessive cash balances frequently come under pressure from institutional investors to return capital to shareholders. Shareholders are concerned that having stockpiles of cash may lead management to engage in value-destroying activities, such as

- Expensive and poorly conceived takeovers
- Value-reducing investments
- Perquisite consumption, i.e., the misuse of cash for the direct personal gain of managers[16]

Empirical evidence — The costs of excess cash

All the value-destroying activities are ultimately reflected in lower shareholder returns. Studies have documented a substantial discount on excess cash held in a company's account. Researchers have shown that investors think that $1 in the company's cash account has an average value of only 80 to 90 cents.[17] For poorly governed companies, the fear that this cash will be misused is even higher, and the value of $1 falls to 30 to 40 cents.

8.6   EMPIRICAL EVIDENCE ON DIVIDEND PAYOUTS

Overall, too high retention of earnings leads investors to discount the value of the company's cash holdings. As a result, the firm value will be less than the sum of its cash holdings and the present value of its expected future free cash flows. In order to prevent this, a company has to convince the market that cash will be profitably reinvested. Typically, the market trusts young companies with valuable growth opportunities to invest cash profitably. On the other hand, mature companies with healthy free cash flows and limited growth opportunities should pay dividends or repurchase shares. In **Figure 8.3**, we present evidence on the payout ratios of large companies around the world.

---

[15] See Opler, Pinkowitz, Stulz, and Williamson (1999) and Ferreira and Vilela (2004).

[16] See Jensen (1986).

[17] Pinkowitz, Stulz, and Williamson (2006) estimate the marginal value of cash. They find that the relation between cash holdings and firm value is much weaker in countries with poor governance standards. Similarly, Dittmar and Marth-Smith (2007) show how the value of cash holdings (as assessed by investors) is substantially lower in poorly governed firms.

FIGURE 8.3: Payout ratios around the world as of 2012.

Europe – Euro Stoxx 50 companies

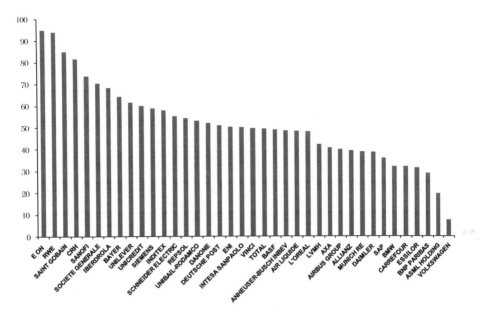

USA – Dow Jones 30 companies

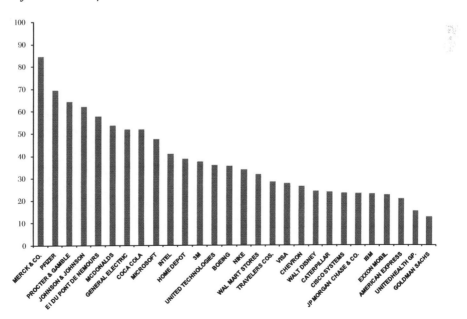

Rest of the World

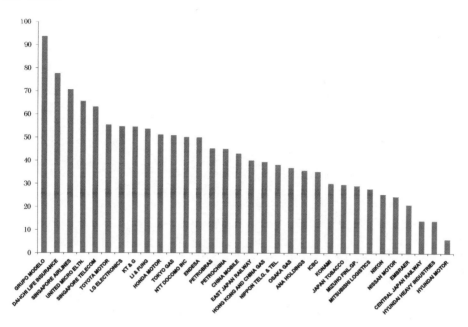

Source: Datastream and IMD research.

Corporate payout policies vary considerably around the world. In general, higher-growth companies tend to pay lower dividends. We observe several high-growth companies, for instance technology companies, that pay low dividends. We should not expect these types of young and growing companies to pay dividends, because the growth opportunities are strong, and investors are better off allowing the company to reinvest all the profits generated in a certain year internally. Conversely, companies in more mature and established industries pay higher dividends.[18] That is typically the case with utilities and telecom companies.

In addition to growth, several other drivers of dividend payouts have been identified. Some of the most important ones are size and profitability.[19] Larger and more profitable companies pay higher dividends. Also, research has found that dividend payouts are related to the quality of corporate governance. Weak governance strengthens the investor interest in higher cash payouts. That is, in countries where governance is poor, shareholders force

---

[18] DeAngelo, DeAngelo, and Stulz (2006) find that the propensity to pay dividends is positively related to the ratio of retained earnings to total equity, a proxy for the firm's life-cycle stage.

[19] Denis and Osobov (2008) find that the propensity to pay dividends is higher among larger, more profitable firms and those for which retained earnings constitute a large fraction of the total equity.

company managers to pay dividends, as they do not trust that the money will be well spent if it stays inside the company.[20] Strong controlling shareholders (usually associated with family companies) are also positively related to the decision to distribute dividends.

8.7 RETURNING MONEY TO SHAREHOLDERS THROUGH SHARE BUYBACKS

Share buybacks (or repurchases) represent a more flexible way of returning money to shareholders.[21] More than 95% of buyback programs worldwide are through an open-market program, whereby the company announces the buyback program, and then repurchases shares in the open market (stock exchange) over a period of time (typically one to two years).[22] There are some guidelines to be followed in order to prevent stock price manipulation. For instance, in many jurisdictions, companies may not purchase more than 25% of the daily trading volume.

Reasons for a buyback

- Distribute excess cash to shareholders.
- Combat the dilutive effect of stock options given to the company's executives.
- Change the capital structure.
- Offset the company's stock options program (including long-term incentive plans) for its employees.
- Invest in the company when it is undervalued by the market.

All the reasons why companies should pay dividends also apply to share repurchases. But for companies with substantial cash balances, stock buybacks represent an opportunity to provide an extraordinary distribution of cash to shareholders.

The Microsoft payout strategy

Although generating substantial amounts of cash, Microsoft had never paid a dividend to its shareholders until 2003. At the time, the company had more than $40 billion in cash, and legitimate pressures from shareholders to return that cash arose (it was the only Dow Jones 30 company not to pay a dividend at the time).

---

[20] See La Porta, Lopez-de-Silanes, Shleifer, and Vishny (2000).

[21] Since the late 1990s, buybacks have become the largest form of payout for US firms. Large share repurchases started later in Europe than in the US (von Eije and Megginson, 2006), but are nowadays a common practice around the world.

[22] The alternative to the open-market purchase is a self-tender offer; the firm offers its shareholders the opportunity to sell their shares back to the company, over a short time window, at a pre-specified price.

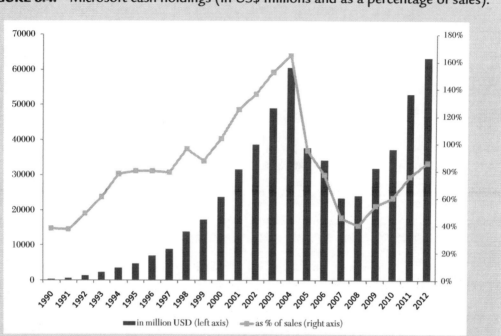

FIGURE 8.4:   Microsoft cash holdings (in US$ millions and as a percentage of sales).

■ in million USD (left axis)   ◆ as % of sales (right axis)

The company then initiated a dividend payment (originally a quarterly dividend of US$0.08, together with a buyback plan of up to US$30 billion. CEO Steve Ballmer explained, "We are confident in our long-term ability to grow revenue, profits, and shareholder value … We will continue to make major investments across all our businesses, and maintain our position as a leading innovator in the industry, but we can now also provide up to $75 billion in total value to shareholders over the next four years."

Overall, this payout was then clearly communicated to investors as a growth story (as opposed to a lack of investment ideas for the future), where excess cash was being generated.

Repurchasing shares may be a more tax-efficient way of returning capital to shareholders when the capital gains tax rate is less than the dividend tax rate. However, taxes are highly dependent on the company's environment and its shareholders, so it is difficult to generalize. Also, the majority of executives agree that taxes are a second-order consideration when designing payout policies.[23]

---

[23] See Brav, Graham, Harvey, and Michaely (2005). See also DeAngelo, DeAngelo, and Skinner (2009) for a comprehensive review of the academic research on corporate payout policy.

A share repurchase reduces the number of outstanding shares, and thus increases the EPS. Changes in the EPS should not be confused with value creation. Indeed, despite changes in the EPS, the intrinsic value of the company remains unchanged.

8.7.1 Buybacks Provide Flexibility

Besides the direct cash impact of returning money to shareholders, there are also other factors at work in buybacks. First and foremost, share buybacks provide an alternative to dividends for companies with volatile cash flows. Indeed, a company with volatile cash flows cannot afford to pay a high dividend, as it may have to reduce it the following year. Because companies and investors prefer stable dividends, a share buyback program in this situation would allow companies to temporarily disburse high levels of cash, while preserving the capability to discontinue the buyback program in a year when the company's operations are not as profitable and cash flows are lower.[24]

This is an important distinction relative to dividends. Share buybacks represent a temporary, one-off event that allows the company to get rid of excess cash and distribute its earnings to shareholders. But it does not commit the company to providing similar payouts in the future.

KEY LEARNING POINT ✓

Share buybacks provide flexibility, and they are usually associated with a positive stock price reaction.

The empirical evidence is clear. Share buyback announcements are associated with positive stock returns (3% on average).[25] That means that shareholders usually view repurchases as a positive event in the life of the company.

However, this is the average announcement return. There are some rare cases in which the market actually reacts negatively to a share buyback announcement. This is again due to the signal that the buyback sends to shareholders. For some companies, a buyback signals that the management has run out of ideas, and the company no longer has attractive investment

---

[24] See Jagannathan, Stephens, and Weisbach (2000).

[25] Several researchers have analyzed the abnormal stock market return at the announcement of a repurchase program. See, for instance, Bradley and Wakeman (1983), Ikenberry, Lakonishok, and Vermaelen (1995), and Chan, Ikenberry, and Lee (2004).

opportunities available. Investors interpret this as a bad sign, and they reduce their expectations of the company's future cash flows, growth rates, and profitability, which ultimately translates into a lower stock price.

Stock buybacks do not always lead to price increases

In May 2005, Vodafone announced changes to its payout policy. The mobile phone company announced that it would buy back GBP 4.5 billion worth of shares, and decided to double its dividends. Despite these decisions, the stock price decreased substantially that day, eroding more than GBP 5 billion in its market capitalization. In other words, investors did not associate this buyback with a great deal. One possible explanation for this apparently puzzling reaction resides in the growth expectations. By distributing all this money among investors, Vodafone signaled to investors that it was no longer a high-growth company, which led to a revision in its valuation and multiples.

TABLE 8.3:   Differences between dividends and share buybacks

Dividends	Share Buybacks
Stable — should not vary widely from year to year.	Discretionary — useful for companies with volatile cash flows.
Dictatorial — all shareholders must receive them, even if they don't want to.	Democratic — allow a choice; if investors do not want to receive cash, they simply do not sell their shares.
Higher taxes — usually taxed at a higher rate than capital gains.	Lower taxes — on capital gains (usually).
Signals confidence in the future — given their stable nature, it reflects confidence in being able to keep dividends at that level in the future.	Reflects lower growth opportunities — may signal that the company's management does not know what to do with the money.
Does not impact the EPS, as the number of shares is unchanged.	Increases the EPS, as the number of shares decreases.

Additionally, by investing in buying their shares, managers signal that they believe the stock is undervalued. Brav, Graham, Harvey, and Michaely have surveyed managers, and found that 75% mentioned market undervaluation of their company's stock as the number one factor that might cause them to consider repurchasing shares in the future.

Also, by returning cash to shareholders, managers signal a commitment that they will not engage in wasteful investments. This commitment to rewarding shareholders when there are not enough profitable investment opportunities, rather than keeping excess cash inside the company, is well received by shareholders.

BP in 2013

On March 23, 2013, BP announced an $8 billion share buyback. This buyback came after the sale of a stake in a Russian unit that left the company with substantial amounts of cash. The buyback was well received by investors (with a positive stock price reaction of 2.5%), who generally considered it good news and a sign that the company puts the interests of shareholders first. The chairman of BP said that this buyback "allows shareholders to see benefits in the near term, from the value we have realized by reshaping our Russian business."[26]

8.7.2   Once a Buyback Has Been Decided, Should a Company Try to Time the Market?

No. It is difficult, and ultimately costs the company a lot of money. As Warren Buffett said: "… Many companies now making repurchases are overpaying departing shareholders at the expense of those who stay …. Buying dollar bills for $1.10 is not good business for those who stick around."[27]

Managers sometimes have the desire to buy low and sell high. That is, they try to time the stock repurchases, in order to buy shares in periods when the shares are undervalued. However, markets are volatile, and this is obviously a difficult strategy to implement. Indeed, research finds that managerial overconfidence often leads executives to buy back shares at peak prices. For instance, while the stock market rose between 2005 and 2008, buyback programs were large and frequent. However, during the stock market downturn of 2009/2010, the majority of companies withheld their buyback programs.

Buyback timing is difficult

"… It would have been wiser to wait. We're sorry." JP Morgan CEO, James Dimon apologizing to shareholders on October 13, 2011, for the $8 billion in buybacks done earlier in that year at a high price.[28]

The JP Morgan example reflects the academic research in the field. On average, companies buy when they should not.[29] That is, companies pay disproportionally large amounts when the stock is high and reduce their purchases when the stock is low. This has an unfortunate consequence. The company is disproportionally rewarding the shareholders who sell in the

---

[26] See Chazan and Oakley (2013).

[27] Warren Buffett, letter to shareholders, March 1, 2000.

[28] See Kopecki (2011).

[29] See Jiang, Bin, and Koller (2011) and Bonaime, Hankins, and Jordan (2013).

buyback program, at the expense of those loyal shareholders who do not tender their shares. The loss to non-selling shareholders has been estimated in the range of 2% to 3% in annual stock returns.

A more efficient way of buying back shares

Follow an income-averaging approach that smoothens repurchasing activities across time. This dollar-cost averaging strategy provides companies with 2% to 3% higher returns than market timing attempts:

Step 1) Determine the overall amount of money available for buyback.

Step 2) Every month, buy the same amount (in dollar terms) of shares, without trying to time the market.

Overall, companies should use buyback programs when they have more cash than they require. Once the decision is taken, they should just gradually implement their buyback over a period of time, and should not try to beat the market during that period.

SUMMARY

Payout policy is a very important component of financial policy, as it closes the circle of finance and returns capital to investors. It determines what part of the company's profits flows to shareholders and what part is retained by the company for reinvestment. Dividends are the regular payouts that companies make to equity holders. Share buybacks represent an alternative way for companies to return money to shareholders. No formula exists to calculate the company's optimum dividend and buyback amounts. But this chapter covers the main drivers of these choices, with supporting empirical data and research:

When no interesting investment opportunities exist, companies should pay dividends to shareholders rather than keeping the accumulated past profits in the company's cash account.

Excessive amounts of cash are typically valued at a discount by investors, who fear that the cash will be misused.

When the company is growing and significant value creation opportunities exist for new projects and businesses, dividends should be kept to a minimum.

For low-growth companies, where not many positive NPV projects exist, dividend payout ratios should be high.

Companies should balance dividends with share buybacks.

Dividends should be stable, and once initiated, should be continued at the same level. Similarly, once a company increases dividends, the expectation is that it will keep them at that higher level into the future.

Share buybacks can be used for one-off distributions of excess cash to shareholders. Buybacks thus provide flexibility for irregular payments that do not commit the company to keeping them forever at that level.

Buybacks signal confidence in the stock price.

Given the importance of stable dividends, companies with more volatile earnings should use buybacks more often.

It is important that the payout be consistent with the type of shareholders the company has as well as its growth stage and financing policy. Before considering the different ways to return money to shareholders, managers must consider the future funding requirements of the company, cash balances, and cash flow forecasts. And managers must know that dividend and buyback announcements frequently have significant implications for the company's stock price. Overall, payout policies should be set in a way that remunerates investors, but also preserves financial flexibility for growth opportunities.

REFERENCES

Baker, M., and J. Wurgler, 2004, A Catering Theory of Dividends, *Journal of Finance*, Vol. 59, Iss. 3:1125–1165.

Bonaime, A.A., K.W. Hankins, and B.D. Jordan, 2013, Is Payout Flexibility Good for Shareholders? Evidence from Share Repurchases, Working paper, 1 May. Available at SSRN: http://ssrn.com/abstract=1977654 or http://dx.doi.org/10.2139/ssrn.1977654.

Bradley, M., and L. Wakeman, 1983, The Wealth Effects of Targeted Share Repurchases, *Journal of Financial Economics*, Vol. 11 (April):301–328.

Brav, A., J. Graham, C. Harvey, and R. Michaely. 2005, Payout Policy in the 21st Century, *Journal of Financial Economics*, Vol. 77, Iss. 3:483–527.

Chan, K., D. Ikenberry, and I. Lee, 2004, Economic Sources of Gain in Stock Repurchases, *Journal of Financial and Quantitative Analysis*, Vol. 39, Iss. 3:461–479.

Chazan, G., and D. Oakley, 2013, "BP to Use TNK-BP Cash for $8bn Buyback," *Financial Times*, 22 March.

DeAngelo, H., L. DeAngelo, and D. Skinner, 2008, Corporate Payout Policy, *Foundations and Trends in Finance* Vol. 3, Iss. 2–3:95–287.

DeAngelo, H., L. DeAngelo, and R. Stulz, 2006, Dividend Policy and the Earned/Contributed Capital Mix: A Test of the Life-Cycle Theory, *Journal of Financial Economics*, Vol. 81, Iss. 2:227–254.

Denis, D., and I. Osobov, 2008, Why Do Firms Pay Dividends? International Evidence on the Determinants of Dividend Policy, *Journal of Financial Economics*, Vol. 89, Iss. 1:62–82.

Dittmar A., and J. Marth-Smith, 2007, Corporate Governance and the Value of Cash Holdings, *Journal of Financial Economics*, Vol. 83, Iss. 3:599–634.

Ferreira, M.A., and A.S. Vilela, 2004, Why Do Firms Hold Cash? Evidence from EMU Countries, *European Financial Management*, Vol. 10, Iss. 2:295–319.

Ikenberry, D., J. Lakonishok, and T. Vermaelen, 1995, Market Underreaction to Open Market Share Repurchases, *Journal of Financial Economics*, Vol. 39:181–208.

Jagannathan, M., C.P. Stephens, and M.S. Weisbach, 2000, Financial Flexibility and the Choice between Dividends and Stock Repurchases, *Journal of Financial Economics*, Vol. 57, Iss. 3:355–384.

Jensen, M., 1986, Agency Costs of Free Cash Flow, Corporate Financing, and Takeovers, *American Economic Review*, Vol. 76, Iss. 2:323–329.

Jiang, B., and T. Koller, 2011, The Savvy Executive's Guide to Buying Back Shares, *McKinsey Quarterly*, October.

Kopecki, D., 2011, JPMorgan's Investment Bank Revenue "Flat," Chief Dimon Says, *Bloomberg*, 7 December.

La Porta, R., F. Lopez-de-Silanes, A. Shleifer, and R. Vishny, 2000, Agency Problems and Dividend Policies around the World, *Journal of Finance*, Vol. 55, Iss. 1:1–33.

Miller, M., and F. Modigliani, 1961, Dividend Policy, Growth, and the Valuation of Shares, *Journal of Business*, Vol. 34, Iss. 4:411–443.

Opler, T., L. Pinkowitz, R. Stulz, and R. Williamson, 1999, The Determinants and Implications of Corporate Cash Holdings, *Journal of Financial Economics*, Vol. 52, Iss. 1:3–46.

Pinkowitz L., R. Stulz, and R. Williamson, 2006, Does the Contribution of Corporate Cash Holdings and Dividends to Firm Value Depend on Governance? A Cross-Country Analysis, *Journal of Finance*, Vol. 61, Iss. 6:2725–2751.

von Eije, H., and W. Megginson, 2008, Dividends and Share Repurchases in the European Union, *Journal of Financial Economics*, Vol. 89, Iss. 2:347–374.

Key Principles for Company Valuation

The value of a company depends not only on the cash flows it provides to its investors but also on the timing and the risk of those cash flows.

Valuation is a key skill for managers who are considering spinning off part of their venture, looking to buy a new asset or company, or planning to sell a stake in the company to outside investors.

Importantly, valuation techniques allow managers to focus their attention on the main drivers under their control, such as operational efficiencies, that impact the value of the company.

9.1   VALUATION MAP

There are two general ways of valuing companies: by discounted cash flows (the DCF method) or by comparison with other companies (also called multiples analysis or relative valuation). And within each of these broad categories, several variants exist.

Discounted Cash Flows	Relative Valuation
Free cash flows to the firm	Price-earnings ratio
Free cash flows to equity	Enterprise value-to-EBITDA
Adjusted present value	Enterprise value-to-sales
Dividend discount model	Price-to-book ratio

In the discounted cash flow method, the main elements are the cash flows and what cost of capital (or discount rate) to use. In the relative valuation method, the key elements are an appropriate sample of benchmark companies and the correct computation of the chosen multiples. In this chapter, we provide further details on these methods.

9.2   VALUING A BUSINESS USING DISCOUNTED CASH FLOWS

The value of a company depends on the cash flows it generates. The same holds true for a proposed investment project, whether it is a capital expenditure, a new product launch, an entry into a new market, or a replacement of a machine. There is an old saying: "Cash is a fact, profit is an opinion." In a DCF valuation, it is thus important to distinguish between profits and cash flows.

Profit (or income) is different from cash flow for a variety of reasons. For instance, booking a sale usually translates into more income. Usually, however, customers obtain trade credit, and only after some time is the cash actually collected. One other major reason for the difference between cash flow and income is the way fixed assets are treated. In accounting terms, the value of a building or car (any kind of fixed asset) depreciates over time. Thus, each year there is an accounting item that reflects how much depreciation the accounting tables allow for those fixed assets. However, in reality, cash is paid when the car is bought. And from then on there are no cash flows related to the acquisition of the car. This implies that when computing cash flows, we have to undo several accounting statement entries to clear them of virtual transactions that have no cash flow implications.

The most common method of company valuation using discounted cash flows is free cash flow to the firm (FCFF), which is covered in detail in this section. With this method, we attempt to determine the enterprise value, or value of the company, by discounting[1] all the cash flows over the life of the company. Then, we can estimate the equity value by subtracting the debt value from the resulting enterprise value. Alternatively, we can use the free cash flow to equity method (FCFE),[2] adjusted present value (APV), or the dividend discount model, which represent slight modifications of the main method described in this chapter — the FCFF method.

We now present a detailed overview of the key steps of company valuation using the FCFF method:

- Define free cash flows to the firm
- Forecast future cash flows and calculating the forecasting period
- Estimate the growth in perpetuity
- Determine the appropriate cost of capital

---

[1] The terms *discounting* and *present value* are used interchangeably.

[2] In the case of the FCFE, we focus on the cash flows (CFs) to equity holders only after all debt-related cash flows have been deducted (new debt issues, interest payments, and amortization of debt). The FCFE is then discounted at the cost of equity. It is important that the cost of equity reflect the appropriate business and financial risk. Also, similar to the FCFF method, a careful analysis of the terminal value should be performed.

9.2.1 Defining Free Cash Flows to the Firm (FCFF)

The free cash flow to the firm (FCFF) represents the cash generated by the company that is available to all capital providers after taxes have been paid and investment needs have been met. This cash can be used to return money to shareholders (either through dividends or share buybacks), repay debt, acquire other companies, reward key employees with extraordinary bonuses, and so on.

The FCFF is also called the unlevered cash flow because it represents the total amount of cash available for distribution to all suppliers of capital, including debtholders. It can also be interpreted as the free cash flow that a company without debt (unleveraged company or all-equity company) would have.[3]

The FCFF is defined for each year as

$$FCFF = EBITDA - \Delta NWC - Taxes - CAPEX \tag{9.1}$$

or

$$FCFF = Unlevered\ Net\ Income + Depreciation - CAPEX - \Delta NWC \tag{9.2}$$

| EBITDA is the earnings before interest, taxes, depreciation, and amortization generated by the company.
| ΔNWC is the annual changes in net working capital.
| Taxes is the amount of taxes to be paid, assuming there are no debt-related tax shields. Tax = EBIT × Tax rate, or EBIT × t. EBIT is earnings before interest and taxes.
| CAPEX is the capital expenditures.
| Unlevered net income is equal to EBIT × (1 – Tax rate). The unlevered net income is also called the net operating profit after taxes (NOPAT).
| Depreciation includes all non-cash operating expenses used for tax purposes, including depreciation, depletion, and amortization.

There are thus two alternative routes to arrive at the FCFF. Using formula (9.1), we start with the EBITDA and subtract changes in the net working capital (ΔNWC). EBITDA less ΔNWC represents the operating cash flows.[4] We then need to subtract the taxes to be paid, as well as the necessary capital expenditures to arrive at the FCFF.

With formula (9.2), we start with the unlevered net income[5] and then add back depreciation expenditures, because these are non-cash expenses recognized only for tax purposes.

---

[3] Interest payments are tax deductible from pre-tax income, which effectively lowers the cost of debt (tax shields). The tax advantage of debt is intentionally excluded from the FCFF calculation. In this way, we avoid double-counting the tax shields, because they are incorporated in the weighted average cost of capital (WACC).

[4] Indeed, the EBITDA is close to the operating cash flow, but not exactly the same owing to working capital account movements related to trade payables, receivables, and inventory.

[5] The unlevered net income represents the profit generated by the company if it does not have any debt-related payments (or the associated tax shields on debt). It equals EBIT × (1 – Tax rate).

Then, as with formula (9.1), we still need to subtract the capital expenditures in the period, as well as the additional investments in the net working capital. The results are identical when both formulas are used correctly.

In the FCFF method, we do not include any debt-related payment in the cash flows. The cost of debt and its associated tax shields are considered in the cost of capital and thus impact the company valuation through the discount rate.

9.2.2   Forecasting Future Cash Flows

In order to estimate the future FCFF, we need to generate projected income statements and balance sheets for future years (also called pro forma accounting statements), so that we can compute the different items needed for the FCFF.

It is common to start with sales. Forecasting a company's sales for future years requires market research analysis as well as competitive positioning, which allow us to compute sales growth rates into the future.

Then, assumptions related to the operating profit margin must be made. We must forecast how the cost of goods sold and general expenses will evolve. It is sometimes assumed that these costs represent a certain percentage of sales. It is also important to consider that in future years margins might be higher or lower than in the past for reasons such as

- Capacity utilization
- Unit labor cost
- Inflation
- Competition — local and foreign

Once we have these assumptions regarding sales and various costs, we can compute the projected EBITDA for each year.

The net working capital also needs to be estimated. It can be defined as a percentage of sales or a fixed amount per customer, or it can be based on monthly terms (e.g., one month of credit to customers, two months of inventories). It is important always to look at changes in the net working capital from one year to the next.

Depreciation, although not a cash item, must also be estimated. Above all, depreciation will impact taxes. Depreciation reflects past capital expenditures made by the company and the average useful life of equipment.

Another key item of the FCFF is the amount of capital expenditures. This represents the investment required to support the company's capacity to generate goods and services according to the planned revenue projections. For companies with no growth, it is common to assume that capital expenditure equals depreciation. If CAPEX equals depreciation, the company is only replacing its assets but not growing beyond its current capacity. In addition, we can assume that the net working capital is constant and, thus, on an annual basis, the company will not change its receivables, inventory, and payables. As a consequence, there is no required investment in working capital on an annual basis. In this case, the free cash flow equals the unlevered net income (or NOPAT). However, it is important to remember that for companies that are growing, capital expenditure is likely to be growing as well. And it is typically the case that CAPEX is higher than depreciation, which means that the overall net assets grow over time.

Overall, we need to have forecasts for each year for each of the components of the FCFF formulas (9.1) and (9.2). These cash flow forecasts should be based on sound industry and company analysis and should reflect industry trends, market research data, competitive pressures, and company strategy. Obviously, good-quality inputs are essential to generate accurate FCFF forecasts and, ultimately, a trustworthy company valuation.

Consider a company with the following financials:

- Previous year revenues = $10,000.
- Estimated revenue growth = 5%, 4%, and 3% over the next 3 years, respectively.
- Cost of goods sold (COGS) = 50% of sales.
- Selling, general, & administrative expenses (SG&A) = 15% of sales.
- The effective tax rate = 30.0%.
- Net working capital requirements = 5% of sales.
- Current assets = $2,000. Additional capital expenditures are planned according to the following table:

	XXX1	XXX2	XXX3
CAPEX	$300	$294	$284

- For accounting purposes, the company uses a 10% annual depreciation rate.

Regardless of the method chosen to compute the FCFF, we must always prepare a pro forma income statement in order to determine the amount of taxes to be paid, as well as other important components of the FCFF.

In this case, given the above assumptions, revenues grow at 5%, 4%, and 3%, respectively, and the income statement will be as follows:

(in $)	XXX1	XXX2	XXX3
Revenues	10,500	10,920	11,248
COGS	5,250	5,460	5,624
SG&A	1,575	1,638	1,687
EBITDA	**3,675**	**3,822**	**3,937**
Depreciation	200	210	218
EBIT	**3,475**	**3,612**	**3,718**
Taxes (EBIT × tax rate)	1,043	1,084	1,115
Unlevered net income	**2,433**	**2,528**	**2,603**

Given that the company will always require 5% of sales in working capital, the working capital requirements for each year are as follows.

(in $)	XXX1	XXX2	XXX3
Net working capital (NWC)	525	546	562
Changes in NWC	−25	−21	−16

Note that, for valuation purposes, only the yearly changes in the NWC account are relevant. If the NWC increases from one year to the next, that means an additional investment must be made (which explains the negative sign in the second row). In the first year of the forecast, the company needs to have $525 as NWC (5% of year 1 sales). But the company has always required 5% of sales in the NWC account. Because the previous year sales was $10,000, the NWC was $500. This means that only an additional $25 must be invested in the NWC during year 1 of the forecast. Similar reasoning applies to the other years. For instance, in year 2, the company needs $546 as NWC (5% of year 2 sales). This means that there is an additional investment of $21 in the NWC.

Under formula (9.1), the FCFF can be computed as follows.

(in $)	XXX1	XXX2	XXX3
EBITDA	3,675	3,822	3,937
− Changes in NWC	−25	−21	−16
− Taxes	−1,043	−1,084	−1,115
− CAPEX	−300	−294	−284
FCFF	**2,308**	**2,423**	**2,521**

Alternatively, with formula (9.2), the FCFF can be computed as

(in $)	XXX1	XXX2	XXX3
Unlevered net income	2,433	2,528	2,603
+ Depreciation	200	210	218
– CAPEX	–300	–294	–284
– Changes in NWC	–25	–21	–16
FCFF	**2,308**	**2,423**	**2,521**

Both methods arrive at the same FCFF result of $2,308, $2,423, and $2,521 for year 1, 2, and 3, respectively.

It is important to note that we do not include (or subtract) interest payments, because the objective is to compute the FCFF, which is the cash flow available to pay all owners (or suppliers of capital). All interest and debt-related costs are included in the discount rate — the WACC. Thus, the FCFF is independent of the amount of debt in the capital structure of the company. Changes in the capital structure and, consequently, the tax shield implications of debt, are incorporated in the WACC calculation.

9.2.3 Terminal Value and the Explicit or Forecasting Period

Because companies are usually assumed to have an infinite life,[6] the valuation is usually split into two components: the explicit period (also called the forecast period) and the terminal value (also called perpetuity).

For the explicit period, we compute forecasts of the FCFF for each year. The length of the recommended explicit period varies. There is no absolute truth here. The explicit period depends on our assessment of the prospects for the company's growth. It basically depends on the length of time that we believe the company will be able to grow at a fast rate. But eventually, every company reaches a mature stage, when the terminal value can be computed. For mature companies, it is typical to use five years for the explicit period. For higher-growth companies, where it is reasonable to assume above-average growth for a longer time frame, 10 years can be used. But in certain sectors or companies with even higher growth rates, longer explicit periods could be used.

The terminal value is estimated in the last year of the explicit cash flow period and represents the sum of all the future cash flows that the company is going to generate, in the steady state, thereafter.

---

[6] In some specific cases related to concessions over a certain number of years, this infinite life assumption is obviously not used.

The standard formula for terminal value is

$$TV_t = \frac{FCFF_{t+1}}{WACC - g} = \frac{FCFF_t(1+g)}{WACC - g} \tag{9.3}$$

| TV_t is the terminal value expressed at time t. It is important to remember that it should still be discounted to the present.
| $FCFF_t$ represents the free cash flow to the firm at time t.
| WACC is the weighted average cost of capital.
| g is the constant growth rate that is expected in perpetuity.

The terminal value is equal to the present value of all the cash flows occurring after the explicit period ends. In perpetuity, it is assumed that the company's cash flows will grow at a constant rate (it can also be negative, if we assume a perpetual decline in the FCFF).

Suppose we are interested in computing the terminal value for a company for which we have estimated the first five years of explicit FCFF as follows:

(in $)	XXX1	XXX2	XXX3	XXX4	XXX5
Unlevered net income	2,433	2,528	2,603	2,653	2,706
+ Depreciation	200	210	218	225	229
– CAPEX	–300	–294	–284	–270	–275
– Changes in NWC	–25	–21	–16	–11	–11
Free cash flow to the firm	**2,308**	**2,423**	**2,521**	**2,597**	**2,649**

The assumption is that after year 5, the FCFF is expected to grow in perpetuity at 2% per year. Assume the cost of capital for this company (WACC) equals 9.31%.

We can thus compute the terminal value in year 5, because the company will then grow at a constant rate of 2%.

$$TV_5 = \frac{FCFF_6}{WACC - g} = \frac{FCFF_5(1+g)}{WACC - g} = \frac{2,649 \times (1.02)}{9.31\% - 2\%} = 36,963$$

The terminal value is estimated at $36,963. This terminal value, in the final year of the forecast period (year 5), capitalizes all future cash flows occurring thereafter (from year 6 onward). It is important to remember that this value is, however, computed in year 5, and thus must also be discounted by 5 years to be expressed in present value terms. In this case, the present value of the terminal value (in year 5) equals $23,685.[7]

---

[7] The present value of $36,963 received in five years = $\dfrac{36,963}{(1+0.093)^5}$ = $23,685

9.2.4 Growth in Perpetuity

The free cash flow used in the constant growth formula (formula 9.3) for the terminal value in the above example must be a steady-state cash flow for the year after the forecast period ends. The assumption then is that this cash flow will grow at a constant steady-state rate in perpetuity.

For the terminal value calculation, it is usually assumed that most line items in the financial statement will grow at the expected constant steady-state rate. We must remember that it might be necessary to perform the required calculations for capital expenditures (CAPEX) and the net working capital (NWC) in order to arrive at the final FCFF. CAPEX in the steady state must maintain a certain growth. First, it is necessary to replace assets that are being depreciated. Second, if we assume a certain long-term growth rate for sales, then the assets of the company also have to grow over time. It is important also that this terminal growth be consistent with a sustainable investment and payout policies (section 8.3.1). It is common to assume a certain constant long-term assets/sales ratio, which implies that the operating efficiency of the assets will be maintained in the steady state. Another commonly used alternative is to specify a certain ratio of CAPEX to sales that will be maintained in perpetuity. Alternatively, if we assume growth in revenues when calculating the FCFF but do not allow for growth in CAPEX, we would be assuming an infinite improvement in the efficiency of the assets in place. The same applies to the NWC. If a certain growth is assumed across the company, then the working capital items will also need to grow over time. It is common to assume a certain long-term relation between the NWC and sales: for instance, the NWC is expressed as a certain percentage of sales, which is maintained constant in the long term.

Every company eventually reaches a mature stage. At this point, long-term growth is moderate, and is likely to be close to the inflation rate with some small adjustments for other factors.

It is important to remember that small changes in the growth rate produce large changes in the terminal value. **Table 9.1** shows the present value (that is, already discounted to time 0) of the terminal value for the example above, using different growth rates (WACC = 9.31%).

TABLE 9.1: Present value of the terminal value for different growth rates

(in $)	1.00%	1.50%	2.00%	2.50%	3.00%
Present value of the terminal value	20,839	22,171	23,685	25,421	27,432

Under the base case scenario, where long-term growth is assumed to be 2%, the present value of the terminal value equals $23,685. However, if the long-term growth rate is 1.5%, the terminal value goes down to $22,171. Alternatively, if the long-term growth rate equals 2.5%, the terminal value grows to $25,421.

It is thus advisable to dedicate a substantial amount of time to computing the steady-state growth rate.[8] In perpetuity, no company can grow faster than the overall economy. This means that the growth rate can never be higher than the nominal GDP growth (in the long term). Also, no company can keep growing faster than the overall industry. Finally, the growth rate cannot exceed the cost of capital in perpetuity. In many cases, it is common to assume long-term growth rates of 1% to 2%, that is, close to the inflation rate. But in some sectors (such as fixed-line telecoms), where markets are mature and competitive pressures keep driving margins down, it is sometimes reasonable to assume negative long-term growth rates.

KEY LEARNING POINT ✓

Perpetuity growth is very important in a DCF valuation, so a substantial amount of time should be dedicated to it and its sensitivities.

9.2.5 Company Valuation by DCF — Putting It All Together

The first step in a company valuation is to estimate the cash flows for each year. Second, we must have a clear measure of the cost of capital. Indeed, the estimated FCFFs are all situated in different times (t) and must thus be discounted to the present, using the company's cost of capital (WACC) as a discount rate. This is valid for any DCF analysis, including capital budgeting and investment decision analysis, and when valuing a company, a division, or an acquisition target.

It is important to remember that the cash flows being discounted are the free cash flows to the firm (FCFF). These are the cash flows available to all providers of capital, that is, equity and debt. Thus, when we discount the FCFF, we obtain the enterprise value, which equals the sum of debt and equity values.

---

[8] Market multiples can also be used to estimate the terminal value (and thus provide a robustness check of the terminal value obtained using the FCFF method). This involves estimating the terminal value using market multiples from publicly traded firms comparable to the company being valued. The triangulation of the terminal value using multiples is often used. Given the considerable importance of the terminal value in a valuation, we must use different approaches to estimate it. Multiples are also useful for obtaining an estimate of the implied growth rate that the market is using in its valuations. It can be helpful to think about this when judging the merits of different long-term growth rates.

$$EV = \sum_{t=1}^{\infty} \frac{FCFF_t}{(1 + WACC)^t} \tag{9.4}$$

| *EV* is the enterprise value, which equals the sum of debt and equity.
| *FCFF_t* represents the free cash flow to the firm at time *t*.
| *WACC* is the weighted average cost of capital.

Because the enterprise value is equal to the value of equity plus the value of debt, to calculate the value of the equity, we subtract the debt from the EV.[9]

$$EV = E + D$$

$$E = EV - D$$

| EV is the enterprise value.
| E is the market value of equity.
| D is the market value of debt.

We are interested in valuing the price per share of a company with the following financials:

- Previous year revenues = $10,000
- Estimated revenue growth = 5%, 4%, 3%, 2%, and 2% over the next 5 years, respectively
- Cost of goods sold (COGS) = 50% of sales
- Selling, general, & administrative expenses (SG&A) = 15% of sales
- The effective tax rate = 30%
- Net working capital requirements = 5% of sales
- Current assets = $2,000. Additional capital expenditures are planned according to the following table.

(in $)	XXX1	XXX2	XXX3	XXX4	XXX5
CAPEX	300	294	284	270	275

- For accounting purposes, the company uses a 10% annual depreciation rate.
- After year 5, the FCFF is expected to grow in perpetuity at 2% per year.
- Number of shares outstanding = 850.
- Total debt = $10,000.
- WACC = 9.31%.

We start by estimating the FCFF for the 5-year forecast period, using the above inputs.

---

[9] Debt is the sum of short-term and long-term debt. If the company has any off-balance-sheet liabilities, they should also be included in the debt computation. For instance, if the company has a deficit in its pension fund, the after-tax unfunded liability is also deducted from the enterprise value to arrive at the equity value. This means that a buyer of the company will have to inject cash into the pension fund to eliminate the underfunding, and of course this reduces the value of the company's equity.

(in $)	XXX1	XXX2	XXX3	XXX4	XXX5
EBITDA	3,675	3,822	3,937	4,015	4,096
– Changes in NWC	–25	–21	–16	–11	–11
– Taxes	–1,043	–1,084	–1,115	–1,137	–1,160
– CAPEX	–300	–294	–284	–270	–275
FCFF	2,308	2,423	2,521	2,597	2,649

After the WACC and the forecast period cash flows have been estimated, we can proceed to the terminal value estimation. We compute the terminal value in year 5, assuming the company will then grow at a constant rate of 2%:[10]

$$TV_5 = \frac{FCFF_6}{WACC - g} = \frac{FCFF_5(1+g)}{WACC - g} = \frac{2,649 \times (1.02)}{9.31\% - 2\%} = 36,963$$

With the terminal value computed, we can proceed to the enterprise value calculation, by discounting all the cash flows (FCFF) at the WACC of 9.31%. The terminal value is computed in year 5, and thus must also be discounted five years to be expressed in present value terms:[11]

$$EV = \frac{FCFF_1}{(1+WACC)^1} + \frac{FCFF_2}{(1+WACC)^2} + ... + \frac{FCFF_4}{(1+WACC)^4} + \frac{FCFF_5 + TV_5}{(1+WACC)^5}$$

$$EV = \frac{2,308}{(1+0.0931)^1} + \frac{2,423}{(1+0.0931)^2} + \frac{2,521}{(1+0.0931)^3} + \frac{2,597}{(1+0.0931)^4} + \frac{2,649 + 36,963}{(1+0.0931)^5}$$
$$= 33,270$$

The EV (sum of the discounted FCFF and the terminal value) is estimated to be $33,270. Because the company has a total debt of $10,000, the value of equity is $23,270:

$$Equity = Enterprise\ Value - Debt = \$33,270 - \$10,000 = \$23,270$$

The total market value of the company's equity is estimated at $23,270. Because the company has 850 shares outstanding, the value per share is

$$Value\ per\ share = \$23,270 / 850 = \$27.38.$$

---

[10] It is important that the cash flow used in the numerator of the terminal value formula be computed when the firm is already in steady-state growth. If not, there would be changes in CAPEX and the NWC that must be taken into consideration. In the example here, the year 5 growth rate is 2%, which is similar to the perpetuity growth rate, so no adjustments are needed.

[11] When using Excel to compute the present value of the cash flows, we can use the NPV (rate; cash flows) formula. It is important to watch out for the timing specifications used by Excel. Specifically, the first cash flow introduced in the formula will be discounted by one year, the second by two years, and so forth.

9.3   VALUATION OF PRIVATELY HELD COMPANIES

When valuing a privately held company or a division of a company, there is no publicly available data to compute its cost of capital. Likewise, beta calculations exist only for publicly traded companies. Thus, to value privately held companies, or divisions of a company (for a possible spin-off), we need to use the "pure play" method, which involves using companies that operate in the same line of business as a benchmark. For instance, how would you compute the cost of equity for a coffee shop that also sells ice creams and is located by the beach?

It is important to consider what risks exist in the business we are interested in evaluating. Then we must find "pure players" (companies that operate exclusively in the same line of business) and obtain their betas. This will give a good indication of the appropriate beta for our cost-of-equity estimation. In the case of the beach bar, the appropriate comparison group could be restaurants or ice cream companies. We could also envision a scenario (for instance, if the bar is in the Caribbean) in which the relevant risks for the beach bar are correlated with the airline industry or the hotel business. In this case, we would obtain betas of players that are exposed to the same types of risks as our company.

KEY LEARNING POINT ✓

When valuing a privately held company, the cost of capital can be estimated by analyzing a sample of pure players in the line of business we are interested in.

It is important that the betas obtained from comparable publicly traded companies be broken down into two components: business risk and leverage (or financial) risk.

9.3.1   The Effect of Capital Structure — Company Risk Varies with Leverage

The way a company balances its financing between equity and debt has an impact on its cost of equity and its beta — in particular, the use of debt financing increases risk. This is obviously true for debtholders — the cost of debt goes up for higher levels of debt use — but it is also true for equity holders. It is important to remember that equity is always the residual claimant on a company's cash flows. The volatility of a company's earnings also increases when a company has a significant amount of leverage. Thus, the cost of equity increases as the company uses higher percentages of debt financing. Conversely, a company without debt is less risky for its equity owners than a highly leveraged company.

Thus, when using the pure play method, we must recognize that different companies may have different mixes of debt and equity. When we use other companies' benchmarks to obtain a beta (or cost of equity) for a specific investment valuation, it is important to remember that debt increases a company's risk, which partly explains the variation in betas across companies in the same business.

The following formula shows the relation between leverage and cost of equity:

$$r^L_{equity} = r^U_{equity} + \frac{D}{E} \times (r^U_{equity} - r_{debt}) \tag{9.5}$$

| r^L_{equity} is the cost of equity of a leveraged company, r^U_{equity} is the cost of equity of an all-equity company (unleveraged, no debt), r_{debt} is the corporate cost of debt, and D/E is the ratio of debt to equity at market value.

According to the formula, a company's debt use increases the financial risk to shareholders. As a consequence, shareholders' required return (cost of equity) will be higher when the company uses higher levels of debt. In practice, formula (9.8) states that the cost of equity of a leveraged company includes compensation for the normal business risk (cost of equity of an unleveraged company), plus compensation for the additional risk that leverage brings to shareholders.

The same relation can be seen in terms of CAPM betas:[12]

$$\beta^L_{equity} = \beta^U_{equity} \times \left(1 + \frac{D}{E}\right) \tag{9.6}$$

Or, reversing it:

$$\beta^U_{equity} = \frac{\beta^L_{equity}}{1 + \frac{D}{E}} \tag{9.7}$$

| β^L_{equity} is the beta of a leveraged company, β^U_{equity} is the beta of an all-equity company (unlevered beta), and D/E is the ratio of debt to equity at market value.

---

[12] The complete formula includes a component related to the beta of debt. A common assumption in practice is that the beta of debt is zero, and thus we can obtain formula (9.6).

According to formula (9.6), the cost of equity is higher for companies with higher levels of debt. The formula[13] can be reversed to estimate an unlevered beta — formula 9.10 — if the observed levered betas for different companies are known,[14] as well as the amount of their outstanding debt.[15]

Suppose we are interested in valuing a privately held company in the airline industry, which uses 40% of debt (and 60% of equity) to finance itself. The company has a rating of A, which translates into a corporate bond spread of 1.5%. The risk-free rate is 4%, and the market risk premium is 5%. In addition, we observe the following data for a group of comparable companies:

Comparable companies	Observed stock beta	Equity ($m)	Debt ($m)
ABC	0.89	40,055	4,481
DSD	1.21	31,867	27,225
KLF	1.11	29,222	4,454
ZBG	1.39	19,078	9,056

For instance, ABC has a beta of 0.89, a market value of equity of $40,055, and a market value of debt of $4,481.

When trying to estimate the cost of equity for our airline based on these comparable companies, we must take into account the fact that they all have different capital structures, and thus their observed betas reflect not only their business risk in the aviation sector but also their differential financial risk. Thus, when using the pure play method to compute the cost of equity, we must adopt the following steps:

1. Obtain the cost of equity (or betas) for comparable companies in the sector:

	Beta
ABC	0.89
DSD	1.21
KLF	1.11
ZBG	1.39

[13] Alternative formulas exist, using $(1 - t)$ in the computation of levered and unlevered betas. The discussion is more theoretical than practical. The theory part — and the reason for the existence of different formulas than the ones recommended here — relies on different assumptions about the risk of the debt tax shields, as well as about the value of debt. In practice, the discussion is not very relevant. Indeed, if we use the same formulas consistently for levering and unlevering the betas, the end result is very similar, regardless of whether $(1 - t)$ is used or not. (For a discussion of the merits of different formulas, refer to the suggested readings at the end of this chapter.)

[14] Betas for stocks can be obtained from various financial services. These betas are levered betas and thus reflect both the business risk and the financial risk of a company based on the company's debt. Some free sites from which betas can be obtained include finance.yahoo.com; finance.google.com; and the *Financial Times* website. Reuters and Bloomberg (main databases of financial data worldwide) also provide betas for companies worldwide.

[15] In practice, we never observe unlevered betas because almost all firms have some amount of debt.

2. Obtain unlevered betas (or cost of equity) for each of the comparable companies:

$$\beta_{equity}^{U} = \frac{\beta_{equity}^{L}}{1 + \dfrac{D}{E}}$$

What we observe for each company is its levered beta (β_{equity}^{L}). Together with its debt-to-equity ratio (D/E) at market values, we can obtain the implied unlevered beta (β_{equity}^{U}).

Comparable companies	Observed stock beta	Equity ($m)	Debt ($m)	D/E ratio	% Debt	Unlevered beta
ABC	0.89	40,055	4,481	11.19%	10%	0.80
DSD	1.21	31,867	27,225	85.43%	46%	0.65
KLF	1.11	29,222	4,454	15.24%	13%	0.96
ZBG	1.39	19,078	9,056	47.47%	32%	0.94

3. Compute the average of the unlevered betas of the comparable companies:

$$\beta_{sector}^{U} = \text{Average of the } \beta_{equity}^{U} \text{ of the different comparable firms}$$

In the above case, the average of the unlevered betas is equal to 0.84.

4. Apply the relevant capital structure of our company (D/E), using the formula below, in which the unlevered beta (or cost of equity) is the average of the unlevered betas of the comparable companies:

$$\beta_{equity}^{L} = \beta_{Sector}^{U} \times \left(1 + \frac{D}{E}\right)$$

| D and E are the debt and equity of our company, both at market values, and β_{equity}^{U} is the average of the unlevered betas of the comparable companies.

If we decide to use 40% of debt and 60% of equity for our company, the levered beta will be

$$\beta_{equity}^{L} = 0.84 \times \left(1 + \frac{0.4}{0.6}\right) = 1.40$$

After obtaining the beta for our company with the appropriate capital structure, we estimate the cost of equity using the CAPM:

$$r_{equity}^{L} = R_f + \beta^{L} \times (Market\ Risk\ Premium)$$

If the risk-free rate equals 4% and the market risk premium equals 5%, then the cost of equity (which is consistent with our target capital structure in point 4 above) is 11%

$$r^l_{equity} = 4\% + 1.4 \times 5\%$$

5. Estimate the WACC using the same capital structure weights as in 4.

Target debt ratio	Target equity ratio	Corporate tax rate	Spread	Cost of debt	Cost of equity	WACC
40%	60%	30%	1.50%	5.5%	11.00%	8.14%

We would then use this estimated 8.14% WACC to discount the forecasted cash flows of our privately held company in the airline industry.

Thus, to value a privately held company taking into account its capital structure, we adopt the pure play method and follow the steps outlined below:

1. Find publicly traded companies that operate in the same line of business that we are interested in.

2. Obtain their cost of equity (or betas).

3. Unlever the observable betas (from the pure players) to remove the effect of their specific capital structure. Average these unlevered betas of the comparable companies to obtain a cleaner estimate of the true business risk of the industry we are considering.

4. Re-lever industry level beta (from 3), using the target capital structure we envision, to obtain the cost of equity for this company — using our own financing mix — and its risk implications (namely, what are the costs of debt and equity that occur if this capital structure is used).

5. Compute the WACC, using the capital structure used in step 4 and the corresponding costs of equity and debt.

In summary, the capital structure of the company must be reflected in the cost of equity, as well as in the weights (of debt and equity) used in the WACC.

KEY LEARNING POINT ✓

The pure play method should be applied in any valuation of privately held companies, or when valuing a company that is going to change its capital structure substantially.

9.3.2 How to Value a Business if the Weights of Equity and Debt Are Not Known

In the above example, we knew already what mix of debt and equity our company will have. However, in many real-life situations, we are interested in valuing a private company, and thus have no idea of what the appropriate D/E ratio is. We typically know the total debt, but not the equity at market value (which is what we are looking for!). This makes it difficult to compute the levered beta (step 4 above), as well the WACC (step 5).

In practice, there are two options for dealing with this circularity problem:

1. Use some multiple of earnings (for instance, price-to-earnings ratio, price-to-book value, or enterprise value-to-EBITDA) as an approximation of the market value of a company's equity. We can then estimate the WACC using the weights of debt and equity given by this approximation.

2. Start by computing the WACC (as well as the levered beta in step 4) using the book values and then discount the cash flows. We thus obtain a first estimate of the market value of the company by discounting the cash flows with a wrongly calculated WACC (because it uses the book value of equity). We then use this estimated market value to recompute the weights of debt and equity in the WACC, and recompute the company value by discounting the cash flows at this new WACC. Repeat this procedure until the WACC (and consequently the company value) does not change. In practice, we need to iterate three to five times until convergence occurs.

In summary, when valuing a privately held company, we must obtain estimates of the cost of equity based on pure players. But then we must adjust the estimates to incorporate the different capital structures across companies. Similarly, when valuing a company in which the capital structure will change, this circumstance should be taken into account. If the company is currently an all-equity company but management plans to shift the mix of debt and equity to a 50-50 mix, computing the WACC (and any of its components, including the cost of equity) under the assumption of no debt would not be correct. We must always compute the cost of equity, reflecting both the business and financial risks needed for the WACC calculation.

9.4   HOW TO DEAL WITH CASH, MARKETABLE SECURITIES, AND UNCONSOLIDATED SUBSIDIARIES

Up to now, we have assumed that the value of a company comes from the future cash flows it generates. This is correct. But if a company also has a huge amount of cash in the bank, this surely adds to its value. Analysts often use the following formula for the enterprise value:

$$\text{Enterprise Value} = \text{Equity} + \text{Debt} - \text{Cash} \qquad (9.8)$$

This can be interpreted in terms of the value of equity:

$$\text{Equity} = \text{Enterprise Value} - \text{Debt} + \text{Cash} \qquad (9.9)$$

$$\text{Equity} = \text{Enterprise Value} - \text{Net Debt} \qquad (9.10)$$

| Net Debt is equal to Total Debt – Cash.

Formula (9.9) simply states that the value of the equity is equal to the discounted value of the FCFF (enterprise value) minus the debt, plus any cash that the company has.

Suppose that in the example valuing the price per share above (section 9.2.5), the company had $50,000 in the bank (in addition to the estimated cash flows). Surely this would mean that the value of the equity of that company is much higher than the previously computed value. An equity holder would not only be entitled to the future cash flows (which we estimated at $33,270 in present value terms) but also to use the cash right now.

In this case, the value of equity would be

$$E = \$33,270 - \$10,000 + \$50,000 = \$73,270$$

This implies a value per share of $73,270 / 850 = $86.20.

KEY LEARNING POINT ✔

Cash holdings can be added at the end of the valuation, to determine a final value.

The same principle applies to marketable securities the company may have invested in or to other non-consolidated investments in other companies. These investments (or their returns) will not show up in the FCFF calculations.

For instance, if company A owns 20% of an unconsolidated subsidiary B, the discounted FCFF of company A will include only its operating performance, CAPEX, etc. But the value (or the cash flows) of the 20% stake in its subsidiary B is not included there. So, if we are valuing company A, we must acknowledge this and correct its equity value. One option is to add the value of the 20% stake in the subsidiary (which can itself be valued by the DCF or by using its market value if it is a publicly traded company).

$$\text{Equity}_A = \text{EV}_A - \text{Net Debt}_A + (\text{Value of 20\% of B's Equity}) \qquad (9.11)$$

| Equity_A is the value of the equity of company A.
| EV_A is the enterprise value of company A, obtained by discounting its FCFF.
| Net Debt_A equals debt – cash of company A.

An alternative method would be to include the cash flows received from subsidiary B (in the form of dividends) in the FCFF calculation for company A and then discount them to the present.

This idea can be illustrated with a real estate example. Suppose we are valuing a company A, which also has a 10% investment in an apartment building. We have two options:

1. Include the expected cash flows to be received from renting the apartments (10% of the full rental income net of any potential costs) in the FCFF calculation going forward.

2. Add the current market (selling) value of the 10% stake in the apartment building to company A's valuation estimates.

But we cannot do both! Including the cash flows from the rental income and then adding the sales value of this stake would obviously be a mistake.

KEY LEARNING POINT ✔

When valuing a company that has unconsolidated subsidiaries (that do not appear in the cash flow estimations), we must add their estimated value to the final valuation calculation.

9.5 VALUATION USING COMPARABLE COMPANIES — MULTIPLES

Up to now, we have been focusing on valuation by discounting cash flows. Alternatively, it is also common when valuing a company to analyze comparable companies' trading multiples as a benchmark. This involves analyzing various multiples (see below) that companies in the same industry are trading at. A number of different multiples are commonly used:

- Price-earnings ratio (PER) = P/EPS (or Value of equity[16]/Net income)

- Enterprise value to EBITDA = EV/EBITDA

- Price-to-book ratio = Market price per share/Book value of equity per share

- Dividend yield = Dividends per share/Price, or Total dividends paid/Value of equity

- Price-to-sales ratio = P/Sales

The rationale for a multiple analysis is to see how much the market is currently paying for an asset with similar characteristics as the one we are interested in valuing.

Multiples are widely used when valuing small companies for which cash flow estimates are not very reliable.[17] In addition, multiples are frequently used as complements to a DCF valuation in M&As and IPOs when it is important to know "how much the market is paying for similar companies."

9.5.1   Steps in a Multiple-Based Valuation

When using multiples to value a company, we follow these steps:

1. Choose a multiple (EV/EBITDA, PER, etc.)

2. Choose a list of comparable companies.

3. Compute the multiple for each of the comparable companies, and average them.

4. Multiply the average multiple of the peer group by our company's relevant indicator (EBITDA, for instance, if the chosen multiple is the EV/EBITDA).

We want to value a company with the following financials:

- EBITDA = $40 million
- Net income = $20 million
- Net debt = $80 million
- Shares outstanding = 100 million

And we have identified a peer group of comparable companies that are currently trading at a multiple of EV/EBITDA of 8.0x, and at a multiple of PER of 14.5x.

---

[16]   The value of equity is the market capitalization in the case of publicly traded companies. Market capitalization is obtained by multiplying the price per share by the number of shares outstanding.

[17]   For instance, in some sectors there is a rule of thumb whereby small companies are traded at a certain multiple (150%, for instance) of their annual sales.

EV/EBITDA analysis

Taking 8.0× as a benchmark, our company's EV should be

$$EV = \$40 \text{ million} \times 8 = \$320 \text{ million}$$

Because the debt equals $80 million, this means that the equity value, based on comparable companies, should be close to $240 million ($320 million – $80 million). Thus, the EV/EBITDA analysis suggests a value per share of $2.40 ($240 million/100 million shares).

PER analysis

Taking 14.5 × as a benchmark for the PER, our company's equity value should be

$$\text{Value of equity} = \$20 \text{ million} \times 14.5 = \$290 \text{ million}$$

Thus, the PER analysis suggests a value per share of $2.90 ($290 million/100 million shares).

As seen in the above example, different multiples will result in different estimates of value. This is common, and that is why multiple valuations should be handled with care and must always be combined with a fundamental DCF valuation.

9.5.2   Multiples and Terminal Value Estimates

Market multiples can also be used to estimate the terminal value (and thus provide a robustness check of the terminal value obtained by using the FCFF method). Specifically, instead of computing the terminal value as

$$TV_t = \frac{FCFF_{t+1}}{WACC - g}$$

we can compute it using the EV/EBITDA multiple of comparable companies.

Suppose comparable companies have an EV/EBITDA multiple of 7. This means that the enterprise value of those companies is seven times their EBITDA (on average). Thus, we can apply this multiple to the company being valued:

$$TV_t = 7 \times EBITDA_t$$

| $EBITDA_t$ is the EBITDA of the company being valued in year t.

This triangulation of the terminal value using multiples is often used. Given the considerable importance of the terminal value in a valuation, we must use different approaches to estimate it. Multiples are also useful for obtaining an estimate of the implied growth rate that the market is using in its valuations. It can also be helpful to think about this when judging the merits of different long-term growth rates.

9.5.3 Which Multiple to Choose?

Multiples have sometimes been wrongly used because they are simpler to apply than the DCF method. Indeed, for a multiples valuation, we only need to observe the current data and ratios of our company alongside a number of reference peers. Care should be taken when using multiples, particularly in relation to timing of earnings (whether EPS, net income, or EBITDA) and differences in accounting standards. For instance, if we use the EV/EBITDA multiple, we must ensure that all the EBITDAs are comparable, are measured in the same time period, and use similar accounting standards (if not, the EBITDA numbers need to be adjusted).

KEY LEARNING POINT ✔

When computing multiples for different companies, it is important to watch out for differences in accounting standards and the timing of the data used.

The choice of multiple will affect what peer group is selected. Consider two airlines, where one airline owns its planes, whereas the other leases them. In this case, comparisons based on the EV/EBITDA multiple would be erroneous: The airline that owns its airplanes will have a much higher EBITDA because the cost of the planes will appear in the depreciation charges (thus the cost of the planes will appear below the EBITDA line). Conversely, the airline that leases planes will have a lower EBITDA because the cost of the planes would appear above the EBITDA line. Thus, different capital structures, business models, and asset intensity may make some comparisons of multiples inaccurate.

In practice, perhaps the most commonly used multiple is EV/EBITDA. Its advantage is that it allows comparisons of companies with different leverage (it does not include interest, which EPS does), controls for different depreciation regimes, and is sometimes positive, whereas EPS may be negative. Above all, it focuses on EBITDA, which is a good proxy for operational cash flow (as long as there are no large working capital fluctuations).

And in addition, different industries tend to have certain well-established multiples that are commonly used. For instance, in the oil sector, a commonly used multiple is EV/Reserves, which relates the enterprise value to the total amount of reserves the company has. In the specific case of oil companies, EBITDA shows the current profitability, but typically, the future of these companies (and thus the future EBITDAs) is related to their proven reserves.[18]

KEY LEARNING POINT ✓

EV/EBITDA is the most commonly used multiple, but different sectors do use other multiples.

9.5.4   Multiples Are Related to a Company's Fundamentals

We need to be careful when identifying a group of comparable companies before using a multiple as a benchmark for valuation. It is absolutely vital to consider the details of each company. In principle, multiples are higher for companies that are more profitable, grow more, or have lower risk. Therefore, it is not correct to say that a company is overvalued just because its value reflects a higher multiple than the average in the market for companies in the same industry.

KEY LEARNING POINT ✓

If a company has a higher multiple than the market (or industry), this does not mean it is overvalued.

---

[18] In the late 1990s, most dot-com-related firms had negative earnings, EBITDAs, and, mostly, negligible revenues. When analysts tried to use multiples, some creativity was needed. The multiple that become the standard was the "price per click," whereby companies were evaluated based on the number of clicks from visitors on their website (even if there was no business model behind it to convert clicks into cash flows!). We have to be cautious about using sector-specific multiples that are unrelated to earnings or cash flows and, above all, that allow a whole sector to be overvalued relative to the overall market.

Formula (9.12) shows the breakdown of the PER for a stable growth company:

$$PER = \frac{P_0}{EPS_1} = \frac{\dfrac{EPS_1\left(1 - \dfrac{RE}{Earnings}\right)}{r - g}}{EPS_1} = \frac{1 - \dfrac{RE}{Earnings}}{r - g} = \frac{1 - \dfrac{RE}{Earnings}}{r - ROE \times \dfrac{RE}{Earnings}} \quad (9.12)$$

| PER is the price-earnings ratio, which is the ratio of P_0 (the current price) to EPS_1 (the forecasted earnings per share next year).
| RE is the retained earnings.
| Earnings is the net income of the company.
| g is the growth rate.
| r is the appropriate discount rate (cost of equity, because we are discounting dividends to equity holders).
| ROE is the return on equity, defined as Earnings/Equity.

Thus, the breakdown in formula (9.12) shows how a high-growth company may have a very high PER, and this is justifiable based on its fundamentals (margins/ROE, growth, cost of capital). Indeed, by increasing g, the whole ratio becomes bigger.

Similarly, by increasing r, the ratio becomes smaller. This means that riskier companies, which have a higher cost of capital, should have lower multiples.

KEY LEARNING POINT ✓

Companies with lower risk, higher growth, or higher margins tend to have higher multiples than their peers.

9.5.5 The Number of Companies to Include in the Peer Group

It is therefore common to find, even in the same industry, very different multiples for companies with different business risk, costs, and growth potential. This is an important concern whenever a multiples-based approach to valuation is used. We should not blindly take the average of the multiples of all companies in a sector and use that as a benchmark. Indeed, this is a common mistake in many valuations, which base their multiples on a large number of companies, most of which are not really relevant peers. It is preferable to have a smaller group (less than 10) of carefully chosen comparable companies than a larger group of randomly chosen and very diverse companies.

As we have shown above, it is important to differentiate the benchmark companies based on their fundamental multiple drivers. In the end, when using a multiples approach, we are trying to value a company by using comparable companies as a benchmark. This means that the benchmark companies should be as similar as possible to our company in terms of products, as well as risk, growth, and margins.

KEY LEARNING POINT

It is preferable to have a narrower peer group (with a selected group of companies with similar risk, growth, and margins) than a very wide one, with disparate companies (even though they are in the same industry).

9.5.6 Key Assumptions in a Multiples Valuation

A multiples-based valuation uses a reference group of companies and, based on their valuations, tries to infer the value of the company we are interested in valuing. Multiples are used in everyday life, for instance, in real estate transactions. It is common for real estate agents to talk about price per square meter and apply this "multiple" to houses in a certain city. In the sections above, we have sounded a note of caution about the appropriate choice of a peer group. Indeed, in real estate deals, we also try to assess the price paid in the market for comparable houses with similar characteristics.

Valuation using multiples requires far fewer calculations than a DCF valuation. But this simplicity comes at a cost: It completely ignores whether or not the peer companies are fairly priced. Indeed, this point is often forgotten. When we apply a multiple based on other companies, we are effectively assuming that these companies are fairly priced and that a similar multiple will apply in our case. However, this reasoning leads to a procyclical behavior, in which companies' valuations will be higher using multiples when the whole stock market is inflated.

FIGURE 9.1: Evolution of the PER in the US.

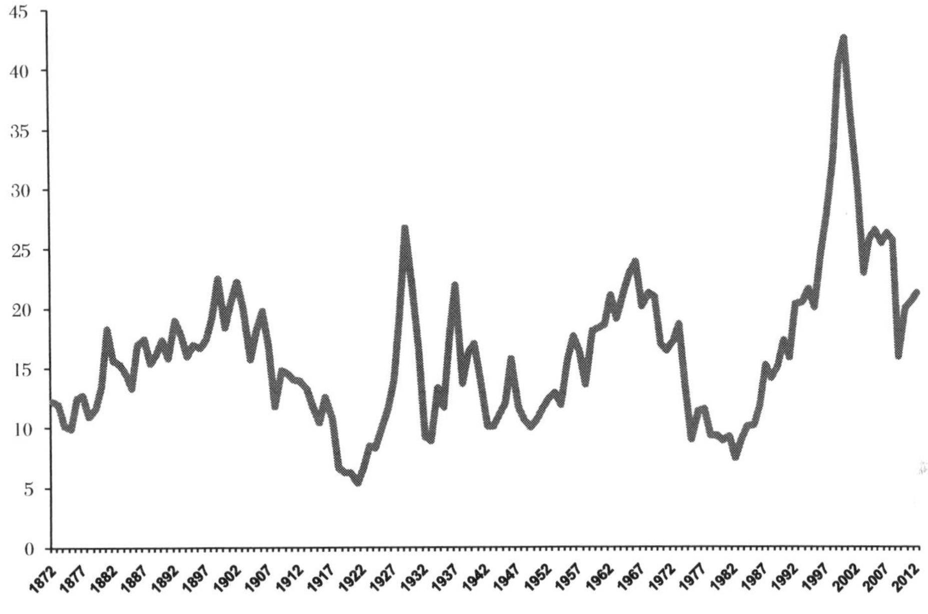

Source: Robert Shiller and Datastream.

Figure 9.1 shows the evolution of the PER in the US over the last 140 years. The market multiple fluctuation can be clearly seen. For instance, in the late 1990s, at the end of the dot-com bubble, the average PER in the market was above 40. Three years later, it was less than half that value.

This means that if we are valuing a company using multiples, the same company (with exactly the same cash flows and fundamentals) will have a value twice as large when the market is high relative to when the market is low. This pro-cyclical behavior leads investors who use multiples to overpay when the market is inflated, relative to the fundamental value or cash flows they are receiving in exchange.

Overall, valuation using multiples is only a comparison of relative value. If the peer group is incorrectly valued, then the resulting multiples valuation will also be inaccurate.

KEY LEARNING POINT ✓

Market multiples can vary greatly over time, and thus significantly affect valuations.

SUMMARY

The valuation of companies is an important but difficult subject. In this chapter, we have looked at the different methods used to value a company. We have provided a detailed description of the DCF method and discussed many practical issues regarding its implementation. We have also shown how multiples can be used to estimate the value of a company and discussed some practical issues and pitfalls regarding their application.

The DCF method of valuation is the recommended method for company valuation. It has the advantage of being a forward-looking metric that focuses on cash flow but recognizes the time value of money as well as risk.

A company valuation needs to take into account the cost of capital and the financing structure of the company. An important point is that the cost of capital is not dictated by the management. It is, rather, the rate of return demanded by the investors who finance a company by buying either company bonds (debtholders) or stocks (equity holders). The WACC is thus a market-value concept that the management needs to know in order to make good decisions for a company's owners. For privately held companies or for divisions of a larger company, the appropriate discount rate must be estimated using comparable companies as a reference.

Finally, as soon as any valuation is complete, the next step is a sensitivity analysis. No valuation is right in an absolute sense, but there are countless wrong ones. There are many assumptions behind any valuation. For managerial decision making, it is vital to know their impact and what the real drivers of value in a company are.

The DCF method allows us to understand the economics of a business. If required, we can explicitly incorporate different information or special insights into the valuation. For instance, we can easily include expected operating efficiency gains in the valuation, or even test a variety of different business models for the company, thereby making it possible to assess the merits (and value) of several proposed managerial actions.

In general, it is recommended to value companies using both the discounted cash flow and the multiples methods. When they give comparable results, it is reassuring for our estimates. And when they differ substantially, we can try to learn what is driving this difference, and refine our analysis.

Value Creation through Mergers and Acquisitions

Mergers and acquisitions (M&As) are important events in the life of any manager and company. This chapter focuses on the strategic and economic considerations in M&As, with a special emphasis on the key drivers of successful acquisition strategies.

Valuation is a key tool for understanding whether a particular merger will add value for shareholders. Thus, this chapter covers concepts such as

- Value creation through M&As. For whom do mergers create value?
- Valuation by discounted cash flows (DCF) in M&As
- Types of synergies and how to consider them
- Appropriate discount rates in an M&A setting
- Valuation using multiples and other market transactions as a reference

It is noteworthy that the principles here also apply to divestitures and spin-offs. Indeed, when a company has taken the strategic decision to divest a business or assets, it must know how to create value from this transaction. This means that the seller must understand the acquirer's motivation and how to get the most out of the deal.

10.1   THE MARKET FOR M&As

Many companies' strategic growth plans involve expansion. Regardless of whether it is domestic or overseas expansion, M&As are usually an important part of the implementation of that strategy.

M&As are one of the biggest moves a company can make, and often involves venturing into new territories (from either a geographical or a product standpoint). A lot of value can be created if they are well executed, but it requires hard work. Indeed, merger success depends on deal structure and rigorous work.

The M&A market is empirically characterized by merger waves – peaks of heavy M&A activity, followed by quiet periods. **Figure 10.1** provides a historical perspective, by showing the number of US deals from 1887 to 2005.

FIGURE 10.1: Merger waves.

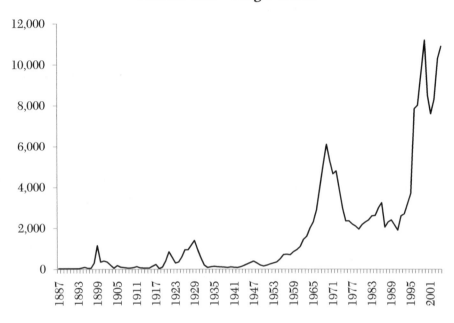

Source: Kummer and Steger (2007).

Empirical evidence has identified several explanations for the unevenness of M&As over time[1]:

- *Economic expansions and rising stock markets* are associated with higher M&A activity. The phenomenon of procyclical mergers is well established.[2]

- Merger waves occur in periods of rapid *credit expansion*.[3]

- Merger waves occur as a response to *innovations and technological shocks*, which occur across different industries.[4]

---

[1] See Andrade, Mitchell, and Stafford (2001) and Betton, Eckbo, and Thorburn (2008) for two surveys of the merger market.

[2] See Shleifer and Vishny (2003), Rhodes-Kropf and Viswanathan (2004), and Rhodes-Kropf, Robinson, and Viswanathan (2005), who argue that merger waves are driven by misvaluation in financial markets.

[3] Maksimovic, Phillips, and Yang (2013) suggest that merger and acquisition waves are driven mostly by the participation of public firms (and not so much by privately held firms).

[4] Harford (2005) finds that merger waves occur in response to specific "industry shocks that require large-scale relocation of assets. Schlingemann, Stulz, and Walkling (2002) find that firms are more likely to sell assets in periods of high industry liquidity. Eisfeldt and Rampini (2006) identify liquidity as the reason why asset sales are procyclical.

Research has also analyzed the evolution of the market for cross-border M&As.[5] In addition to the above factors, this research highlights the importance of geography, culture, institutions, investors, and exchange rate movements.

KEY LEARNING POINT ✓

Mergers tend to occur in waves — peaks of heavy M&A activity, followed by quiet periods.

10.1.1 What Are Hostile Takeovers?

Most mergers are negotiated by the two companies' top management and boards of directors. When an agreement is reached, it is called a "friendly deal." A hostile takeover is one that is not friendly toward the target company's management.

A hostile takeover occurs when the friendly approach fails. In this case, the acquirer goes over the heads of the target company's management and board and appeals directly to its shareholders, who are ultimately the ones who should decide whether a particular price is good enough for them to sell or not. Although this is called a hostile takeover, it is never hostile toward shareholders.

10.2   THE REASONS FOR M&As

There are several good reasons for M&As, such as[6]:

- *Increasing product range*: Combining two companies can improve the end offer to consumers and give the merged entity a stronger product portfolio, from which it generates gains.

---

[5] Rossi and Volpin (2004) show that firms in lower-corporate-governance countries are more likely to be targets of cross-border mergers. Ferreira, Massa, and Matos (2009) investigate the role of institutional investors in the market for M&As: a higher percentage of foreign institutional shareholders increases the probability that a merger is cross-border. Erel, Liao, and Weisbach (2012) find that cross-border mergers are more likely when countries are geographically close and trade more with one another. They also find that countries whose currencies appreciate are more likely to have acquiring firms, whereas countries whose currencies depreciate are more likely to be targets. Ahern, Daminelli, and Fracassi (2012) show that cross-border mergers are more likely if countries share a common religion, common language, and are closer in terms of many cultural variables.

[6] Hoberg and Phillips (2010) show that acquirers who merge with target firms that have complementary products achieve product range expansion, higher operating profitability, and sales growth. Bena and Li (2013) look at the technological overlap between merger partners and find it to be an important source of synergies. Akdogu (2009) looks at the telecommunications sector and finds that firms can gain a competitive edge through acquisitions.

- *Increasing distribution range*: Combining two companies can enlarge the distribution range and geographical scope of activities, thus allowing for cross-selling of products and services.

- *Increasing manufacturing capabilities*: This happens when the target company has some technological edge that can be better leveraged as part of a combined and bigger company.

- *Reducing unit costs*: Often, deals are justified by the generation of cost synergies, whereby the final cost of goods or services can be reduced if two companies are merged.

- *Greater pricing power*: Deals can be justified based on improvements in the competitive positioning, if they ultimately lead to better pricing power.

ABB-Baldor: In 2010, ABB announced its acquisition of the US electric motor manufacturer Baldor. Significant synergies were identified based on the potential from cross-selling through each other's distribution network. The Baldor sale enabled ABB to establish a presence in the US. Also, the deal allowed Baldor to take advantage of ABB's global distribution. In addition, the deal allowed for better portfolios to be offered to the customers, given that the two companies had complementary product lines.

Disney-Pixar: In 2006, Disney acquired Pixar for $7.4 billion, and made it a Disney subsidiary. The merger of Disney and Pixar generated substantial synergies. After the merger, the two companies could collaborate freely and easily. This led to more launches of blockbuster movies. After the merger, Pixar moved to biannual film launches (including *WALL-E*, *Up*, *Cars 2*), which was unthinkable before the merger. And getting integrated advertising, marketing, and merchandising with Disney certainly proved successful.

Exxon-Mobil: In 1999, Exxon and Mobil signed a $81 billion merger agreement that formed ExxonMobil. It became the largest company in the world. The merger allowed for substantial synergies to be achieved in two areas: operating synergies (increases in production and sales, decreases in unit costs, and the ability to combine complementary operations) and capital productivity improvements (efficiencies of scale, cost savings, and sharing of best management practices). There were also technology synergies as both companies owned proprietary technologies that could be used profitably in each other's oil and gas fields.

Despite many examples of "good" M&As, they also occur for the *wrong reasons*:

- Ego
- Empire building
- "Strategic" acquisitions

These wrong reasons are frequent and, to a certain extent, correlated. Indeed, many deals that destroy value occur because of empire-building strategies in which CEOs are often interested in creating a large conglomerate, whether or not synergies exist. In addition, ego tends to play a significant role in the failure of M&As. Overconfident CEOs are prone to pursuing risky deals and tend to pay too much.[7] Finally, in many situations, there is simply no economic rationale for the deal or the price paid. In these cases, a rational analysis of the benefits of the merger does not justify the premium paid for the acquired company. It is common in these situations to see justifications such as "This deal is strategic for us, we'd be crazy not to do it." Some managers have a tendency to believe that once a deal is called "strategic," it creates value for their shareholders — this is not the case at all.

Daimler-Benz and **Chrysler:** In 1998, German automaker Daimler-Benz and the American auto manufacturer Chrysler merged in a $36 billion deal. At the time, it was the largest purchase of a US company by a foreign buyer in US history. Nine years later, Daimler sold the American brand for just $7 billion. In the merger's first year, DaimlerChrysler delivered $1 billion in savings by combining purchasing and back office functions. But following those quick wins, there were significant coordination problems between Daimler and Chrysler, and a total lack of post-merger synergy in engineering as well as in research and development. "You had two companies from different countries with different languages and different styles come together, yet there were no synergies. It was simply an exercise in empire-building by Jürgen Schrempp (Daimler-Benz CEO in 1998).[8] The sharing of parts, components, and vehicle architecture did not materialize, and Chrysler losses began cumulating, until it was finally divested.

Sprint and **Nextel:** In 2005, Sprint paid $36 billion for a majority stake in telecom company Nextel. The idea behind the deal was to quickly merge customers and catch up with Verizon and AT&T. However, incompatible wireless technologies and cultural clashes made that impossible. There was an exodus of Nextel executives after the merger, thousands of layoffs, billion dollar losses, and the company's stock plummeted.

America Online and **Time Warner:** In 2000, AOL purchased Time Warner for $164 billion at the high of the dot-com bubble. Shortly after this megamerger, the dot-com bubble burst, causing a significant reduction in the value of the AOL division. This led to the 2002 losses of $99 billion, the largest annual loss ever reported by a company. In addition, the combined company did not implement content convergence of mass media and the Internet, and AOL executives' know-how in the Internet sector did not translate to capabilities of running a media group with 90,000 employees.

Quaker Oats and **Snapple Beverage:** In 1994, Quaker Oats acquired Snapple for a purchase price of $1.7 billion. Twenty-seven months later, Quaker Oats sold Snapple for $300 million, or a loss of $1.4 billion. Quaker Oats' management thought it could leverage its relationships with large retailers; however, the majority of Snapple's sales came from smaller channels, such as gas

[7] Malmendier and Tate (2008) document that acquirer CEO overconfidence negatively affects acquirer abnormal returns and has a positive effect on firm acquisitiveness. Fernandes, Ferreira, Matos, and Murphy (2013) find that CEO pay is higher in firms with more US acquisitions. Fu, Lin, and Officer (2013) also highlight a governance issue: acquirer CEOs extract substantial rewards for themselves despite the poor performance their shareholders have to suffer. Goel and Thakor (2009) develop and test a model that shows how envious CEOs are more likely to engage in mergers and pay higher acquisition premiums than less envious CEOs. Additionally, Masulis, Wang, and Xie (2007) find that acquisitions that destroy the most value are made by managers who are entrenched, and where the firm's governance is weaker.

[8] Source: Dave Healy, analyst from Burnham Securities.

stations. The acquiring company also changed Snapple's advertising campaign, in which its previously popular ads were replaced with inappropriate marketing signals to customers. At the same time, its rivals Coca-Cola and Pepsi launched a number of competing products that ate away at Snapple's positioning in the beverage market. By the time Snapple was divested, it had suffered a 40% reduction in revenues compared to when it was a stand-alone company.

HP and **Autonomy:** In 2011, Autonomy was acquired by Hewlett-Packard (HP) for $11 billion. One year later, HP wrote off $8.8 billion of Autonomy's value. HP's chief executive and Autonomy founder are among eight defendants of a class action suit that accuses those who oversaw the deal of conducting "cursory due diligence on a polluted and vastly overvalued asset." The HP chairman and its longest-serving directors resigned from the company following the write-down.

10.2.1 When Do M&As Create Value?

M&As are a key element of many companies' strategies to maximize value and create sustainable competitive advantage. Yet, more than 50% of acquisitions fail, and deals that were supposed to create great value for the company end up destroying value. Why?

Acquisitions are complex and difficult to execute and manage successfully. Furthermore, in an M&A, the buyer always pays a premium to the target company's shareholders. It is precisely because this premium is usually too high (overpayment) that, ex-post, mergers destroy value.

KEY LEARNING POINT ✓

If the price paid is too high relative to the fundamental value, the deal destroys value for the buyer.

Valuation thus plays a key part in explaining whether a merger will create value or not. The value of a company depends not only on the cash flows it provides to its investors but also on the timing and the risk of those cash flows. Creation of value for the buyer implies that some of the benefits from the deal will be appropriated by the shareholders of the acquiring company. The idea behind value-creating M&As is

$$\text{Value (A+B)} > V(A) + V(B) \tag{10.1}$$

| V(A+B) = Value of a company created by combining A and B
| V(A) = Value of the independent company A
| V(B) = Value of the independent company B

Value is created through M&As whenever the value of the merged company is greater than the sum of the two stand-alone companies. This typically happens in the cases described above as "good reasons for M&As." However, depending on the amount for which the target company is ultimately acquired, the gains from the M&A will be split unevenly among the buyer's and the seller's shareholders. Indeed, even if a merger creates value, it is possible that it destroys value for the acquirer if the price paid was too high. This is the key problem with most M&As that fail: a lack of understanding, ex-ante, of the economics of the business of the target company and of the value that could be created by merging the two companies. In these cases, the mergers were typically performed by the acquirer for the "wrong reasons" above. Given the importance that valuation plays in separating the winners from the losers in the M&A world, this chapter describes the main methods used to value companies in an M&A setting.[9] The main analysis is based on a free cash flow to the firm/discounted cash flow (FCFF/DCF) approach, but other methods, such as comparable deal multiples and peer multiples in the market are also analyzed.

10.2.2 Empirical Evidence

For many decades, there have been studies on the value created by M&As for bidder and target companies. The overwhelming evidence suggests that the majority of the merger gains are passed on to the target shareholders through the premium paid. And on average, research typically found that there are negative returns for the acquiring companies during the period around the announcement of the M&A, which can be interpreted as value destruction.[10] Additionally, several studies analyzed the long-term returns to shareholders of acquiring companies and tend to find negative returns to the acquirers.[11]

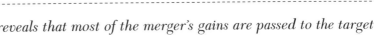

KEY LEARNING POINT ✓

Empirical evidence reveals that most of the merger's gains are passed to the target shareholders, through the high price paid.

---

[9] For further insights into company valuation methods, see chapter 9.

[10] See Andrade, Mitchell, and Stafford (2001) and Betton, Eckbo, and Thorburn (2008) for surveys of the voluminous literature on the gains from M&As.

[11] See Loughran and Vijh (1997) for an analysis of long-term returns following M&As.

But there are some deal characteristics that are associated with higher and lower returns to M&As. Empirical research suggests that the value created by mergers depends on a number of factors:[12]

- *Company size:* Larger companies typically make worse deals. Bidder announcement returns are negatively related to company size.

- *Leverage:* Leveraged companies typically make better deals. Bidder announcement returns are positively related to the bidder pre-acquisition leverage.

- *Diversification:* Mergers that focus on the company's core activity enhance stockholder value, whereas diversifying mergers typically destroy value.

- *Deal size:* When the deal size is large relative to the acquirer's size, the returns are more negative.

- *Payment method:* Cash payments are associated with a positive stock price reaction for the acquirer company. Stock-for-stock exchanges tend to generate lower returns for the buyer.

- *Cash flow level:* Cash-rich companies make worse deals. High levels of free cash flow induce empire-building acquisitions, and there is an empirical negative relationship between bidder returns and the cash-flows-to-equity ratio

- *Whether the company is public or private:* Private companies make better deals, with higher synergies captured, than publicly traded companies.

- *Cultural differences:* Greater cultural differences between the countries of origin of the companies are associated with worse-performing M&As.

10.3   VALUATION IN M&As

The most common method of company valuation in an M&A setting is the free cash flow to the firm (FCFF) method. In this method,[13] we attempt to determine the enterprise value, or value of the company, by discounting all the cash flows over the life of the company. Then, we can estimate the equity value by subtracting the debt value from the resulting enterprise value. In the FCFF method, it is usually assumed that a company has an infinite

[12] See Asquith, Bruner, and Mullins (1983), Morck, Schleifer, and Vishy (1990), Lang, Stulz, and Walkling (1991), Maloney, McCormick, and Mitchell (1993), Schwert (2000), DeLong (2001), Andrade, Mitchell, and Stafford (2001), Moeller, Schlingemann, and Stulz (2004), Moeller, Schlingemann, and Stulz (2005), Dos Santos, Errunza, and Miller (2008), Martynova and Renneboog (2011), Ahern, Daminelli, and Fracassi (2012), among others, for analysis of the different determinants of merger returns.

[13] Alternatively, we can use the free cash flow to equity method (FCFE), which is only a slight modification of the main method described in this chapter — FCFF. In the case of FCFE, we focus on the cash flows (CFs) to equity holders only after all debt-related cash flows have been deducted (new debt issues, interest payments, and amortization of debt). The FCFE is then discounted at the cost of equity. It is important that the cost of equity reflect the appropriate business and financial risk.

life. Thus, the analysis is performed in two (or sometimes more) parts: 1) an explicit forecast period and 2) a terminal value. In the forecast period, we make explicit forecasts of different items in the FCFF. The terminal value is estimated at the end of the forecast period and summarizes the present value of all future cash flows from that period onward.

When valuing a company by FCFF in an M&A setting, the potential sources of value from combining the two companies, or synergies, are key determinants of the valuation. Importantly, company valuation by the DCF method allows explicitly for the computation of the value of the synergies. Under the DCF model, it is common to consider two scenarios: stand-alone value and value with synergies.

10.3.1 Stand-Alone Value

The stand-alone valuation involves forecasting the cash flows that the target company is able to generate on its own. These base cash flows should not include any of the benefits that might result from the merger. We must forecast the cash flows of the target company based on its business plan, a competitive analysis of the market, and the overall growth of the sector and the economy. We perform the following steps:

1. We obtain, for each year, the FCFF of the target company, according to current management plans, which should be consistent with industry trends and competitive positioning.
2. We discount these cash flows at the weighted average cost of capital (WACC) of the target company, which then gives us the stand-alone enterprise value.
3. We obtain the value of the equity of the company by subtracting the net debt value from the resulting enterprise value.

It is important to put aside the time necessary for this stand-alone calculation.

The stand-alone value can be compared to the market value of the target if it is publicly traded and may allow for an assessment of whether the target company is under- or overvalued in the market. Generally, under capital market efficiency, this stand-alone value should not differ much from the current market value of the target (assuming it is publicly traded). In most situations, it is unlikely that the target is substantially under- or overvalued, and thus calibration of the stand-alone model allows the acquirer to understand some of the investors' perceptions of the target company.[14] Thus, the stand-alone valuation provides a floor in terms of the value that the bidder should pay in a negotiation setting. Also, rational

---

[14] For instance, some of the key inputs in any valuation are the discount rate and the perpetuity growth rate. By performing a market valuation, we can reverse-engineer the market estimates of these critical inputs using our stand-alone model.

shareholders of the target company should never agree to sell their company for less than the stand-alone value.

10.3.2 Value with Synergies

The idea behind most M&As is that the synergies between the two companies will operate in such a way that the cash flows generated by the target company will be higher after the merger takes place. When a bidder is considering making an offer for a particular target company, it needs to consider what the possible sources of value are and how much they are worth. Having built a stand-alone valuation, we can add to it the various synergies. Indeed, by combining the two companies, there could be increases in revenue, as well as cost savings from optimizing operations, purchasing, overheads, and the like. Once we incorporate all these operating synergies into the cash flows, we obtain the FCFF with synergies. By discounting the FCFF with synergies at the cost of capital, we obtain the full value of the target company, assuming all the synergies will materialize.

The main sources of synergies are usually the following:

- *Cost of goods sold:* When two entities merge, there are often economies of scale, and the different functional strengths can be optimized. This allows the combined company to become more cost-efficient. There can also be potential cost savings related to purchasing activities because the merged entity may be able to negotiate better conditions with its suppliers.

- *SG&A:* There is usually a certain degree of overlap in administrative and selling expenses between the acquiring and target companies. For instance, in the case of two publicly traded companies, the combined entity will require only a single investor relations department, one CEO, a combined HR department, and so on. Thus, it is reasonable to assume a reduction in SG&A for the target company in most M&As. The level of SG&A reduction depends on the degree of overlap (including geographical) between the acquiring and target companies. Indeed, if the two companies are located in distinct regions, the potential for cost cutting based on combining structures is reduced. However, if the companies are in the same region and sector, combining them generates significant synergies.

- *CAPEX:* Merging companies can translate into benefits in terms of CAPEX. This is frequently the case with M&As in the pharmaceutical industry, where a combination of the R&D of two companies usually allows for significant cost savings in terms of CAPEX because of the overlapping portfolio of drugs under development.

- *Sales*: Revenue synergies are related to possible cross-selling of products and services. Companies can obtain higher growth in new or existing markets owing to the combination of the two companies, for instance, by leveraging each other's distribution networks or presenting a better end-to-end solution to their customers. By presenting a better and more complete product (and service) portfolio, the new entity might be able to increase its revenues (relative to the two stand-alone companies). It is also possible to obtain revenue synergies owing to the greater pricing power due to reduced competition and higher market share.

- *Net working capital*: There can be better use of inventory, an impact on payment terms with suppliers, or different trade credit terms as a result of a merger. This will also impact the value with synergies.

- *Taxes*: There are often financial gains to be explored related to tax optimization (for instance, goodwill amortization). Tax benefits can arise by taking advantage of tax laws and through better use of past net operating losses. If a profitable company acquires a company that has been accumulating losses, the acquiring company might be able to reduce its tax burden. Also, a company can sometimes increase its amortization and depreciation charges after an acquisition, thereby saving taxes and increasing its value.[15]

Real-world synergies

Synergies vary from one deal to another. For instance, in the case of the merger of Glaxo with SmithKline Beecham in 2000, R&D and revenue synergies were key:

"When we at SmithKline Beecham look at acquisitions, we do focus on revenues because our production costs, once we've developed a drug, are minimal. So if we can increase revenues, we're in great shape. And what really drives revenues in the drug business is R&D; there are enormous opportunities in the new technologies now being developed. When we looked at merging with Glaxo, for example, we were talking about synergies in R&D. By merging the two organizations, we probably could save in the neighborhood of $500 million. That's $500 million more a year we could reinvest in the R&D itself, and that's where the merger's real benefit would be."[16]

In other instances, the biggest driver behind a merger is cost synergies, which are made possible through more efficient use of the assets. For instance, in 2008, Delta Air Lines and Northwest Airlines announced a merger agreement to form what was at the time the largest commercial airline in the world. Cost synergies from more effective aircraft utilization were the key driver for the deal. Indeed, the deal was expected to generate more than $500 million of combined savings, through a more comprehensive route system (and therefore better utilization of both companies' airplane fleets) and cost synergies from reduced overheads and improved operational efficiency.

---

[15] Devos, Kadapakkam, and Krishnamurthy (2009) empirically analyze 264 large mergers. They estimate the average synergy gains of mergers to be 10.03% of the combined equity. When they decompose the gains into operating and financial synergies, they find that mergers generate most value by improving resource allocation rather than by reducing tax payments.

[16] Jan Leschly, CEO SmithKline Beecham, May 2000.

Arriving at reasonable numbers for the different synergy components requires rigorous analysis of both companies' operations and businesses. After the synergies have been identified, it is common to assume that they will be achieved gradually, normally in two or three years. The rule of thumb is that if a synergy has not been implemented within three years of the merger, it is because it is no longer there! Once the merger is concluded, it is vital to base the post-integration plan on the forecasted synergies before the merger. Indeed, it is these synergies that define the price to be paid and, ultimately, the value creation of the merger. If they are not adequately pursued in the post-merger period, the merger will obviously not create value for the acquirer.

After obtaining the FCFF with synergies, we discount it using the WACC and obtain the enterprise value of the target, assuming the full value of the synergies[17] to generate the *value with synergies*.

This value with synergies represents the full value of the target company for the acquirer's shareholders if all the planned synergies are implemented. Thus, it also represents the upper limit that a value-maximizing buyer should pay for that particular company. Of course, most bidders do not want to give all the benefits of the merger to the sellers of the acquired company.

KEY LEARNING POINT

Value creation for the acquirer shareholders is only achieved when the price paid for the target company is below the company's full value with synergies.

How these synergies are split between the two parties – buyer and seller – is one of the major issues for negotiation. Indeed, we should aim for a situation in which the synergies are split (not necessarily equally) between the shareholders of the target and acquiring companies. This occurs when the purchase price is above the stand-alone value and is below the value with synergies (see **Figure 10.2**). In this case, value is created for both buyer and seller.

---

[17] Getting from the enterprise value to equity value is a straightforward exercise:

$$\text{Enterprise Value} = \text{Equity} + \text{Debt} - \text{Cash , or}$$
$$\text{Equity} = \text{Enterprise Value} - \text{Debt} + \text{Cash.}$$

FIGURE 10.2:   Value with synergies — value creation for buyer and seller.

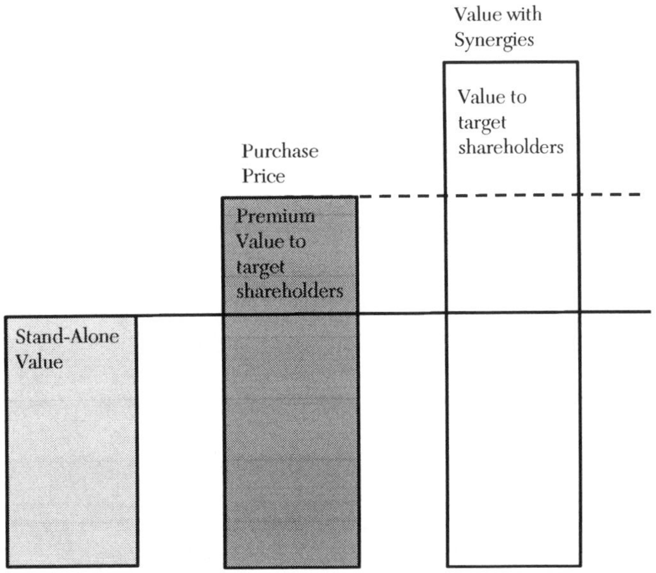

It is precisely because the value with synergies is higher than the stand-alone value that it is normal for a buyer to pay a premium to the target shareholders. It is important to remember that the premium can be higher when there are significant synergies and lower when the synergies are minimal.

However, if the buyer pays a price above the value with synergies, all the benefits of the merger will go to the target shareholders. In this case, the merger will be a value-destroying investment for the shareholders of the acquiring company.

KEY LEARNING POINT ✓

If the seller accepts a price that is below the value with synergies, then it is a win-win situation. If not, the buyer should simply walk away and avoid wasting shareholders' money.

Besides the buy/no buy decision, the purpose of the valuation analysis is to support negotiators. If we know our value boundaries and conduct a sensitivity analysis,[18] we enhance our flexibility to respond to new ideas that may appear at the negotiating table.

10.3.3 WACC Calculation in an M&A Setting

The basic principle of discounting is that the discount rate should compensate investors for the risk involved in the cash flow forecasts. In an M&A setting, the cash flows that are being analyzed – and that the buyer is ultimately interested in acquiring – are the cash flows of the target company. Thus, the appropriate discount rate (or cost of capital) to use is the one of the target company.

KEY LEARNING POINT ✓

When in doubt, always look at where the money is going, rather than where it came from.

If the target and the acquirer are in the same industry, geography, and product lines, they are likely to be exposed to the same business risk. In this case, unless there are striking differences in the capital structures of the two companies, it is acceptable to use the WACC of the acquirer as the discount rate. However, in most situations, the target company's WACC provides a more appropriate discount rate, because it reflects the risk premium that investors demand for incurring the risks involved in the target company's cash flows.

It is important to remember that capital structure matters and that more indebted companies have higher costs of equity (and betas). Thus, if the target company is substantially more leveraged than the acquirer or a typical company in the industry, its cost of equity is also likely to be higher.

If the acquired company is privately held, we must estimate its cost of equity using comparable companies, following the "pure play" method.[19] In this method, we obtain information on the appropriate discount rate by using information on other companies in the target's industry to obtain a reliable estimate of the business and financial risk of the target company.

---

[18] See section 4.5 for an application of sensitivity analysis.

[19] See section 9.3.

Suppose company Buyer is considering buying company Target. Both Buyer and Target are in the same industry and there are significant expected synergies from this transaction.

Prior to the merger, Target has the following financials:

- Previous year revenues = $10,000.
- Estimated revenue growth = 5%, 4%, 3%, 2% and 2% over the next 5 years, respectively.
- Costs of goods sold (COGS) = 50% of sales.
- Selling, general & administrative expenses (SG&A) = 15% of sales.
- The effective tax rate = 30.0%.
- Net working capital requirements = 5% of sales.
- Current assets = $2,000. Capital expenditures are planned according to the table below:

(in $)	XXX1	XXX2	XXX3	XXX4	XXX5
CAPEX	300	294	284	270	275

- For accounting purposes, the company uses a 10% annual depreciation rate.
- After year 5, the FCFF is expected to grow in perpetuity at 2% per year.
- Number of shares outstanding = 850.
- Total debt = $10,000.
- WACC = 9.31%.

Using the above inputs, we can estimate the FCFF for the 5-year forecast period of Target on a stand-alone basis.

(in $)	XXX1	XXX2	XXX3	XXX4	XXX5
EBITDA	3,675	3,822	3,937	4,015	4,096
Changes in NWC	−25	−21	−16	−11	−11
Taxes	−1,043	−1,084	−1,115	−1,137	−1,160
CAPEX	−300	294	−284	−270	−275
Free cash flow to the firm	2,308	2,423	2,521	2,597	2,649
Terminal value					36,963
Present value (PV) FCFF	2,111	2,028	1,930	1,819	25,382

These estimates assume the stand-alone scenario for the growth of sales over time, the cost of goods sold, and SG&A. For instance, the first year EBITDA of $3,675 is computed using the revenues of $10,500 (prior year $10,000 + 5% growth), minus the COGS and SG&A associated with these revenues (COGS = 50% of revenues, SG&A = 15% of revenues). Because the NWC is constant at 5% of sales but sales is growing, every year some additional investment in the NWC should be made. Then we have to consider the taxes the company pays each year, based on the above assumptions. Finally, we subtract the CAPEX planned for each year to obtain the FCFF for each year.

It is important to remember that the appropriate discount rate is that of Target, i.e., the risk of the cash flows being bought (the WACC for Target is 9.31%). According to these FCFF, the value of Target on a stand-alone basis is

Valuation summary stand-alone		
PV of visible period	$9,586	28.8%
PV of terminal value based on DCF	$23,685	71.2%
Enterprise value	**$33,270**	100%
– Net debt	$10,000	
Value of equity	**$23,270**	
Value per share	**$27.38**	

Thus, on a stand-alone basis, the enterprise value (EV) of Target is close to $33,270. The EV is the value of the whole company for its suppliers of capital (debt and equity). Because Target has a net debt (debt – cash) of $10,000 million, the value of the equity stake is valued at $23,270. As Target has 850 shares outstanding, the price per share is $27.38 ($23,270/850) under the stand-alone plan.

Introducing synergies into the model

Under the new management of Buyer, Target's operations will become more efficient, and it will also improve its distribution capabilities. Suppose that the incremental sales due to improved distribution capabilities is $500 next year (and the above growth rates remain unchanged). There are also cost synergies: COGS will be reduced to 48% of sales (from 50%) and, owing to economies of scale, SG&A will be reduced by 1% to 14% of sales (down from 15%).

The FCFF analysis allows us to place a value on these synergies. Specifically, we can model Target including synergies and then compare this to the stand-alone valuation.

According to the above synergies, the pro forma income statement of Target with synergies is

(in $)	XXX1	XXX2	XXX3	XXX4	XXX5
Revenues	11,000	11,440	11,783	12,019	12,259
COGS (without depreciation)	5,280	5,491	5,656	5,769	5,884
SG&A	1,540	1,602	1,650	1,683	1,716
EBITDA	**4,180**	**4,347**	**4,478**	**4,567**	**4,659**
Depreciation	200	220	229	236	240
EBIT	**3,980**	**4,127**	**4,249**	**4,332**	**4,418**
Taxes = (EBIT × Tax rate)	1,194	1,238	1,275	1,299	1,325
Unlevered net income	**2,786**	**2,889**	**2,974**	**3,032**	**3,093**

As a result of the merger, sales is higher ($11,000 vs $10,500) and the costs are lower (COGS and SG&A are both reduced as a result of more efficient operations post-merger), which results in a higher EBITDA. Thus, given these potential synergies, we can compute the DCF value with synergies.

(in $)	XXX1	XXX2	XXX3	XXX4	XXX5
EBITDA	4,180	4,347	4,478	4,567	4,659
Changes in NWC	–50	–22	–17	–12	–12
Taxes	–1,194	–1,241	–1,278	–1,303	–1,329
CAPEX	–300	–294	–284	–270	–275
Free cash flow to the firm	**2,636**	**2,790**	**2,899**	**2,983**	**3,042**
Terminal value					**42,453**
Present value FCFF	2,411	2,335	2,219	2,089	29,152

Thus, the value of Target with synergies can be computed as the NPV of the FCFF above.

Valuation Summary with Synergies		
PV of visible period	$11,005	28.8%
PV of terminal value based on DCF	$27,202	71.2%
Enterprise value	**$38,207**	
– Net debt	$10,000	
Value of equity	**$28,207**	
Value per share	**$33.18**	

Using the same WACC as before (9.31%), we obtain an enterprise value (EV) of $38,207. This compares with the previous value of $33,270. The difference between them is attributable to the synergies that have been generated by a more efficient and productive Target post-acquisition. This EV can be converted into a price per share of $33.18 ($28,207 / 850 shares outstanding). In this case, the total value of the synergies, in present value terms, is given by the difference in EV with and without synergies:

EV with synergies	$38,207
EV stand-alone	$33,270
Value of synergies	$4,936

The value creation potential of the above merger is valued at approximately $5 billion, or $5.81 per share. How this value is shared between the buyer and the seller depends on the final offer price. Obviously, Buyer would not want to offer Target 100% of the synergies (thus paying $33.18

per share). At that price, the NPV of the synergies is all paid to Target shareholders (who sell their shares), and there is no value creation for Buyer, even if all the projected synergies are achieved.

For instance, if Buyer is willing to split the synergies 30/70 (thus paying Target shareholders 70% of the synergies), it will offer a price between the two values (the stand-alone value and the value with synergies) $27.38 and $33.18.

Premium Analysis	
PV of 100% of synergies	$4,936
100% synergies per share	$5.81
Stand-alone value per share	$27.38
% of synergies for Buyer	30%
% of synergies for Target	70%
Offer per share	$31.44
Premium	15%

Given the above example with a 30/70 split of synergies, a $31.44 price per share represents a 15% premium over the previous stock price.

If Buyer offers $27.38, the premium is 0%. In this case, Buyer is offering Target shareholders 0% of the synergies' value and keeps 100% for itself.

Alternatively, if Buyer offers $33.18 per share to Target shareholders (a 21% premium), it is not keeping any of the value from the synergies for itself.

KEY LEARNING POINT ✓

Higher synergies allow for a higher premium to be paid, while still creating value for the buyer.

10.4   OTHER VALUATION APPROACHES

DCF is generally the preferred valuation method in most M&As, because it allows for an explicit valuation of the synergies. However, a number of alternative valuation methods exist to complement a DCF analysis, including current market capitalization, market and transaction multiples, and previous premiums paid.

10.4.1 Current Market Capitalization of the Target

When talking about an acquisition price, the current market capitalization of the target is typically the floor, i.e., the lowest acceptable price. Indeed, it is unusual for the board of directors of a target company to agree to being taken over at a value per share lower than the current market price on the stock exchange.[20] A premium is usually paid, and this premium should be (as seen above) a function of the value of the synergies. In mergers with substantial synergies, the premium paid can be larger and still create value for the acquirer.

10.4.2 Market Multiples

When valuing a company, it is common to analyze comparable companies' trading multiples as a benchmark. This involves analyzing various multiples that companies in the same industry are trading at.

The main multiples used are EV/EBITDA, the price-to-earnings ratio, and the price-to-book ratio. The logic behind a multiple analysis is to see how much the market is currently paying for an asset with similar characteristics to the one being valued.

Before we can use a multiple as a benchmark for valuation, it is essential to identify a group of comparable companies and to consider the details of each one. It is common to obtain multiples from a list of comparable companies and then average them. In doing so, it is important to watch out for outliers. Also, the selection of comparable companies is not a trivial task. Indeed, multiples are often higher for companies with[21]

- Higher growth
- Higher margins
- Lower risk

This is an important consideration whenever a multiples-based approach to valuation is used. We should not blindly take the average of the multiples of all companies in a sector and use that as a benchmark. Indeed, this is a common mistake in many valuations, when

---

[20] Indeed, according to Baker, Pan, and Wurgler (2012), target shareholders are unlikely to accept prices below the maximum stock price over the past year.

[21] See section 9.5 for a more detailed analysis of valuation based on multiples.

the multiples are based on a large number of companies, the majority of which are not really relevant peers.[22]

KEY LEARNING POINT ✓

It is important to carefully select the relevant peers in a multiple's valuation. Multiples are higher for companies that are more profitable, grow more, or have lower risk.

Ultimately, when using a multiples approach, we are trying to value a target company by using other companies as a benchmark. This means that these benchmark companies should be as similar as possible to our company.

10.4.3 Transaction Multiples

In an M&A situation, it is common to analyze, as a benchmark, comparable transactions that have already taken place in the same industry. This involves analyzing the multiples (PER, EV/EBITDA, etc.) paid by acquirers in previous transactions. This is commonly referred to as "what the market is paying."[23] Of course, for comparability, the more recent the deal, and the more similar the transaction is to the one under consideration, the more relevant the deal multiple.

The same caveats as with market multiples apply to transaction multiples. In addition to an appropriate comparison group, it is also important to consider the details of each transaction. In principle, higher multiples occur when there are significant gains from combining two companies. This suggests that, depending on the synergies involved,[24] the multiples may differ across deals. Also, common practice dictates that privately held companies are typically valued at a discount relative to publicly traded ones.[25]

---

[22] It is possible to use regression analysis to generate appropriate multiples based on larger groups of companies. In this case, we would try to identify how much multiples vary with respect to a number of determinants (for instance, growth, profitability, and risk). With this approach, the statistical regression analysis will check for firm differences in those determinants and estimate how much they impact the observed multiples in the market. Finally, we can apply the regression estimates to the reality of the specific company we are interested in to come up with an appropriate multiple.

[23] These multiples from past transactions tend to be higher than market multiples, as they already include a premium paid over the market value of the companies.

[24] These, in turn, depend on the relative efficiency of the two companies, the geographical overlap, potential for cost optimization, etc.

[25] Officer (2007) finds that privately held firms are typically valued at a 15% to 30% discount (lower premium) relative to comparable publicly traded targets.

10.4.4 Previous Premiums Paid

It is also common to analyze premiums paid in previous transactions. The premium is typically defined as the offer price (how much the buyer is offering for each share of the target company) divided by the pre-announcement stock price of the target company. It is important to adjust for possible "run-ups" that may have occurred in the pre-announcement days (often due to information leaks). For this reason, the premium is typically measured over the stock price 30 days (or one week) prior to the announcement.

As with transaction multiples, it is important to consider the details of each transaction. In principle, higher premiums will be paid when there are significant gains from combining two companies. This suggests that, depending on the synergies involved, the premiums may differ across deals.[26]

The empirical evidence on M&As suggests that the average premiums paid fluctuate between 15% and 40% for most mergers. However, it is also clear that many mergers do not create value for the acquirer.[27] This means that the acquirer's shareholders lose money on M&As because the acquirer overpays. Even if all the synergies are successfully implemented after the merger, there is no value creation for the acquirer, who has paid a high premium and offered more than 100% of the value of the synergies to the target company's shareholders.

KEY LEARNING POINT ✓

If there is overpayment, value for the buyer is certain to be destroyed.

10.5   HOW TO PAY FOR THE DEAL

Once a proper valuation has been achieved, an important question arises: How are we going to pay?

---

[26] Betton, Eckbo, and Thorburn (2008) report an average 43% premium paid over the pre-merger price for US deals from 1980 to 2005. But these premiums vary substantially across companies. Bris and Cabolis (2008) show how premiums also vary across countries: acquisitions of firms in weaker-governance countries by firms in stronger-governance countries have a higher premium. Bargeron et al. (2008) show that publicly traded acquirers pay higher premiums than privately held companies do. Alexandridis, Fuller, Terhaar, and Travlos (2013) show that acquirers pay larger premiums for smaller targets.

[27] Bradley, Desai, and Kim (1988), Andrade, Mitchell, and Stafford (2001), and Campa and Hernando (2004) report positive average returns from M&As, suggesting that they create positive synergies. However, the gains go primarily to the target's shareholders.

A bidder can pay using two methods: cash or stock (or a mix of the two). In a cash deal, the bidder pays the target shareholders the agreed price in cash; in a stock deal, the bidder issues new shares and offers them to the target company shareholders. The target shareholders deliver the shares to the target company and, in exchange, receive new shares from the acquiring company. In this case, the price offered needs to be converted into an exchange ratio: the number of acquirer shares to be paid in exchange for each target share.

The form of payment is heavily influenced by the interests of the target shareholders and the financial constraints of the acquirer. For the acquirer, a payment in cash must be financed with cash the company has in its balance sheet or through new issues of debt and/or equity. Of course, this raises issues related to financing and capital structure. For instance, new issues of debt may impact the company's credit rating.

From the target's perspective, cash and stock deals can have different tax exposures. Often, in a cash deal, target shareholders have to pay taxes immediately on any capital gains. In a share deal, the taxes are usually deferred until the target shareholders sell the shares they have received in exchange (acquirer shares). There are numerous reasons (besides taxes) that may lead the seller to prefer cash or shares, depending on the circumstances. For instance, many small family-owned companies are acquired by larger multinationals. In this case, the typical reason for selling is lack of succession (following the founder's death, for instance), and the family simply wants to cash out and not be a shareholder in a large multinational company (in which they would have only a small percentage of shares).[28]

More importantly, cash and share payments have different risk implications. In a cash deal, the target shareholder receives a fixed amount and does not incur any risk if the realized synergies do not materialize. In contrast, by accepting payment in shares, the target shareholders will effectively become shareholders of the new combined company. This means that they will have a stake in the future of the new company. If the synergies are greater than expected, the stock price of the company should rise, and the target shareholders will ultimately benefit. However, if the merger fails to realize significant synergies or the future profitability of the new company takes a hit, the target shareholders will suffer. This means that while a share deal can be risky for target shareholders, it can also bring potential rewards if the merged entity becomes profitable.

---

[28] Ownership structure explains why Faccio and Masulis (2005) find that most European bids are entirely cash financed. Similarly, Moschieri and Campa (2009) find that only 9% of European deals are exclusively paid in stock. Netter, Stegemoller, and Wintoki (2011) report that in the US, approximately 50%–65% of the deals are paid in cash. However, once we look at publicly traded targets, the picture is reversed, and the majority of the deals are financed with stock. Payment methods also vary over time. Shleifer and Vishny (2003) show how when firms are overvalued (stock market boom), managers undertake mergers to exchange their overvalued shares for real assets.

> ## KEY LEARNING POINT ✓
>
> *Receiving payment in shares can be risky for the seller. But the seller also can enjoy potential rewards if the deal (and its integration) is successful.*

10.5.1 Can the Payment be Contingent on Some Future Performance Metrics?

Earnouts, also referred to as contingent payments, are present in some M&A deals, typically in small private company acquisitions.[29] Earnouts are essentially options on the future performance of the target company. An earnout is a plan that involves triggers on payments to the seller. The triggers are based on specific agreements for measuring progress and take the form of a legal contract. This enables the buyer to pay a fixed amount today and then, in the future, pay additional sums of money to the seller if certain performance metrics are achieved (typically a two-year period). Earnouts are also frequently used together with management retention schemes.

Earnouts are particularly useful when there are strong disagreements about future performance (and thus the estimated cash flows) between the buyer and the seller. The seller is frequently more optimistic about the performance of its company than the buyer. This, of course, gives rise to substantial differences in valuations. If both parties agree on a higher valuation if performance goals are met, they can make that valuation differential contingent on meeting those targets. For the buyer, the earnout helps to manage risk. Additional payments only occur if the business performs well in the future or the synergies are realized. For the seller, the earnout can provide additional payments (relative to what a risk-averse buyer would pay) if the performance targets are met.

The difficulty of using earnouts derives from the post-acquisition integration and also the complexity of defining goals. Indeed, once the deal has been completed, it sometimes becomes difficult to assess the performance of the acquired entity, because it is now part of the buyer's operations and integrated into a larger combined company. And finally, the seller is often simply not interested in having any position or contingent claim on the combined company: sometimes the seller just needs cash!

---

[29] Empirically, research has shown that approximately 4% of the announced deals involve earnouts, and these tend to be concentrated on privately held targets, smaller deals, by smaller acquirers. See Cain, Denis, and Denis (2011) for evidence on earnout contracts in acquisitions.

KEY LEARNING POINT ✓

Earnouts are used in a small number of deals, typically when the target is a small, privately held, and young company, where the value is more uncertain.

10.6   THE ROLE OF INVESTMENT BANKS IN M&As

Investment bankers are key stakeholders in many M&A deals. For investment banks, M&As represent one of the most important sources of fee-based income (see **Table 10.1** for a league table).

TABLE 10.1:   The top 25 investment banks worldwide in 2013

Rank	Financial advisor	Value($ million)	Number of deals
1	Goldman Sachs & Co	616,588	402
2	JP Morgan	552,594	302
3	Morgan Stanley	539,278	329
4	Bank of America Merrill Lynch	537,253	234
5	Barclays	361,762	207
6	UBS	317,070	200
7	Deutsche Bank	262,673	201
8	Citigroup	239,886	224
9	Credit Suisse	213,873	247
10	Lazard	195,526	271
11	Guggenheim Securities LLC	143,276	15
12	Rothschild	138,104	265
13	Paul J Taubman	130,100	1
14	Centerview Partners LLC	105,217	34
15	Moelis & Co	103,521	113
16	BNP Paribas SA	98,407	124
17	Evercore Partners	86,848	121
18	RBC Capital Markets	80,208	145

19	Wells Fargo & Co	62,855	54
20	Jefferies LLC	54,912	116
21	HSBC Holdings PLC	53,867	78
22	LionTree Advisors LLC	48,457	8
23	Nomura	46,866	140
24	Macquarie Group	46,331	122
25	PricewaterhouseCoopers	34,924	424

Source: SDC.

In the league tables, the world's biggest banks are ranked for M&A advisory work based on the value of the deals (i.e., enterprise value, including net debt) they were involved in, as advisor of either the target or the acquirer. Goldman Sachs, the leader, was involved in 402 deals in 2013, as advisor of either the target or the acquirer. And the deal value (measured using the enterprise value) of all these deals was $616 billion. The position of different banks in the league tables helps them secure future business, as it is a measure of their experience and reputation.[30]

The average fee is estimated to be less than 1% of the deal value. And the percentage fee is a decreasing function of the transaction value.[31]

However, it should also be clear that the incentives for the investment bank are not always fully aligned with those of the buyer. The investment bank is paid upon completion of the deal, and the fee is directly proportional to the deal size. This means that even if the deal does not create value for the buyer, it still pays the investment bank fees. This does not mean we should not use investment banks. On the contrary, we *must* use them in most cases that involve publicly traded companies. But we must be sure always to seek advice from objective experts and avoid conflicts of interest.

The reality is that most M&As are driven by international investment banks that are not necessarily going to be engaged in the operational realities of the deal or be responsible for the implementation or achievement of the promised synergies. Managers who simply outsource the valuation to an investment bank may be risking their company's money and jeopardizing potential opportunities for significant value creation for their shareholders.[32]

---

[30] Bao and Edmans (2011) show that top-performing advisors in the past continue to provide better advice for the next several years.

[31] Golubov, Petmezas, and Travlos (2012) report an average advisory fee of 0.65% in the case of public firm acquisitions. Furthermore, they show that fees (as well as the return of the deal to the bidder) increase with the investment bank's reputation. See also McLaughlin (1990).

[32] Bodnaruk, Massa, and Simonov (2009) find that the investment bank advising the bidder often builds up a stake in the target prior to the announcement and earns substantial profits. And the size of this stake is negatively related to the post-merger losses of the bidding firm. Evidence to the contrary is found by Griffin, Shu, and Topaloglu (2011), who find no evidence that client information is exploited for trading purposes.

CEOs, CFOs, and other top executives of acquiring companies need to be involved at the earliest possible stage of any merger and understand how valuations are made, so that they can maximize the creation of value for their shareholders. It is also important to make sure that they steer their organizations into identifying and assessing valuable opportunities and risks.

KEY LEARNING POINT

Managers should involve themselves in the valuation, and should not leave it as a "detail" to be performed by the investment banker alone.

Rapidly gaining an understanding of opportunities across the two companies, knowing where to increase revenues and reduce costs, and the like, are fundamental. This stage should provide the rationale for the valuation and deal structure. And it should always be linked to the post-merger integration plan.

10.7 WHAT HAPPENS AFTER THE M&A HAS BEEN COMPLETED?

Once the deal has been signed, the post-merger period begins. At this stage, the buyer has paid a premium to the seller and now has control of the target company.

For many companies, the post-merger integration process begins once the deal has been signed off. This is a mistake. It should be clear by now that the post-merger integration process begins with rigorous pre-merger planning. As soon as the closure of the deal is announced, the post-merger integration process should aim to achieve the pre-merger plans and thus needs to engage different parts of the organization.

It is essential at this stage not to forget what was done in the pre-merger period, namely, the valuation and the synergies that were planned in the value-with-synergies model. We know that the merger will only create value for the acquirer provided those synergies (or more) are indeed implemented in the post-merger period.

KEY LEARNING POINT

The post-merger integration should focus on the items that most justify the valuation of the target company — and hence the premium paid.

Execution is vital, and key implementation decisions must be made rapidly. Speed is of the essence, and not losing external focus is key. Once a company has decided to sell, several problems with customers, suppliers, and employees can arise. It is important to realize this and act accordingly. For example, companies need to keep customers on board, which necessitates fast communication. Also, it is important to engage employees quickly and to make them part of the solution.

Continuity is important. One of the most common mistakes in the M&A world is to dissociate the deal phase from the post-merger period, which explains why most acquirers fail to create value from their acquisitions. For instance, business units or divisions should not be allowed to define the integration approach in isolation. This means that operational managers should be involved from an early stage, because they are closest to the business and know more about the value of the integration strategies/synergies.

Real-world integration

In the case of the previously mentioned Delta Air Lines and Northwest Airlines merger in 2008, the valuation and thus the rationale for the deal hinged on a number of identified synergies. One year after the deal, the original plan of $500 million in synergies had been exceeded (they achieved close to $700 million in one year).

SUMMARY

In this chapter, we have demonstrated tools that allow companies to assess a business opportunity in a more comprehensive and integrated way. Success is measured by how well executives represent the shareholders of their company in an M&A situation.

Value creation through M&As requires a thorough understanding of valuation principles and their application to the target company. The DCF method of valuation is the recommended method for company valuation in an M&A setting. It has the advantage of being a forward-looking metric that focuses on cash flow but also recognizes the time value of money and risk.

Importantly, the DCF method allows for the incorporation of expected operating synergies in the valuation, thereby allowing an evaluation of the merits of the acquisition.

Years of research have shown that, on average, M&As destroy value for buyers. This average number indicates that the majority of bidders overpay relative to what they are buying. That is why valuation and a thorough identification of the sources of value from an M&A are so important. Valuation conducted in the pre-deal period is vital as it identifies value creation opportunities — the drivers of value creation. In addition, valuation tools are essential for devising negotiation strategies, and they help bring about focus in the post-M&A period. The post-merger integration should focus on the items that most justify the valuation of the target company — and hence the premium paid.

Value creation for the acquirer shareholders is only achieved when the price paid for the target company is below the company's full value with synergies. This principle is violated in many cases and leads, ex-post, to significant value destruction as a result of the M&A. Over-payment represents value destruction for the buyer. This value destruction does not mean that the merger is not right or does not make sense. It also does not mean that the synergies between the two companies do not exist or are insignificant. It simply means that even if all the synergies do materialize, the price paid to the seller has already included all the value from the synergies.

M&As that destroy value often start with the wrong approach. The buyer sets out with the objective of closing a deal (for example, "this is strategic for us"), then agrees on a price that makes the seller happy, then finds out what is needed to achieve that price, seeking confirmatory evidence of synergies, and the like. This is a mistake. A bottom-up approach should be taken, starting with a clear understanding of the potential sources of value creation from the deal, setting a time frame for them (and later making people accountable for them) and, finally, taking all this into account when valuing the target company. If the seller accepts a price that is below the value with synergies, then it is a win-win situation. If not, the buyer should simply walk away and avoid wasting shareholders' money.

M&As are important components of many companies' growth strategies. By improving the M&A process and focusing it on value creation, companies increase their chances of success rather than ending up as another statistic on the long list of post-merger failures.

REFERENCES

Alexandridis, G., K. Fuller, L. Terhaar, and N. Travlos, 2013, Deal Size, Acquisition Premia, and Shareholder Gains, *Journal of Corporate Finance*, Vol. 20 (April):1–13.

Akdogu, E., 2009, Gaining a Competitive Edge through Acquisitions: Evidence from the Telecommunications Industry, *Journal of Corporate Finance*, Vol. 15, Iss. 1:99–112.

Andrade G., M. Mitchell, and E. Stafford, 2001, New Evidence and Perspectives on Mergers, *Journal of Economic Perspectives*, Vol. 15, Iss. 2:103–120.

Ahern K., D. Daminelli, and C. Fracassi, 2013, Lost in Translation? The Effect of Cultural Values on Mergers around the World, *Journal of Financial Economics*, forthcoming.

Asquith, P., R.F. Bruner, and D.W. Mullins, Jr., 1983, The Gains to Bidding Firms from Merger, *Journal of Financial Economics*, Vol. 11, Iss. 1–4:121–139.

Bao, J., and A. Edmans, 2011, Do Investment Banks Matter for M&A Returns? *Review of Financial Studies*, Vol. 24, Iss. 7: 2286–2315.

Bargeron, L., F.P. Schlingemann, R.M. Stulz, and C.J. Zutter, 2008, Why Do Private Acquirers Pay So Little Compared to Public Acquirers?, *Journal of Financial Economics*, Vol. 89:375–390.

Baker, M., X. Pan, and J. Wurgler, 2012, The Effect of Reference Point Prices on Mergers and Acquisitions, *Journal of Financial Economics*, Vol. 106, Iss. 1 (October):49–71.

Bena, J., and K. Li, 2013, Corporate Innovations and Mergers and Acquisitions, *Journal of Finance*, forthcoming.

Betton, S., B.E. Eckbo, and K.S. Thorburn, 2008, "Corporate Takeovers," in B.E. Eckbo (ed.) *Handbook of Corporate Finance: Empirical Corporate Finance*, Vol. 2, Elsevier/North-Holland, Ch. 15:289–427.

Bodnaruk, A., M. Massa, and A. Simonov, 2009, Investment Banks as Insiders and the Market for Corporate Control, *Review of Financial Studies*, Vol. 22, Iss. 12:4989–5026.

Bradley, M.D., A.S. Desai, and E.H. Kim, 1988, Synergistic Gains from Corporate Acquisitions and Their Division between the Stockholders of Target and Acquiring Firms, *Journal of Financial Economics*, Vol. 21:3–40.

Bris, A., and C. Cabolis, 2008, The Value of Investor Protection: Firm Evidence From Cross-Border Mergers, *Review of Financial Studies*, Vol. 21, Iss. 2: 605–648.

Cain, M.D., D.J. Denis, D.K. Denis, 2011, Earnouts: A Study of Financial Contracting in Acquisition Agreements, *Journal of Accounting and Economics*, Vol. 51, Iss. 1:151–170.

Campa, J.M., and I. Hernando, 2004, Shareholder Value Creation in European M&As, *European Financial Management*, Vol. 10, Iss. 1:47–81.

Delong, G., 2001, Stockholder Gains from Focusing Versus Diversifying Bank Mergers, *Journal of Financial Economics*, 59, Iss. 2:221–252.

Devos, E., P.-R. Kadapakkam, and S. Krishnamurthy, 2009, How Do Mergers Create Value? A Comparison of Taxes, Market Power, and Efficiency Improvements as Explanations for Synergies, *Review of Financial Studies*, Vol. 22, Iss. 3:1179–1211.

Dos Santos, M.B., V. Errunza, and D. Miller, 2008, Does Corporate International Diversification Destroy Value? Evidence from Cross-Border Mergers and Acquisitions, *Journal of Banking and Finance*, Vol. 32:2716–2724.

Eisfeldt, A., and A. Rampini, 2006, Capital Reallocation and Liquidity, *Journal of Monetary Economics*, Vol. 53:369–399.

Erel, I., R.C. Liao, and M.S. Weisbach, 2012, Determinants of Cross-Border Mergers and Acquisitions, *Journal of Finance*, Vol. 67, Iss. 3:1045–1082.

Faccio, M., and R.W. Masulis, 2005, The Choice of Payment Method in European Mergers and Acquisitions, *Journal of Finance*, Vol. 60:1345–1388.

Ferreira, M.A., M. Massa, and P. Matos, 2009, Shareholders at the Gate? Institutional Investors and Cross-Border Mergers and Acquisitions, *Review of Financial Studies*, Vol. 23:601–644.

Goel, A.M., and A.V. Thakor, 2010, Do Envious CEOs Cause Merger Waves?, *Review of Financial Studies*, Vol. 23, Iss. 2:487–517.

Golubov, A., D. Petmezas, and N.G. Travlos, 2012, When It Pays to Pay Your Investment Banker: New Evidence on the Role of Financial Advisors in M&As, *Journal of Finance*, Vol. 67:271–312.

Griffin, J.M., T. Shu, and S. Topaloglu, 2012, Examining the Dark Side of Financial Markets: Do Institutions Trade on Information from Investment Bank Connections?, *Review of Financial Studies*, Vol. 25:2155–2188.

Harford, J., 2005, What Drives Merger Waves?, *Journal of Financial Economics*, Vol. 77, Iss. 3:529–560.

Hoberg, G., and G. Phillips, 2010, Product Market Synergies and Competition in Mergers and Acquisitions: A Text-Based Analysis, *Review of Financial Studies*, Vol. 23, Iss. 10:3773–3811.

Kummer, C., and U. Steger, 2008, Why Mergers and Acquisition (M&A) Waves Reoccur: The Vicious Circle from Pressure to Failure, *Strategic Management Review*, Vol. 2:44–63.

Lang, L.H.P., R.M. Stulz, and R.A. Walkling, 1989, Managerial Performance, Tobin's Q, and the Gains from Successful Tender Offers, *Journal of Financial Economics*, Vol. 24:137–154

Loughran, T., and A.M. Vijh, 1997, Do Long-Term Shareholders Benefit from Corporate Acquisitions?, *Journal of Finance*, Vol. 52:1765–1790.

Maksimovic, V., G. Phillips, and L. Yang, Private and Public Merger Waves, *Journal of Finance*, forthcoming.

Malmendier, U., and G. Tate, 2008, Who Makes Acquisitions? CEO Overconfidence and the Market's Reaction, *Journal of Financial Economics*, Vol. 89:20–43.

Maloney, M.T., R.E. McCormick, and M.L. Mitchell, 1993, Managerial Decision Making and Capital Structure, *Journal of Business*, Vol. 66:189–217.

Martinova M., and L. Renneboog, 2011, The Performance of the European Market for Corporate Control: Evidence from the Fifth Takeover Wave, *European Financial Management*, Vol. 17, Iss. 2: 208–259.

Masulis, R.W., C. Wang, and F. Xie, 2007, Corporate Governance and Acquirer Returns, *Journal of Finance*, Vol. 62:1851–1889.

Micah, O., 2007, The Price of Corporate Liquidity: Acquisition Discounts for Unlisted Targets, *Journal of Financial Economics*, Vol. 83:571–598.

Moeller, S.B., F.P. Schlingemann, and R.M. Stulz, 2004, Firm Size and the Gains from Acquisitions, *Journal of Financial Economics*, Vol. 73:201–228.

Moeller, S., F. Schlingemann, and R. Stulz, 2005, Wealth Destruction on a Massive Scale? A Study of Acquiring Firms in the Recent Merger Wave, *Journal of Finance*, Vol. 60:757–82.

Morck, R., A. Shleifer, and R.W. Vishny, 1990, Do Managerial Objectives Drive Bad Acquisitions?, *Journal of Finance*, Vol. 45:31–48.

Moschieri, C., and J.M. Campa, 2009, The European M&A Industry: A Market in the Process of Construction, *Academy of Management Perspectives*, Vol. 23, Iss. 4:71–87.

Netter, J.M., M. Stegemoller, and M. B. Wintoki, 2011, Implications of Data Screens on Merger and Acquisition Analysis: A Large Sample Study of Mergers and Acquisitions from 1992–2009, *Review of Financial Studies*, Vol. 24:2316–2357.

Rhodes-Kropf, M., and S. Viswanathan, 2004, Market Valuation and Merger Waves, *Journal of Finance*, Vol. 59, Iss. 6:2685–2718.

Rhodes-Kropf, M., D.T. Robinson, and S. Viswanathan, 2005, Valuation Waves and Merger Activity: The Empirical Evidence, *Journal of Financial Economics*, Vol. 77, Iss. 3:561–603.

Rossi, S., and P.F. Volpin, 2004, Cross-Country Determinants of Mergers and Acquisitions, *Journal of Financial Economics*, Vol. 74, Iss. 2:277–304.

Shleifer, A., and R.W. Vishny, 2003, Stock Market Driven Acquisitions, *Journal of Financial Economics*, Vol. 70:295–311.

Schlingemann, F.P., R.M. Stulz, and R.A. Walkling, 2002, Divestitures and the Liquidity of the Market for Corporate Assets, *Journal of Financial Economics*.

Schwert, G.W., 2000, Hostility in Takeovers: In the Eyes of the Beholder?, *Journal of Finance*, Vol. 55:2599–2640.

Derivatives and Risk Management

Derivatives are financial weapons of mass destruction, carrying dangers that, while now latent, are potentially lethal.

Indeed, at Berkshire, I sometimes engage in large-scale derivatives transactions in order to facilitate certain investment strategies.

Warren Buffett
(Berkshire Hathaway CEO's letter to shareholders, 2002)

Derivatives are an important class of financial instruments (or securities) whose prices are determined by the prices of other (underlying) securities.

This chapter highlights the contradictory nature of Buffett's statements above. Although derivatives have frequently been misused and caused significant harm to many companies, when used correctly they can be very useful and a source of great value.

This chapter introduces the main types of derivatives (futures, forwards, options, and swaps[1]), and discusses

- Why companies use derivatives
- What happens when companies hedge risks
- How derivatives are traded

---

[1] But the detailed explanation (including possible strategies, pricing, trading mechanics) of each of these derivatives is the subject of the next two chapters.

11.1   THE MAIN CATEGORIES OF DERIVATIVES AVAILABLE TO FIRMS

Derivatives can be characterized broadly by

- The specific type of derivative product
- The underlying risk or asset they refer to and the way they are traded
- How they are settled

11.1.1   Different Types of Derivative Products

In terms of products, there are three main categories:

- Futures and forwards
- Options
- Swaps

In a futures (or forward) contract, two parties agree today on the terms under which a certain trade will occur in the future. The parties are a buyer and a seller. The buyer agrees to pay a pre-specified price for a certain asset at a certain date. The seller agrees to deliver the asset for the pre-specified price on the agreed date. Both parties are obliged to fulfill their part in the contract.

In the case of an option, the buyer of the option (to buy) has the right, but not the obligation, to buy the asset. That is, if at the maturity of the option the buyer can find the same asset at a cheaper price in the market, he will not exercise the option. In exchange for this right, the buyer must pay a price (or premium) to the seller.

A swap is a contract between two parties to exchange cash flows. In a swap, each party undertakes to make a series of payments based on the underlying value of a particular variable such as interest rate, commodity price, equity index, or foreign exchange rate. For instance, in an interest rate swap (IRS), one of the most liquid interest rate derivatives, two parties agree to exchange cash flows based on a specified notional[2] amount. Each party agrees to pay either a fixed or a floating rate for a specified maturity.

---

[2] A notional amount is the face amount that is used to calculate payments made on a particular derivative instrument.

11.1.2 Underlying Risks

Derivatives exist on a variety of underlying assets. But the majority of contracts are related to interest rates, foreign exchange, equity-linked (index or stocks), commodities, or credit default swaps (CDSs).

TABLE 11.1: The amount outstanding of derivatives related to the various asset types

($ billion)	Exchange	Over-the counter (OTC)	Total
Interest rate	52,343	494,018	546,361
Foreign exchange	343	66,645	66,988
Equity-linked (index or stocks)	3,762	6,313	10,075
Commodities		2,993	2,993
Credit default swaps		26,931	26,931
Others		42,028	42,028
Total	56,448	638,928	695,376

Source: Bank of International Settlements, 2012.

Table 11.1 shows that in 2012 the amount outstanding of derivatives was close to $700 trillion. Given this large size (for comparison, the market capitalization of all stocks worldwide was less than $50 trillion), derivatives markets are usually very liquid.

Derivative contracts are typically designed for professional users, companies, and institutional investors. They can be traded on an exchange or on an over-the-counter (OTC) market. In the case of exchange-traded derivatives, the contracts that are traded have to be standardized. For OTC contracts, no standardization is necessary because contracts are traded directly between the two parties without the involvement of an exchange. In these cases, it is a bilateral trade in which both parties agree on a particular settlement of the derivative contract in the future.

Overall, OTC markets account for approximately 90% of the total global derivatives market. The flexibility and customization of the OTC market explain its popularity. Indeed, for the majority of assets, organized exchanges offer very limited maturities (less than two years) with sufficient liquidity. This is not the case in OTC markets, in which derivative positions can be contracted for periods up to 10 years. The OTC derivative contracts can be tailor-made in terms of the underlying size, maturity, settlement procedures, and many other features. But given their bilateral nature, OTC contracts are subject to the credit risk of the counterparty. Some of the more common OTC contracts (for example, interest rate swaps) include a plethora of standardized contract parameters, which include procedures for counterparty risk mitigation — such as collateralization.[3]

In contrast, exchange-traded derivatives are standardized, but also liquid. This means that it might sometimes be easier to close or cancel a position in an exchange-traded contract (provided there is enough liquidity[4]) than in an OTC one.[5]

KEY LEARNING POINT

Exchange-traded derivatives are standardized in terms of amounts, maturities, and other terms. Conversely, OTC derivatives are tailor-made to the particular needs of the company.

11.1.3 How Derivatives Are Settled

When a derivative contract matures, it can be settled physically or in cash (which is most common).

Say, for instance, that the contract is a futures contract on 10 tons of frozen orange juice at a pre-specified price of $500 per ton. The buyer is said to have a long position in this futures contract; i.e., he is obliged to buy the asset at the pre-specified conditions.[6] If at maturity, the spot price for frozen orange juice is equal to $700 per ton, the buyer will be happy. He can buy the juice at $500 per ton and not at the market price of $700 per ton.

The physical settlement would consist of the seller bringing the orange juice to a pre-specified location and being paid $5,000 (10 tons × $500). The buyer would be saving $2,000 compared with market prices on the same day.

Alternatively, the buyer and the seller may agree on a cash settlement. In this case, the seller simply transfers $2,000 to the buyer's account, and the contract is then settled. Because a physical settlement usually carries significant transaction costs, it is not surprising that fewer

---

[3] *Collateral* refers to the assets that are pledged by the parties involved in an OTC derivative contract. A wide range of possible assets can be used as collateral, but the most common ones are cash and government securities.

[4] Not all derivatives contracts are liquid. For example, some out-of-the-money (see chapter 13) options of smaller firms can be very illiquid.

[5] In many cases, there is effective competition between exchanges and OTC broker–dealers. For all derivatives categories, exchanges offer products that may protect against exactly the same risk (provided there is enough liquidity).

[6] A long position means that you have invested or bought something. A short position is equivalent to selling.

than 2% of all transactions are physically settled (many contracts do not even allow for physical settlement anymore).

KEY LEARNING POINT ✓

Most derivative contracts are settled in cash, and do not actually need any physical delivery.

11.1.4 The Origins of Derivatives Markets

Derivatives are not a recent invention. Indeed, there are records of derivatives being used several thousand years ago:

- Contracts for the future delivery of goods were frequently used in Mesopotamia as well as in Roman and Greek times.
- Around 600 BC, Thales the Milesian used options on olive presses.
- Forward contracts were traded on tulip bulbs in the early 1600s.
- Futures contracts were traded on the Yodoya rice market in Osaka, Japan, around 1650.

But it was only after the 1970s that derivatives came into extensive use worldwide, for several reasons. First, computer power became more widespread, which enabled complex models and computations to be solved quickly and efficiently. Then, in 1973, Fischer Black and Myron Scholes published their paper, "The Pricing of Options and Corporate Liabilities," which established a rigorous methodology for determining option prices (Black and Scholes, 1973). Until then, the value of derivatives was subject to discussions on the appropriate discount rate and risk to be used to value them. Black and Scholes, along with Robert Merton, showed that derivatives payoffs can be replicated by holding a portfolio of the underlying asset and the risk-free rate. The so-called hedged position could then be valued without any specific assumption about risk — just using the concept of arbitrage.[7] In 1997, Robert Merton and Myron Scholes received the Sveriges Riksbank Prize in Economic Sciences in Memory of Alfred Nobel (commonly referred to as the Nobel Prize in Economics) for "a new method to determine the value of derivatives."[8]

---

[7] Arbitrage involves the simultaneous purchase and sale of an asset in order to profit from a difference in the price. Specifically, it consists of making money: 1) today, 2) without risk, and 3) without using capital.

[8] Fischer Black, the other developer of the pricing methods, died in 1995.

11.2 WHY AND WHEN COMPANIES SHOULD USE DERIVATIVES

Companies can use derivatives to protect themselves from uncertain changes in the price of different assets they are exposed to (such as foreign exchange rates, interest rates, commodities prices, etc.).

You manage a US-based business that exports to Japan. Your company is going to receive ¥100 million in 6 months. The current exchange rate is $1 = ¥80. But the relevant exchange rate is that which will occur 6 months from now. If in 6 months the dollar depreciates and the exchange rate becomes $1 = ¥50, the amount of yens received converts into $2 million. However, if the dollar appreciates to $1 = ¥100, the amount to be received in dollars equals $1 million. If your company decides to do nothing, it is therefore exposed to the foreign exchange risk, because the final amount of dollars (the currency of interest for the company) to be received fluctuates according to the $/¥ exchange rate.

A foreign exchange future allows you to fix the exchange rate for a transaction that will occur in the future. You can agree with the bank to exchange $1 for ¥82 in 6 months. So, if you are to receive ¥100 million from your operations in 6 months, you are guaranteed $1.22 million (¥100 million divided by the guaranteed forward rate of ¥82 per dollar).

The company can also decide to use a foreign exchange option. In this case, the company has the right to convert at a pre-specified exchange rate, but only if it is advantageous. The option thus allows the company to protect itself against negative outcomes, while retaining the upside. However, hedging using options is more expensive, as a premium must be paid in order to start the derivative contract.

Risk management is often referred to as *hedging* and consists in the reduction — or even elimination — of risk. For non-financial companies, derivatives and their hedging possibilities provide a number of benefits and, if used effectively, they allow for more stable streams of revenues and earnings.

Derivatives use by industrial corporations

Duke Energy, an electricity company whose key input is natural gas, can use derivatives markets to hedge against fluctuations in the spot[9] prices of this commodity. Therefore, during the period of the derivative contract, regardless of whether the price of gas goes up or down, the company would have locked in a fixed value for the cost of its raw materials.

An agriculture producer can use derivatives markets to hedge its production. Without derivatives, an orange producer will have to wait until the oranges have been harvested and sold before knowing how much revenue will be made that year. Using commodity derivatives, the producer can

---

[9] The spot price is the price at which an asset is traded in the market at that moment.

hedge his revenues and lock in, perhaps at the beginning of the year, a certain fixed amount of revenue. Similarly, Tropicana, which buys oranges for its juices, can benefit by hedging its raw material costs, and thus avoid potential price risk.

A telecom company is currently borrowing at a floating rate. To mitigate the risk of rising interest rates, the company can use an interest rate swap. This means the company can effectively convert a floating rate obligation into a fixed-rate debt, thus eliminating any uncertainty regarding future interest payments.

Patek Philippe, a Swiss watchmaker that exports to the US, is subject to a foreign exchange risk. That is, the company knows how many dollars it will receive in a certain export contract. But because the company is Swiss and its costs are in Swiss francs, it will be subject to a foreign exchange risk. In order to hedge against this risk, the company can use foreign exchange futures or options. Ultimately, if it wants, it can completely eliminate any exposure to currency movements.

Overall, research has found a number of reasons why companies should use derivatives for risk management[10]:

- *Ability to focus on the core business:* By using derivatives to hedge some risk exposures (foreign exchange, interest rates, and commodities), companies can focus on their core business instead of trying to beat or forecast financial market variables.

- *Reduction of bankruptcy and financial distress costs:* By hedging risks with derivatives, companies may be able to reduce the likelihood of financial distress. As seen in Chapter 5, there are significant costs attached to financial distress.

- *Stabilization of earnings and cash flows:* Risk management can reduce volatility and stabilize earnings. This is positive, as in general, the market likes prudence and predictability. Also, the lower volatility allows companies to take on more debt, and thus they benefit from significant tax savings.

- *Increased managerial flexibility*[11]*:* By lowering their risk, companies improve their ability to take strategic options to grow their business. Indeed, risk management activities

---

[10] Froot, Scharfstein, and Stein (1993) show that risk management can add value through the firm's investment policy, particularly when external capital is costly. Guay (1999) analyzes decisions to initiate derivatives programs, and finds that firm risk declines following derivatives use. Haushalter (2000) studies the oil and gas industries, and finds companies manage risk to alleviate financial contracting costs. Graham and Rogers (2002) show that firms hedge to increase debt capacity and take advantage of the tax deductibility of interest. MacKay and Moeller (2007) show that hedging adds value when revenues are concave in product prices or when costs are convex in factor prices. Campello et al. (2011) show how hedging with derivatives has significant effects on firm financing and capital investment decisions, increases value, reduces the costs of financial distress, and eases the access to credit. Similarly, Bartram, Brown, and Conrad (2011) find evidence that the use of derivatives reduces risk and increases value.

[11] DeMarzo and Duffie (1995) suggest that risk management activities provide a positive signal of managerial ability to outside investors. Tufano (1996) suggests that risk management can also be influenced by management objective of lower risk. Mello and Parsons (2000) examine how different hedging strategies, their liquidity, and cash flow timing problems affect firm value. An optimal hedge is one that maximizes a firm's financial flexibility. Adam, Dasgupta, and Titman (2007) demonstrate the value of hedging as a strategic tool in competitive settings.

with derivatives can protect companies from unforeseen events that could force them to delay (or even stop) their strategic investment plans.

The academic evidence suggests that risk management activities using derivatives can add significant value in many settings. Access to these risk management instruments has positive and significant effects on firm value, profitability, investment, financing, and risk.[12]

KEY LEARNING POINT ✓

Risk management can lead to an increase in firm value.

The advantages of hedging (and thus hedging's impact on company's value) depends on the types of risks to which the company is exposed. Hedging may be less relevant whenever investors can themselves easily hedge their exposures. For instance, an investor cannot easily hedge the currency risk of a multinational company, as the sources of risk are complex, and not easy to quantify from the outside. On the other hand, an investor can identify an oil company's price exposure (to the oil price) from its financial reports and hedge it. In this case, hedging by the company does not confer a special advantage because investors can hedge on their own.[13] Additionally, investors take positions in oil producers to gain exposure to oil prices. In this case, hedging will insulate the company from oil price movements, but that is not desired by investors — it is the core business of the company to be exposed to oil price fluctuations.

Overall, companies are often better off eliminating certain types of risk and devoting their management time to their operations and the growth of their business, rather than speculating on the evolution of exchange rates, interest rates, or commodities prices (unless this is their core business activity). In this chapter, and also in the next two chapters, we cover many different types of derivatives, with a focus on how non-financial corporations can use them to mitigate risks and create value for their shareholders.

---

[12] Allayannis and Weston (2001) show evidence of a positive relationship between the use of currency derivatives and firm value for a sample of multinationals exposed to currency risk. Carter, Rogers, and Simkins (2006) show that jet fuel hedging is positively related to airline firm value. Pérez-Gonzáles and Yun (2013) find that the introduction of weather derivatives increases investment and values for weather-sensitive electric and gas firms. Similar evidence is found by Cornaggia (2013) in the agricultural industry.

[13] Jin and Jorion (2006) examine a sample US oil and gas producers and document insignificant effects of risk management on valuation.

Hedging jet fuel cost at Southwest

In the airline industry, it is often difficult to pass higher fuel prices on to passengers by raising ticket prices owing to the highly competitive nature of the industry. And most airlines want to prevent significant increases in operating expenses (which would impact their bottom line profitability).

Fuel hedging has been key to Southwest's success. Indeed, Southwest chose to hedge fuel prices in the late 1990s. Using different derivative strategies, Southwest has locked in the prices it pays for large amounts of jet fuel years ahead of time.

From 1998–2008, it has saved $3.5 billion (above what it would have paid at the industry's average price for jet fuel). That is more than 80% of the company's profits over those 10 years.[14]

Southwest's hedging strategy has allowed the company to keep fare increases much lower than those of most other carriers, and gain substantial market share.

11.3   ABUSES OF DERIVATIVES AND THEIR IMPLICATIONS

Derivatives markets are typically associated with low transaction costs — the cost of investing in an asset is much higher than the cost of buying a futures contract. Given the low transaction costs,[15] and because the value of derivative securities depends on the price of the underlying assets, they can be useful tools for speculating in financial markets.[16]

As discussed, companies can use derivatives for risk management (hedge or insure against certain risks). But some companies have also used them differently. Indeed, when companies use derivatives for speculation, they are making a financial "bet" on some asset price.

The large losses some companies have incurred with their derivative position have frequently hit the newspaper headlines.

However, the fact that many companies have lost money with derivatives does not invalidate their usefulness. Indeed, in the above cases the management started using derivatives to take directional bets in the direction of some market. And many of the companies in **Table 11.2** were shaken by heavy losses on derivatives speculations, and ultimately went bankrupt as a result of their failed derivatives bets.

---

[14] *Source: USA Today*, July 24, 2008.

[15] Futures and forwards are cheap, but options can be expensive (a premium must be paid ex-ante). More on this in the next two chapters.

[16] Speculation is the practice of using risky assets in an attempt to profit from fluctuations in their market value. Bodnar, Hayt, and Marston (1998), Faulkender (2005), Géczy et al. (2007), and Chernenko and Faulkender (2011) show evidence of the use of derivatives for speculation.

TABLE 11.2: Sample of companies that posted heavy losses due to derivative contracts

Country	Company	Derivative Used (main type)	Year
Chile	Codelco	Copper, silver, gold futures	1993
Germany	Metallgesellschaft	Oil Futures	1993
Japan	Showa Shell Sekiyu	FX Forwards	1993
Japan	Kashima Oil	FX Forwards	1994
United States	Procter & Gamble	Interest Rate Derivatives	1994
Singapore	Barings Bank	Nikkei Futures	1995
Japan	Sumitomo Corporation	Copper Futures	1996
United States	Long Term Capital Management	Interest Rate and Equity Derivatives	1998
China	China Aviation Oil	Oil Futures and Options	2004
United States	Amaranth Advisors	Gas Futures	2006
Brazil	Aracruz	FX Options	2008
France	Société Générale	European Index Futures	2008

China Aviation Oil in 2005

China Aviation Oil (CAO) had a monopoly of jet fuel supply to Chinese airports. The company drew public attention in 2005, when its losses due to derivatives became public. Subsequently, this led to the collapse of the company, and the arrest of its CEO, Chen Jiulin, for fraud.

In the beginning, CAO traded futures and swaps as hedging instruments, to manage the risk in its business of acquiring oil. Later, the company started to enter into speculative option trades to profit from upward market movements in oil prices. At first, this strategy generated positive payouts, as oil prices were going up. However, as the tide turned, things got ugly. By then, the company had multiplied the size of its speculative activities, and the open exposures were huge. The losses were further exacerbated as the company sold a large number of risky option contracts to generate premium income, in an attempt to cover existing losses on closed positions. Similar practices had been followed by Nick Leeson, which led to the collapse of Barings Bank in 1995.

Controladora Comercial Mexicana

In 2008, Controladora Comercial Mexicana (CCM), Mexico's third largest retailer, employing over 40,000 people, filed for bankruptcy. The company had lost more than $1 billion in its trades of foreign exchange derivatives, following a large depreciation of the Mexican peso. Traditionally, CCM used derivatives to hedge exchange rates, owing to its purchase of non-food goods (for instance, electronics) in US dollars. The main motive of these derivatives transactions was to counter the uncertainty related to commercial operations. But in 2008, as the Mexican peso was appreciating versus the US dollar, CCM's treasury department decided to place additional bets against the US dollar. CCM entered into foreign exchange derivatives with six different banks. These positions had nothing to do with the company's traditional business, and were not operations related. At first, CCM generated some gains from these contracts. But then, in October of 2008, as the financial crisis spread, investors began pulling money out of emerging markets. As a result, the Mexican peso began to plummet. Despite posting strong operating results in Q3 2008, on October 9, 2008, CCM filed for bankruptcy owing to its heavy losses in derivatives.

Aracruz Celulose

Aracruz Celulose, the world's biggest eucalyptus-pulp maker, announced in December 2008 losses of over $2 billion owing to currency losses on derivatives trades and a strengthening dollar. Aracruz originally used the contracts to secure profits from exports. But as the Real approached a nine-year high, its management began speculating that the currency would continue to appreciate. But then it began to slump with surprising rapidity (the currency lost more than 20% of its value in 2 months), which led the Brazilian company to post $2.5 billion in losses due to this trade, and to the resignation of its CFO.

Procter & Gamble

In 1994. Procter & Gamble (P&G) posted one of the largest losses ever suffered by an American company owing to speculative derivative positions. Like most multinational companies, P&G used swaps to hedge itself against swings in international interest and currency rates. Then its treasurer decided to up the bets by entering into a complex and speculative contract with Bankers Trust, betting on a decrease in German and US interest rates. At first, no one asked any questions, as the market was going up and they were making money. But that highly leveraged swap turned out to be an expensive bet, when the Federal Reserve Board announced on February 4, 1994, that it was raising short-term rates for the first time in five years.

The above examples highlight that some precautions must be taken when companies enter into derivative positions:

- Assess the risks posed to the business before entering into any derivative position.
- Establish proper risk management procedures.
- Ensure that senior management can provide adequate oversight.
- Monitor open derivative positions frequently.
- Analyze the risk profile of the derivative products and the appropriateness of their use.

Many non-financial companies around the world have misused derivatives. What is a soap or pulp manufacturing company doing in the foreign exchange market speculating with billions of dollars? P&G's business is consumer goods products, not highly leveraged swaps. Aracruz's business is eucalyptus pulp, not speculating on the Real–USD exchange rate using options. Top managements of non-financial (and obviously also financial) companies have a responsibility to understand and monitor derivatives markets when their companies are involved in them. And if they do not or cannot understand both the risks and the rewards of these products, then they should not use them at all.

SUMMARY

Derivatives are important not only for financial companies but also for non-financial companies. The value of a derivative contract always depends on some underlying asset, which can be a stock, a commodity, a stock index, an exchange rate, an interest rate, and so on.

There are three main categories of derivatives: futures and forwards, options, and swaps. Most derivative contracts are traded in the OTC market, which allows further customization of the terms. The specific details of each of these derivatives, their use, and their pricing are examined in the next two chapters.

Derivatives can be very useful in order to hedge against the possibility of loss in certain business environments. The evidence suggests that risk management can lead to an increase in company value, as it allows managers to focus on the core business, reduces the uncertainty and volatility of cash flows, and increases managerial flexibility.

However, if companies enter into positions that are not connected with their underlying business activity, much trouble can result. The evidence suggests that most non-financial companies have no expertise in predicting market prices of exchange rates, interest rates, commodities, etc. But many managers have historically been tempted to take a view. The problem is that these bets often turn out to be costly, and can end up in disaster. Companies should hedge appropriately, to reduce their risk exposure to some market variables. But they should not allow their derivatives' positions to become disconnected from their operational realities; otherwise, they can turn into gambles on the direction of the market. Companies and their managers should stick to running their business operations, and use derivatives only to hedge risks that can and should be hedged. They should not get carried away and begin to operate profit centers in their treasury desks that deal with derivatives.

REFERENCES

Adam, T., S. Dasgupta, and S. Titman, 2007, Financial Constraints, Competition, and Hedging in Industry Equilibrium, *Journal of Finance*, Vol. 62:2445–2473.

Allayannis, G., and J. Weston, 2001, The Use of Foreign Currency Derivatives and Firm Market Value, *Review of Financial Studies*, Vol. 14:243–276.

Bartram, S.M., G.W. Brown, and J. Conrad, 2011, The Effects of Derivatives on Firm Risk and Value, *Journal of Financial and Quantitative Analysis*, Vol. 46:967–999.

Black, F., and M.S. Scholes, 1973, The Pricing of Options and Corporate Liabilities, *Journal of Political Economy*, Vol. 81:637–659.

Bodnar, G.M, G.S. Hayt, and R.C. Marston, 1998, Wharton Survey of Financial Risk Management by U.S. Non-Financial Firms, *Financial Management*, Vol. 27:70–91.

Campello, M., C. Lin, Y. Ma, and H. Zou, 2011, The Real and Financial Implications of Corporate Hedging, *Journal of Finance*, Vol. 66, Iss. 5:1615–1647.

Carter, D., D.A. Rogers, and B.J. Simkins, 2006, Does Hedging Affect Firm Value? Evidence from the U.S. Airline Industry, *Financial Management*, Vol. 35:53–87.

Chernenko, S., and M. Faulkender, 2011, The Two Sides of Derivatives Usage: Hedging and Speculating with Interest Rate Swaps, *Journal of Financial and Quantitative Analysis*, Vol. 46:1727–1754.

Cornaggia, J., 2013, Does Access to External Finance Improve Productivity? Evidence from a Natural Experiment, *Journal of Financial Economics*, Vol. 109:419–440.

DeMarzo, P.M., and D. Duffie, 1995, Corporate Incentives for Hedge and Hedge Accounting, *Review of Financial Studies*, Vol. 8, Iss. 3:743–771.

Faulkender, M., 2005, Hedging or Market Timing? Selecting the Interest Rate Exposure of Corporate Debt, *Journal of Finance*, Vol. 60:931–962.

Froot, K.A., D.S. Scharfstein, and J.C. Stein, 1993, Risk Management: Coordinating Corporate Investment and Financing Policies, *Journal of Finance*, Vol. 48:1629–1658.

Géczy C., B. Minton, and C. Schrand, 1997, Why Firms Use Currency Derivatives, *Journal of Finance*, Vol. 52:1323–1354.

Graham, J.R., and D.A. Rogers, 2002, Do Firms Hedge in Response to Tax Incentives?, *Journal of Finance*, Vol. 57:815–839.

Guay, W.R., 1999, The Impact of Derivatives on Firm Risk: An Empirical Examination of New Derivatives Users, *Journal of Accounting and Economics*, Vol. 26:319–351.

Haushalter, D., 2000, Financing Policy, Basis Risk, and Corporate Hedging: Evidence from Oil and Gas Producers, *Journal of Finance*, Vol. 55:107–152.

Jin, Y., and P. Jorion, 2006, Firm Value and Hedging: Evidence from U.S. Oil and Gas Producers, *Journal of Finance*, Vol. 61:893–919.

MacKay, P., and S.B. Moeller, 2007, The Value of Corporate Risk Management, *Journal of Finance*, Vol. 62:1379–1419.

Mello, A., and J. Parsons, 2000, Hedging and Liquidity, *Review of Financial Studies*, Vol. 13:127–153.

Merton, R., 1973, The Theory of Rational Option Pricing, *Bell Journal of Economics and Management Science*, Vol. 4:141–83.

Pérez-Gonzáles, F., and H. Yun, 2013, Risk Management and Firm Value: Evidence from Weather Derivatives, *Journal of Finance*, forthcoming.

Tufano, P., 1996, Who Manages Risk? An Empirical Examination of Risk Management Practices in the Gold Mining Industry, *Journal of Finance*, Vol. 51:1097–1137.

Management of Corporate Risks with Futures, Forwards, and Swaps

Futures and forward contracts are a special class of financial instruments. Their terms are contracted today, but the trade is only completed at a specific time in the future.

This chapter describes the way they work, why they are useful for companies, possible strategies for using futures and forwards, and their pricing.

Risk management is the main reason for using futures and forwards. But because these instruments are highly leveraged, they can also be used for risky speculative strategies.

This chapter also introduces swaps — derivative contracts between two counterparties to exchange cash flows in the future. Indeed, a swap can be seen as a portfolio of separate forward contracts.

12.1 WHY USE FUTURES OR FORWARDS?

Futures and forward contracts exist for a variety of underlying financial assets/instruments, including interest rates, foreign exchange rates, individual stocks and bonds, and indices. But there are also contracts for non-financial assets such as commodities, and even for the weather.

In terms of exchange trading, the most commonly used futures worldwide are interest rate futures (see **Table 12.1**).

TABLE 12.1: Notional amount outstanding and turnover of various traded futures

	Amounts outstanding		Turnover	
	US$ (billion)	%	US$ (billion)	%
Interest rate	22,683	93.8%	226,695	86.6%
Foreign exchange	231	1.0%	7,343	2.8%
Equity-linked (index or stocks)	1,252	5.2%	27,710	10.6%
Total	24,166		261,748	

Source: Bank of International Settlements, 2012.

KEY LEARNING POINT ✓

The large majority of futures traded in organized exchanges are related to interest rates.

Firms can use futures or forwards to protect themselves from uncertain changes in the price of different assets. This is often referred to as *hedging*, and it reduces or even eliminates risk.

Orange juice futures

Like most farmers, orange producers face a significant market risk because of price fluctuations. For the producer, a downturn in market prices can be financially more devastating than a poor crop (lower quantity than expected). The orange juice derivatives market allows producers (as well as consumers) to hedge their commodity price risk.[1]

The following details pertain to futures contracts traded on the Intercontinental Exchange (ICE Futures US).[2] The contracts are for frozen concentrated orange juice (FCOJ), because oranges are perishable, as is orange juice.

Contract size:	15,000 pounds of orange juice solids (3% or less)
Contract months:	January, March, May, July, September, and November
Settlement:	Physical delivery
Grade/standards/quality:	US Grade A with a Brix value of not less than 62.5 degrees
Delivery points:	Licensed warehouses in Florida, New Jersey and Delaware
Deliverable origins:	US, Brazil, Costa Rica, and Mexico
Price quotation:	Cents and hundredths of a cent per pound

---

[1] Several agricultural contracts exist and are traded on different exchanges, e.g., Chicago Board of Trade, Intercontinental Exchange (ICE), and NYSE Euronext Liffe.

[2] www.theice.com/productguide/ProductSpec.shtml;jsessionid=90E022561F6457FDDB417FAC65F0D461?specId=30.

Each contract calls for the delivery of 15,000 pounds of orange juice, and certain grade/quality standards must be fulfilled. According to the contract, delivery should be to specific locations, and only oranges from certain countries are acceptable. The table shows the summary market report for January 15, 2013.

Contract month	Open#	High	Low	Close#	Volume	Open interest
MAR13	11150	11250	11000	11000	1,223	15,467
MAY13	11290	11290	11070	11095	268	3,765
JUL13	11475	11475	11260	11260	199	1,009
SEP13	11565	11565	11430	11430	21	496
NOV13	11760	11840	11610	11610	122	228
JAN14	11900	11900	11875	11875	10	37
MAR14	0	0	0	0	0	0
MAY14	0	0	0	0	0	0

The Open and Close prices (quoted in hundredths of a cent/pound) reflect the first and last trade in the market. High and Low are the minimum and maximum prices traded during the day. Volume is the total number of contracts to be traded on that day for each maturity, and Open Interest is the total number of futures contracts outstanding. For instance, in the May 2013 contract, the open interest equals 3,765. This means there are 3,765 outstanding contracts holding a long position and a similar number of short positions. The volume and open interest data highlight one key characteristic of most exchange-traded futures — their liquidity is high only for short maturities, but there are no long-term traded contracts with enough liquidity — indeed, beyond one year in this case, there are basically no trades or open interest. This accounts for the popularity of OTC markets, where forward derivative positions can be contracted for periods of more than 10 years.

The March 2013 maturity contract trades on a future price of 11000 hundredths of a cent per pound (using the closing price as a reference). Using the January 15 closing prices as a reference, an orange producer who is expecting a March 2013 crop can lock in a price of $1.10 per pound. To do so, the producer should enter into a short futures contract. That is, in March 2013, the producer would deliver the 15,000 pounds of FOJC and receive $16,500 (15,000 pounds × $1.10/per pound) regardless of what happens to the orange juice spot price. Thus, his short futures contract, or hedge, has locked in a selling price in advance of the actual delivery (or production) date.

There are three possible scenarios when this March 2013 contract matures:

Scenario 1: The spot price in March 2013 equals $1.30/per pound (*Spot price $1.30 > Futures $1.10*). The producer faces losses on the futures short position of $1.10 − $1.30 = −$0.20, so the net total payout is $1.30 + (−$0.20) = $1.10.

Scenario 2: Spot price in March 2013 equals $1.00/per pound (*Spot price $1.00 < Futures $1.10*). The producer realizes gains on the futures short position of $1.10 − $1.00 = $0.10, so the net total payout is $1.00 + ($0.10) = $1.10.

Scenario 3: Spot price in March 2013 equals $1.10/per pound (*Spot price $1.10 = Futures $1.10*). The producer has neither gains nor losses on the futures short position. Thus, the total payout is $1.10.

The above example shows how, regardless of the spot price at maturity, the producer has achieved his goal of securing a fixed price of $1.10 per pound through the short futures position. On the other side of this trade, another investor entered into a long position on this futures contract. The investor with a long position is thus committed to purchasing orange juice on the March delivery date at a price of $1.10 per pound. Various players could be interested in taking this long position, for instance, a juice packer or retailer (who faces the risk of the price of orange juice increasing in the spot market). These consumers can thus offset risk by being long on a futures contract.

At maturity, one of the two parties that entered into a futures contract will lose money. And the other will profit from it. This does not mean that one party was right, and the other was wrong. After all, what if market prices had evolved in the opposite direction? And it also does not mean that the party losing money should not have entered the derivative in the beginning. What is important to remember is why the company entered into a certain derivative position in the first place: to hedge risks, and lock in a cost/revenue for a certain business transaction.

Some other potential examples of hedging using futures and forwards follow.

An Italian importer

Alfa Romeo, an Italian car manufacturer, regularly buys raw materials from Japan. It pays its suppliers in Japanese yen. Its cars are sold mostly in euros and are competitively priced in the market. The company knows that it has a limited capacity to pass exchange rate movements on to its customers. That is, if the price of raw materials stays constant in yen but the yen appreciates, the real euro cost of the raw materials goes up. In this case, the company's margins will go down. The company could enter into foreign exchange futures, going long on yen. It would then be committed to buying yen on a specified date in the future at a current specified exchange rate. All exchange rate uncertainty over the raw materials can be removed in this way.

A Swiss exporter

Patek Philippe, a Swiss watchmaker, exports to the US. It knows how many dollars it will receive in a certain export contract. But since its costs are in Swiss francs, it will be subject to foreign exchange risk. Patek Philippe can use foreign exchange futures to hedge this risk by being short on dollar futures. In this way, the company can eliminate any exposure to currency movements.

An acquisition

Company A has just acquired Company B in the same industry. The seller was a family that wanted to cash out. Company A will have to raise debt to pay for this acquisition. However, the financial closing of the transaction (which is when it will actually have to pay the cash) will only occur one year from now (because of the lengthy competition authority/anti-trust approvals needed to combine A and B). Thus, Company A knows that it will need a loan one year from now. What should it do? Borrow the money right now to make sure it guarantees a certain interest rate on its loan? Wait one year and then shop on the loan market (exposing itself to any interest rate fluctuations over the year)? Alternatively, it could enter into an interest rate futures transaction, which would fix the rate it will have to pay for its loan in the future at the current rates. All interest rate uncertainty can be removed in this way.

KEY LEARNING POINT ✓

Futures allow companies to eliminate the price risk by fixing today the price at which a particular asset will be traded in the future.

12.2 DIFFERENCES BETWEEN FUTURES AND FORWARD CONTRACTS

Both futures and forwards call for the delivery of an asset or commodity at a specified maturity date at an agreed price. Unlike options, where the holder has the right (but not the obligation) to buy or sell an asset, there is an obligation on the part of holders of futures and forward contracts to buy or sell. As in all derivatives markets, there are long and short positions. The trader with the long position commits to buying the asset on the delivery date. The trader with the short position commits to delivering the asset on the specified date. Both parties, long and short, agree on what the price will be when the asset trades on the specified date in the future.

The notional value of most futures contracts is very large. For instance, in foreign exchange futures, the standard euro–dollar contract size is $125,000. However, this does not mean that today's value of a futures contract is significant. Indeed, at the moment the contract is signed, the price is zero for both parties. This is a key feature of futures and forward contracts: neither party pays any money at the start. However, the parties may require some collateral to minimize the credit risk.[3]

---

[3] Also called the *counterparty risk*. This is the risk that the other side of the trade, the counterparty, will not fulfill its part of the deal once the contract matures.

Although futures and forward contracts have fundamentally the same function, there are some differences (see **Table 12.2**). Futures contracts set in advance and standardize the contract size, delivery month, exact date, and procedures for delivery, whereas forward contracts are non-standard bilateral agreements, whereby two parties negotiate the maturity, contract size, and delivery specifications. Thus, forward contracts are traded or negotiated in the so-called over-the-counter (OTC) market.

TABLE 12.2:   Key differences between futures and forwards

	Futures	Forward
Amount	Standardized	Negotiated
Delivery date	Standardized	Negotiated
Counterparty	Clearinghouse	Bank
Collateral	Margin account	Negotiated
Costs	Brokerage and exchange fees	Bid–ask spread
Liquidity	Very liquid	Highly illiquid

One advantage of futures is their potential liquidity. Because futures are standardized contracts, they trade on the secondary market,[4] which allows traders with either a short or a long position to offset their exposure by entering into an opposite trade. Futures contracts also have a daily settlement called *mark-to-market*, which reduces the risk of default by a counterparty, thereby lowering the credit risk.

The main disadvantage of futures contracts is that they are standardized, which means there can be mismatches in maturity or amounts. For instance, the standard expiration date may not match an investor's requirements, or the standard notional contract may not match the amount he or she wishes to hedge. In these cases, forward contracts are more attractive.[5] Indeed, OTC markets account for approximately 90% of the total global derivatives market. The popularity of the OTC market stems from its flexibility and non-standardization. Furthermore, although futures contracts traded on organized exchanges are highly liquid, they offer very limited maturities (less than two years). On OTC markets, however, it is possible to contract forward derivative positions for periods of more than 10 years. **Table 12.3** shows the distribution of OTC derivative positions on interest and foreign exchange rates.

---

[4] Also called *aftermarket*. A secondary market is the market or exchange in which previously issued financial instruments are bought and sold.

[5] From now on, we will use the terms *futures* and *forwards* interchangeably (except later in section 12.4, which deals specifically with the main difference in cash flows between futures and forwards: mark-to-market). The main principles of profits/payoffs, hedging possibilities, and pricing apply to both futures and forwards.

TABLE 12.3: OTC derivative positions (notional amount[6] outstanding)

(US$ billion)	Forwards and swaps		Options	
	< 1 year	**> 1 year**	**< 1 year**	**> 1 year**
Exchange rate	39,985	15,593	8,507	2,587
Interest rate	192,737	250,967	14,179	36,135

Source: Bank of International Settlements, 2012.

KEY LEARNING POINT

Futures trade on organized exchanges, whereas forwards are bilateral contracts between two parties that can be tailor-made to their requirements.

12.3 WHO PROFITS FROM FUTURES AND FORWARD CONTRACTS AT EXPIRATION?

For both futures and forwards, the buyer, or the long party, will pay the agreed pre-specified future price to the seller, or short party. The short party, in turn, will deliver the asset to the long party.

Consider a futures contract on Walmart's stock with a one-year maturity. The current futures price is $100. An investor taking a long position (also called long futures) agrees to buy a share of Walmart at the expiration date for $100. Between the time the contract is signed and the maturity date, the spot price[7] of Walmart fluctuates.

If the price of Walmart is $80 in one year's time (at maturity), the long party suffers a $20 loss. He or she buys a stock of Walmart for $100 (according to the agreed futures price), even though it could be bought in the market at that time for $80. However, if the stock price is $120 at the expiration date, the profit equals $20. Using futures, the investor buys for $100 something that is priced at $120 in the market and thus makes a $20 gain.[8]

---

[6] The notional amount is the nominal or face amount used to calculate payments relative to a derivative instrument.

[7] The daily price of Walmart on the stock exchange.

[8] Importantly, no physical delivery of the stock is required. In order to avoid transaction costs, the buyer and seller simply agree to net out their positions according to the prevailing spot price at that time. This reduces transaction costs, because they do not have to buy or sell the underlying stock.

The total profit at maturity of a long futures position is calculated as follows:

$$\text{Long Futures Profit} = \text{Spot Price} - \text{Futures Price} \qquad (12.1)$$

The long position on the futures contract generates profits when the final spot price is above the futures contract price. But it can also make a loss when the spot price is below the originally agreed futures price. Unlike with options, the long party cannot walk away from the futures contract even if a loss has been generated. He or she is obliged to buy at the futures price whether or not it is above the spot price.

For an investor holding a short position on Walmart futures, the situation is reversed. In this case, he or she has agreed to sell at a price of $100 (short futures). Thus, profits are generated for a short position whenever the spot price is below the futures price at the expiration date. Conversely, if the spot price is above the futures price, the short position will incur losses.

The total profit at maturity of a short futures position is calculated as follows:

$$\text{Short Futures Profit} = \text{Futures Price} - \text{Spot Price} \qquad (12.2)$$

Figures 12.1 and **12.2** plot the profits realized by the long and short side of the futures contract.

FIGURE 12.1:   Long futures on Walmart.   **FIGURE 12.2:**   Short futures on Walmart.

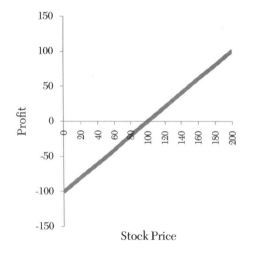

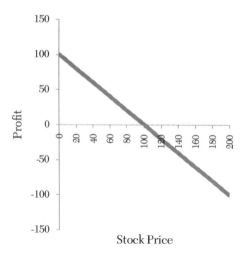

At maturity, the futures profits of the long position are equal to the losses of the short position. For instance, at prices above $100, the long investor makes a profit, while the short investor suffers losses. Conversely, at prices below $100, the short investor makes profits, while the long investor suffers losses. As **Figure 12.2** shows, the payoffs of the seller (short) can be very negative and are not bounded.

In the case of forward contracts, the profits and losses are usually netted at the expiration date, according to the original negotiated agreement. In the case of traded futures contracts, the profits and losses are offset gradually over time (see section 12.4).

12.4   THE MECHANICS OF FUTURES TRADING

An investor can enter into a futures contract with either a long or a short position. The trading is carried out on an exchange or electronic trading platform. Once a buyer and seller have agreed on a trade, a clearinghouse enters the picture.

For trades executed on futures exchanges, the clearinghouse acts as a counterparty to all buyers and sellers. That is, the clearinghouse becomes the buyer for each seller, and the seller for each buyer, so that the counterparty credit risk is reduced.

Whenever an investor wants to exit (or close out) a position, he or she simply needs to reverse the trade on the futures market. For instance, suppose an investor has a long position on a futures contract on a stock index expiring in June. At any time up to maturity, the investor can go back into the market and sell a June futures contract. Once a price has been agreed upon with the prospective buyer, the investor will have a long and a short position on the same contract. The clearinghouse nets, or offsets, the position and considers that from then on the investor no longer has any position in that contract or any remaining exposure. In practice, most futures trades are reversed prior to maturity and therefore do not involve delivery of any assets or commodities.

One of the main differences between futures and forwards is *marking-to-market*. In the case of a forward contract, no funds are transferred until the maturity date, when the contract is eventually settled. In the case of a futures contract, a pay-as-you-go method is followed. Marking-to-market ensures that as the futures price changes, the profits and losses accrue to the investors' accounts immediately.

KEY LEARNING POINT ✓

Marking-to-market is a feature of futures contracts (but not forward contracts); it effectively means that the profits and losses are paid every day.

12.4.1 How Does Marking-to-Market Work?

When a position is established, each party deposits a *margin*[9] with the clearinghouse to absorb potential future losses. The margin is typically a small amount of money represented as a percentage of the notional amount of the futures contract. From then on, the marking-to-market will occur. Each day the profits and losses from the futures contract will be reflected in each investor's account. The party that has opened a long position will collect profits whenever the spot price goes up and incur losses when the spot price decreases. Investors must have a minimum level of funds in their margin accounts; this is called the *maintenance margin* (and the amount is pre-specified in the futures contract). When the balance of the account falls below the maintenance margin, the broker will ask the investor for additional margin funds. This is known as a *margin call*. If the investor does not respond to the margin call and does not deposit new funds in the margin account, the broker will proceed to close the position, thereby avoiding potential credit defaults.

The aim of margins and margin calls is never to put the clearinghouse at risk. All the positions are closed out before the margin account is exhausted.

S&P 500 futures margin account

An investor wishes to enter into a long position on a futures contract on the S&P 500. The current value of the futures price is $1,500. The contract size for S&P 500 futures traded on the Chicago Mercantile Exchange (CME) is $250 × S&P 500 futures price. According to the rules of the CME, the initial margin is $19,250, and the maintenance margin is $17,500.[10]

Suppose that over the next six days, futures prices evolve as in the table below.

Day	Futures price — end of day	Daily gain	Opening balance on margin account	Margin calls/ cash flows	End balance on margin account
1	$1,500			−$19,250	$19,250
2	$1,495	−$1,250	$19,250		$18,000
3	$1,500	$1,250	$18,000		$19,250
4	$1,485	−$3,750	$19,250	−$3,750	$15,500
5	$1,490	$1,250	$19,250		$20,500
6	$1,495	$1,250	$20,500		$21,750

On day 1, the investor enters into a long position on an S&P 500 futures. To do so, he or she must deposit the initial margin in the broker's account.

---

[9] Also called *performance bond*.

[10] Each futures contract has specific requirements for the initial and maintenance margins required to trade it.

On day 2, the S&P drops 5 points (−0.33%). Because the contract is for a notional value of $250 × S&P 500 futures price, the investor loses $1,250 ($250 × 5-point drop) that day. The closing balance of the margin account is $18,000. Because this is above the maintenance margin, nothing happens.

On day 3, the S&P recovers to the original $1,500, and the investor once again has the initial balance of $19,250 in his or her account and records no accumulated gain or loss.

On day 4, the S&P suffers a 15-point drop. This equates to a loss of $3,750. After deducting this loss, the investor's account has $15,500. Because this is below the maintenance margin, he or she will receive a margin call from the broker. The margin call requires the investor to add money to the account.[11] In this case, the investor tops up the account with $3,750, taking it back to the original margin of $19,250. However, if the investor does not add funds, the broker simply closes the contract by selling it in the market.

Finally, on day 6, the investor closes the contract by entering into an offsetting position at a futures price of $1,495. The overall loss is equal to $250 times the difference between the selling price of the contract and the original price paid:

$$\text{Profit/Loss} = \text{Notional} \times (\text{Final Price} - \text{Initial Futures Price})$$
$$\text{Profit/Loss} = \$250 \times (\$1,495 - \$1,500) = -\$1,250$$

If this were a forward contract, the cash would flow only on the last date. At that stage, the long party would pay the short party $1,250. However, in a futures contract, the contract is marked-to-market every day, and the profits and losses are netted daily to the investors' margin accounts.

In this example, the contract was established with an initial margin of close to 5% of the value of the underlying asset.[12] It is important to note the inherent leverage in any futures position, and given the inherent leverage, severe losses can occur even when the index experiences only modest changes.

−$19,250	Originally invested in margin account
−$3,750	Paid in capital owing to margin calls
$21,750	End balance
−$1,250	**Total profit**
−6.5%	Percentage loss (relative to $19,250) original investment

This example also shows how an investor can obtain a −6.5% return on investment by investing in a futures contract when the underlying index changes very little (by only −0.33%).

---

[11] The investor can also reduce the positions or number of contracts, until the minimum requirements are satisfied. Because in this case we are talking about a single contract, no reduction is possible.

[12] The underlying asset is $250 times the value of the S&P 500 futures, that is, on day 1, $250 × $1,500 = $375,000. Because the initial margin is $19,750, it represents approximately 5.3% of the notional amount.

12.4.2 Liquidity and Futures

The fact that futures are marked-to-market can generate margin calls and require large cash outflows. Depending on the liquidity position of the company, this can become a problem. Sudden cash needs (because of large marked-to-market losses) could force the company to raise cash by selling assets or borrowing on unreasonable terms. Also, if faced with a significant margin call, the company might decide to close the contract because the losses are too high given the company's liquidity position. Or if the company does not top up the account, the broker (or exchange) will close it. This means that the company will no longer be hedged. This is a potential weakness of using futures to hedge risks. Overall, by having a futures contract, the company may be hedged against a certain risk (for instance, oil prices), but if it has to cancel the contract early, then it no longer has any protection.

In the case of a forward contract, no such problems would arise, because the payments are only made at maturity. However, as described above, forwards have counterparty risk.

KEY LEARNING POINT

When using futures, investors must be aware of the possibility of sudden cash calls, or margin calls. When using forwards, all the payments are only made at maturity.

12.5 PRICING OF FUTURES AND FORWARDS

In this section, we analyze how futures and forward contracts are priced. There are, in general, two ways to acquire an asset for some date in the future:

1. Purchase it now and store it.
2. Take a long position in futures.

These two strategies must have the same market-determined costs. If they have different costs, arbitrage opportunities are generated.[13] Smart investors can then place appropriate orders and, without any risk, enjoy a profit.

---

[13] Arbitrage consists of making money: (1) today, (2) without risk, and (3) without using capital. It involves the simultaneous purchase and sale of an asset in order to profit from a difference in the price.

The underlying principle in all futures pricing formulas is called the *spot futures parity theorem.* According to this theorem, any position that is perfectly hedged (i.e., without risk) should earn a return equal to the risk-free rate. This relationship can be used to develop futures pricing relationships in different markets using the concept of arbitrage.

Arbitrage example 1

Suppose you want to buy a stock of Walmart. The current spot price is $100. The one-year futures price is $110. The risk-free rate is 5%, and the stock pays no dividends.

There are two alternatives to ensure that you will have the Walmart stock in your portfolio in one year's time:

1) Buy the stock now, and keep it for a year. That is, borrow $100 today for one year. Use the $100 today to buy the stock. In one year, you will have to pay $105 ($100 + 5% interest).
2) Enter into a long position in a futures contract, which means you will pay $110 in a year.

It is obvious that the most economical way to have the stock one year from now is to choose option 1. In this case, you do not need any cash today, and you will have the stock next year for a total of $105.

In a situation like this, the spot–futures parity is broken, and there is a potential arbitrage opportunity. Indeed, investors can buy stocks today with credit (option 1) and enter into a short position on the futures at $110.

The payoffs today and in one year are as follows.

	Today	In one year
Enter into a 1-year loan at 5% rate today	$100	–$105
Buy stock today at $100	–$100	
Hold the stock for one year	+ Stock	
Short futures at $110		$110
Deliver the stock at the end of one year		– Stock
Total cash flow	$0	$5

Thus, with zero cash flow today, you can obtain a profit of $5 next year. This profit is guaranteed, because it does not depend on the Walmart stock price performance.

This is referred to as a cash-and-carry strategy.

Arbitrage example 2

Alternatively, suppose the following conditions prevail. The current spot price is $100. The one-year futures price is $102. The risk free rate is 5%, and the stock pays no dividends.

In this case, a reverse cash-and-carry strategy can be performed. First, you sell the stock today,[14] and deposit the money at 5% interest rate. Then, also today, you go long on a futures contract at the one-year price of $102.

	Today	In one year
Deposit the money in a 1-year deposit at 5% rate	−$100	$105
Sell stock today at $100	$100	
Sell the stock	− Stock	
Long futures at $102		−$102
Receive the stock in one year, according to the futures contract		+ Stock
Total cash flow =	$0	$3

In one year, you use the deposit to pay the futures price and net out the stock position. Doing this guarantees a profit of $3 next year, without any risk and with no capital outlay today.

Both examples above present pure arbitrage opportunities. The return that is achieved is riskless and does not require any investment. It can obviously be replicated or magnified millions of times, unless there is a price correction that would eliminate the arbitrage opportunity. Therefore, we conclude that the only futures price that eliminates arbitrage opportunities is

$$F_0 = S_0 \times (1 + r_f) = 100 \times (1 + 5\%) = 105 \qquad (12.4)$$

| F_0 is the current futures price, S_0 is today's spot price, and r_f is the risk-free rate for the maturity of the futures contract.

At a futures price of $105, no arbitrage opportunity exists. Given the spot price and risk-free rate, this is the only possible futures price that can exist in the market.[15]

---

[14] If you do not have the stock in your portfolio, you can borrow it for one year and execute a short sale. In this case, you will have to return the stock to its original owner after one year.

[15] This is also called *the law of one price*, which says that identical goods must sell for the same price, and that any difference between prices is eliminated by market participants taking advantage of arbitrage opportunities.

12.5.1 Stock Futures

For stocks that pay dividends, or for stock indices, the general pricing formula is

$$F_0 = S_0 \times (1 + r_f) - D = S_0 \times (1 + r_f - d)$$

$$d = {D}\!\Big/\!{S_0}$$

(12.5)

- F_0 is the price of the stock future.
- D is the amount of dividends paid over the duration of the futures contract, and d is expressed as a percentage of the stock price (dividend yield).
- S_0 is the current stock price.
- r_f is the risk free rate.

Calculating the futures price

The spot value of the S&P 500 index is $1,500. The risk-free interest rate is 5%, and the dividend yield is 3%. What is the one-year futures price on the S&P 500?

$$F_0 = S_0 \times (1 + r_f - d) = 1,500 \times (1 + 0.05 - 0.03) = 1,530$$

Thus, today, the price for the one-year futures should be $1,530.

If the futures price is above this, an arbitrage opportunity exists (cash-and-carry trade). Investors then know that the futures price is too high, so their arbitrage strategy must short the futures and long the index (spot).

If the futures price is below $1,530, a similar arbitrage opportunity exists (reverse cash-and-carry trade). Investors then know that the futures price is too low relative to the efficient price, and they should go long on the futures and short on the index (spot).

Importantly, regardless of the S&P 500 performance over the next year, either of these two strategies will deliver guaranteed profits. The only value that eliminates arbitrage opportunities is $1,530. Note that we have not mentioned the word *expectations*.

Many people are surprised to learn that expectations about futures play no role in futures pricing. The futures price of $1,530 does not mean market participants believe the S&P 500 will be priced at that value in a year's time. It is just the only possible futures price, given today's index ($1,500), the risk-free rate, and the dividend yield. Any other futures price would give rise to arbitrage opportunities.

KEY LEARNING POINT ✓

Futures are priced in order to eliminate arbitrage opportunities, and they do not depend on expectations of future market movements.

12.5.2 Interest Rate Futures

Using interest rate futures, investors can lock in an effective interest rate for some future year. Interest rate futures are also priced using arbitrage conditions.

These derivatives are useful whenever investors need to secure an interest rate for a period in the future, for either a forthcoming loan or a deposit.

The general formula for a single-year forward rate agreement is

$$FRA_{t-1,t} = \frac{(1+R_{0,t})^t}{(1+R_{0,t-1})^{t-1}} - 1 \qquad (12.6)$$

| $FRA_{t-1,t}$ is the forward rate agreement, that is, the effective rate that will be guaranteed between year $t-1$ and t.
| $R_{0,t-1}$ is the effective annual yield (interest rate) from now until year $t-1$.
| $R_{0,t}$ is the effective annual yield (interest rate) from now until year t.

You know that in one year you will need to buy a car, for which you will need credit for one year. You know the current market interest rates, but what matters to you is what the one-year rate will be one year from now. You can use interest rate futures to secure an effective future rate today, i.e., lock in how much your financing will cost between year 1 and 2.

Suppose the one-year rate in the market is 5%, and the two-year rate is 6%. The one-year forward rate can be found by using the following parity equation:

$$(1+R_{0,1}) \times (1+FRA_{1,2}) = (1+R_{0,2})^2$$

| $FRA_{1,2}$ is the forward rate agreement, that is, the effective 1-year rate that will be guaranteed between year 1 and 2.
| $R_{0,1}$ is the effective annual yield (interest rate) from now until year 1.
| $R_{0,2}$ is the effective annual yield (interest rate) from now until year 2.

On the left-hand side, we have the two-year return, which is obtained by investing first in a one-year bond and then, after one year, using a forward rate agreement ($FRA_{1,2}$) between year 1 and 2. On the right-hand side, we have the two-year return that is obtained by investing directly in the two-year bond: a guaranteed return of $R_{0,2}$ per year.

Indeed, in order to avoid arbitrage opportunities, the forward rate between year 1 and 2 ($FRA_{1,2}$) has to make the left-hand side of the equation equal to the right-hand side.

That is, using the above example, the forward rate must be

$$1 + FRA_{1,2} = \frac{(1 + R_{0,2})^2}{(1 + R_{0,1})}$$

$$1 + FRA_{1,2} = \frac{(1 + 0.06)^2}{(1 + 0.05)}$$

$$FRA_{1,2} = 7.01\%$$

The above principles can be applied to any kind of forward rate, regardless of the maturities. For instance, what is the one-year rate that should occur two years from now? That is, what is the effective rate you can secure today for an investment between year 2 and year 3? Suppose the two-year rate is currently 5% and the three-year rate is 5.5%.

$$FRA_{2,3} = \frac{(1 + R_{0,3})^3}{(1 + R_{0,2})^2} - 1$$

| $FRA_{2,3}$ = forward rate agreement: the effective 1-year rate that will be guaranteed between year 2 and 3.
| $R_{0,2}$ = effective annual yield (interest rate) from now, until year 2.
| $R_{0,3}$ = effective annual yield (interest rate) from now, until year 3.

which in this case is equal to

$$1 + FRA_{2,3} = \frac{(1 + R_{0,3})^3}{(1 + R_{0,2})^2}$$

$$1 + FRA_{2,3} = \frac{(1 + 0.055)^3}{(1 + 0.05)^2}$$

$$FRA_{2,3} = 6.50\%$$

12.5.3 Foreign Exchange Derivatives

Exchange rates fluctuate constantly. This volatility is a source of concern to anyone involved in foreign trade. Foreign exchange derivatives allow investors to lock in exchange rates for some time in the future.

Investors who have agreed to buy foreign exchange in the future hold a long position. As usual, when the expiration/maturity date arrives, a long position will be profitable whenever the spot price is above the pre-specified futures price.

You agree to buy €100 million in one year at CHF 1.50/€. You are then long in euro forwards. The following figure represents your gain (loss) on this forward contract as a function of the spot exchange rate one year from now.

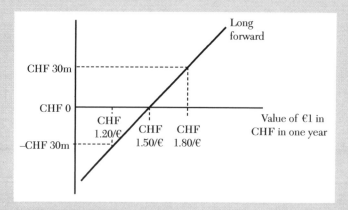

For instance, if in one year, the exchange rate is CHF 1.80/€, then a long position on this contract is profitable. Indeed, using a forward contract, you will buy €100 million in one year at CHF 1.50/€, for a total of CHF 150 million. If you had to go to the market at that time and buy euros at the spot exchange rate of CHF 1.80/€, the total spending would be CHF 180 million. The profit provided by this contract would be CHF 30 million.

A short position in foreign exchange forward contracts has the opposite payoff. In the short case, you as the seller agree to sell €100 million in one year in exchange for Swiss francs at an agreed exchange rate of CHF 1.50/€. If at that time the exchange rate is CHF 1.80/€, the short position incurs losses of CHF 30 million because it could have gained CHF 180 million on the market, but it only gets CHF 150 million because of the forward.

As with stocks and interest rates, foreign exchange forwards are also priced by arbitrage. Indeed, the futures or forward prices for foreign exchange do not depend on expectations; they depend only on the relative ratios of interest rates in both countries.

$$\frac{1+r_{foreign}}{1+r_{\$}} = \frac{f_{foreign/\$}}{S_{foreign/\$}} \qquad (12.7)$$

| $S_{foreign/\$}$ is the spot exchange rate between \$ and foreign market.
| $f_{foreign/\$}$ is the one-year forward rate between \$ and foreign market.
| $r_{foreign}$ is the interest rate in the foreign market.
| $r_{\$}$ is the interest rate in the domestic market.

This is called the *covered interest rate parity relationship*.

Whenever it is violated, arbitrageurs will be able to make risk-free profits in foreign exchange markets by borrowing in one currency, lending in another, and locking the forward rate. This will be a riskless profit (because the foreign exchange forward is used to lock in a future rate) without any investment.

KEY LEARNING POINT ✓

Foreign exchange rate futures prices depend on the interest rates in both countries (not on expectations).

Suppose we want to calculate the appropriate forward rate between the euro and the Swiss franc, given that

- The spot exchange rate is CHF 1.20/€
- The interest rate in € = 4%
- The interest rate in CHF = 1%

We can use the interest rate parity condition in formula (12.7):

$$\frac{1+r_{CHF}}{1+r_{€}} = \frac{f_{CHF/€}}{S_{CHF/€}}$$

$$f_{CHF/€} = \frac{1+r_{CHF}}{1+r_{€}} \times S_{CHF/€}$$

$$f_{CHF/€} = \frac{1+0.01}{1+0.04} \times 1.20 = 1.1654$$

That is, the forward price (the exchange rate agreed today for a euro–Swiss franc transaction that will occur one year from now) must be 1.1654.

The reasoning behind this result is simple. Consider a forward price that equals the spot price (1.20). In this case, investors could lock in the exchange rate for one year from now at the same level as today's spot value. An arbitrage opportunity exists here. Investors can borrow at the cheap rate, deposit at the expensive rate, and make a guaranteed profit. That is, they would borrow in Swiss francs at 1%, deposit in euros at 4%, and generate a riskless spread of 3% over any amount they wanted, and there would be no exchange rate risk because a forward contract at 1.20 was used to convert future euro–Swiss franc flows.

However, if the forward rate is 1.1654, the profitability of this strategy is eroded. In this case, investors cannot make any riskless arbitrage profits by borrowing in one currency and lending in another.

12.6	**HOW TO HEDGE RISKS USING SWAPS**

Swaps are derivative contracts between two counterparties to exchange cash flows in the future. In a swap, each party undertakes to make a series of payments based on the underlying value of a particular variable such as interest rate, commodity price, equity index, or foreign exchange rate. There are two basic types of swaps: interest rate swaps (often referred to as *plain vanilla*) and currency swaps. The cash flows to be exchanged in the future are based on an underlying notional principal (NP) amount. Swaps are part of the OTC market, and they are carried out by swap dealers (intermediaries); companies do not enter into them between themselves.[16]

12.6.1 Interest Rate Swaps

Interest rate swaps (IRSs) are one of the most liquid interest rate derivatives. In an IRS, two parties agree to exchange cash flows based on a specified notional[17] amount:

- One party pays a fixed rate. Every period it pays a fixed interest based on the agreed swap rate.

- The other party pays a variable rate. It pays a floating rate for a specified maturity (or floater).

- The underlying notional amount is never exchanged.

An institution is said to *buy a swap* when it *pays a fixed rate* and receives a variable one (also called *long swap*, or *fixed-rate payer*). The opposite is *selling a swap* (or a *short swap*, or *floating-rate payer*). In this case, the institution commits to paying a variable rate (and receiving a fixed one) for the duration of the swap.[18]

> Company A and Company B have entered into a $100 million IRS for the next five years, with annual payments. In this swap, Company A pays a fixed rate of 4%, and Company B commits to paying a floating rate (Euribor, for instance). Every year, A pays B the fixed 4% rate (which, based on the notional amount, equates to $4 million), and at the same time, B pays A the prevailing floating rate. The two legs of the swap are netted so that only the difference between them is actually paid.

---

[16] For interest rate swaps, there are a large number of standardized contract parameters, which include procedures for counterparty risk mitigation — such as collateralization. Collateralization requires firms to deposit assets as collateral (the most common ones are cash and government securities).

[17] "Notional" refers to the face amount that is used to calculate payments made on a particular derivative instrument.

[18] A swap can be seen as a portfolio of separate forward contracts. Indeed, in a swap contract, someone will deliver a payment based on a fixed rate and receive in exchange a payment based on a floating rate. Both streams of payments can be valued by discounted cash flows.

For instance, if in a particular year Euribor equals 3%, B must pay a total of $3 million (that is, a Euribor of 3% multiplied by the notional amount of $100 million). Because A must pay B $4 million, the net amount equates to a payment from A to B of $1 million.

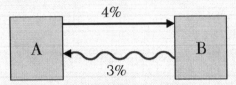

Suppose, now, that variable rates increase in the market, and Euribor in a particular year equals 5%. In this case, B must pay A the net amount of $1 million (the difference between $5 million of the floating leg, less the $4 million of the fixed leg).

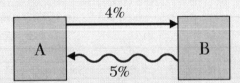

12.6.2 Why Use Swaps?

Companies can enter into a swap to manage risk, as well as to exploit their comparative advantages with respect to the quality spread differentials[19] in different markets. There are often gains from trading swaps, based on each company's comparative advantage. There are thus many reasons to enter into a swap:

- Transform floating rate liabilities into fixed rate liabilities, and vice versa.
- Transform floating rate assets into fixed rate assets, and vice versa.
- Lower borrowing costs and generate higher investment returns.
- Transform the currency behind any asset or liability into a different currency.

12.6.3 Using a Swap to Transform Liabilities

Consider the following situation:

- Company A has an existing floating rate loan.
- Company B has an existing fixed rate loan.

---
[19] Different companies borrow at different rates, fixed and floating, in different markets.

Company A wants to hedge itself against rising interest rates. Currently, all its debt is at a floating rate (LIBOR,[20] for instance), which means interest payments will go up if LIBOR increases. In contrast, Company B has a fixed rate loan and wants to swap it into a floating one. By entering into a swap, they can achieve their objectives.

Company A is buying the swap (long swap) and will receive a floating rate in exchange for a fixed payment every year. Company B is selling a swap (short swap), which means it will commit to paying a variable rate (and receiving a fixed one). Suppose they agree on a $100 million IRS for the next five years, with annual payments. Company A pays a fixed rate of 5%, and company B pays the prevailing LIBOR rate every year.

FIGURE 12.3:   A swap to transform liabilities.

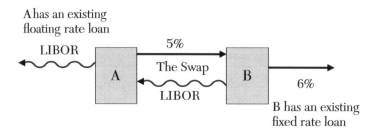

As **Figure 12.3** shows, the result of the swap is that A will pay a fixed rate of 5%, and B will pay LIBOR. Both parties achieve their objectives. Company A effectively converts a floating rate obligation into a fixed rate debt, thus eliminating any uncertainty regarding future interest payments. Company B transforms its debt into a floating rate and will thus benefit from falling interest rates.

12.6.4 Using a Swap to Transform Assets

Consider the following scenario:

- Company A owns an existing floating rate bond that pays LIBOR.
- Company B owns an existing fixed coupon bond (that pays 6%).

Company A wants to hedge itself against possible decreases in interest rates. It thus wants to lock in a fixed rate of return. Conversely, Company B wants to get interest rate exposure and benefit from possible rises in interest rates. An IRS allows these two companies to change their exposures.

---

[20] LIBOR is the London interbank offered rate, and is a widely used benchmark in international transactions.

FIGURE 12.4: A swap to transform assets.

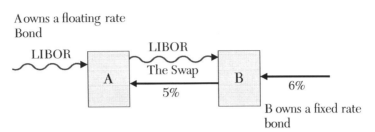

As **Figure 12.4** shows, the result with the swap is that A will receive a fixed rate of 5%, and B will receive LIBOR.

12.6.5 How Swaps Can Lower Borrowing Costs

Two companies can enter into a plain vanilla swap to exploit their comparative advantages with respect to quality spread differentials. Indeed, differential information and institutional restrictions contribute to differences in fixed rate and floating rate markets across companies. As a result, companies will have a comparative advantage in issuing in different markets.

Consider the following scenario:

- Company A can borrow at a fixed rate of 7% or at a floating rate of LIBOR + 25 b.p. (basis points).[21]

- Company B is a lower-rated, riskier company; it can borrow at a fixed rate of 8% or at a floating rate of LIBOR + 75 b.p.

- Company B wishes to borrow at a fixed rate, and Company A wishes to borrow at a variable rate.

Although Company B faces higher rates in both markets, it has a comparative advantage in the floating rate market. It is paying only 50 b.p. more in the floating rate market (its spread is LIBOR + 75 b.p., whereas Company A's spread is LIBOR + 25 b.p.; thus, the difference is 50 b.p.), but it must pay 100 b.p. more in the fixed rate market (Company B pays 8% in the fixed rate market, whereas Company A pays 7%). Company A has a comparative advantage in the fixed rate market because it is paying 100 b.p. less there, compared with 50 b.p. less in the floating rate market.

---

[21] 100 b.p. equals 1%; 1 b.p. equals 0.01%.

By entering into a swap, together with appropriate bond issues, they can achieve their objectives, while lowering their borrowing costs. Because Company A has a comparative advantage in the fixed rate market, it will borrow the notional principal (NP, $100 million, for instance) at a rate of 7%. Company B (also following its comparative advantage) borrows $100 million in the floating rate market, for which it will pay LIBOR + 75 b.p. They will then enter into a swap. Company A will sell a swap (short swap), which means it will commit to paying a variable rate (and receiving a fixed one). Conversely, Company B will buy the swap (long swap), and it will receive a floating rate in exchange for a fixed payment every year. Suppose they agree on a $100 million IRS for the next five years, with annual payments. Company B pays a fixed rate of 7.1%, and Company A pays the prevailing LIBOR rate every year.

FIGURE 12.5:   A swap to lower borrowing costs.

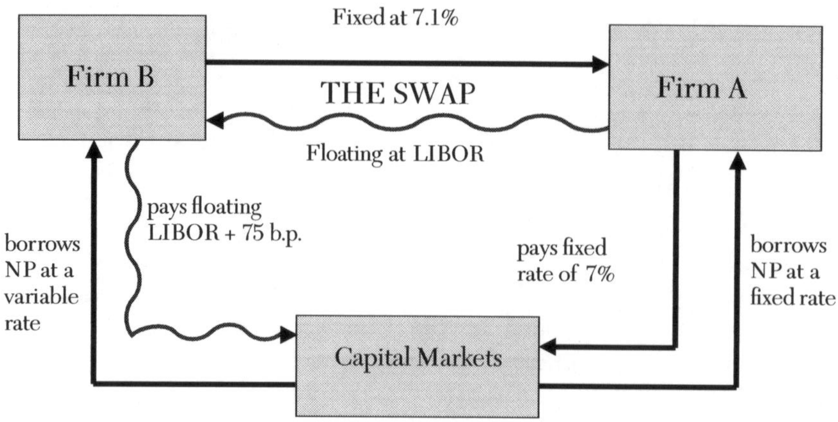

As **Figure 12.5** shows, the net result is that Company B has borrowed at an effective fixed rate of 7.85%.[22] It pays the capital markets LIBOR + 75 b.p. for its floating rate loan. Then through the swap, it pays 7.1% fixed to Company A, but it receives the LIBOR rate. Company B has thus achieved its objectives of borrowing at a fixed rate, but through this mechanism, its effective rate is 7.85%, which is lower than the 8% it would have had to pay if it went straight into the fixed rate market alone.

Company A has borrowed at a floating rate equal to LIBOR − 10 b.p.[23] (It pays a fixed rate of 7% to the market. In the swap, it pays LIBOR to B and receives a fixed 7.1% in exchange.) Both counterparties to this swap have lowered their interest expense by borrowing where they have a comparative advantage and then swapping their loans.

---

[22] 7.85% = LIBOR + 75 bp − LIBOR + 7.1%.

[23] LIBOR − 10 b.p. = 7% − 7.1% + LIBOR.

12.6.6 Currency Swaps

Currency swaps are contracts between two counterparties to exchange principal and fixed rate interest payments on a loan in one currency for principal and fixed rate interest payments (on an equal loan) in another currency. Companies can thus use currency swaps (also called *foreign exchange swaps*, or *FX swaps*) to transform a liability (or cost) in one currency into a liability in another currency.

Suppose a US company (for instance, Walmart) wants to finance capital expenditure of €40 million of its German subsidiary. It could borrow dollars in the US, where it is well known, and exchange the dollars for euros. But this will involve incurring an exchange rate risk: financing a euro project with US dollars. It could borrow euros in the international bond market, but it would pay a premium because it is not as well known abroad. A currency swap is an interesting solution in these circumstances. If it can find a German company with a mirror-image financing need, then a win-win situation is achieved through a currency swap.

If the spot exchange rate is $1.30/€, the US company needs to find a German company (for instance, VW) that wants to finance dollar borrowing of $52,000,000 ($40,000,000 × 1.30). Consider the borrowing costs of the two companies in different currencies:

	$	€
Walmart	8.00%	7.00%
VW	9.00%	6.00%

Walmart pays 1% less to borrow in dollars than VW. But Walmart pays 1% more to borrow in euros than VW. Thus, Walmart has a comparative advantage in borrowing in dollars (and VW a comparative advantage in borrowing in euros).

Because of the transaction costs and the search costs of finding a counterpart, swaps are always conducted through an intermediary (swap bank). Suppose Walmart enters into a swap with a bank, in which it pays a rate of 6.1% in euros and receives a rate of 8% in dollars. VW enters into a swap in which it pays a rate of 8.15% in dollars and receives a rate of 6% in euros. At the same time, each company borrows in its domestic currency, which is where it has a comparative advantage. That is, VW issues bonds in euros, on which it pays 6% interest, and Walmart issues dollar bonds, on which it pays 8% interest. Each company then immediately converts the proceeds of these issues to its chosen currency (given the investment needs, Walmart needs euros and VW needs dollars). **Figure 12.6** shows all the payoffs from these transactions.

FIGURE 12.6:   Currency swap payoffs.

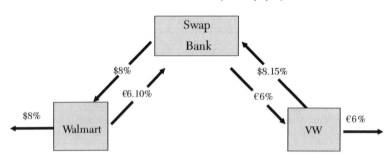

Walmart's net position is to borrow in euros at 6.10%. The 8% in dollars that it receives from the bank is used to pay the interest on its bonds issued in the US, which have an interest rate of 8%. Overall, this rate of 6.1% on its euro borrowing is substantially lower than what Walmart could achieve on its own (7%).

VW's net position is to borrow in dollars at 8.15%. It pays 8.15% in dollars to the bank and receives 6% in euros in exchange (which is used to pay for the euro-denominated bond). Overall, this rate of 8.15% on its dollar borrowing is substantially lower than what VW could achieve on its own (9%).

The quality spread differential (QSD) gives the potential gains from the swap (which can be shared between the counterparties and the swap bank):

$$QSD = \$(\text{Company A} - \text{Company B}) - €(\text{Company A} - \text{Company B}) \qquad (12.8)$$

| $\$(\text{Company A} - \text{Company B})$ is the difference in dollar borrowing costs between the two companies, and $€(\text{Company A} - \text{Company B})$ is the difference in the euro borrowing costs.

In this particular case:

$$\$(\text{Walmart} - \text{VW}) = 8.0 - 9.0 = -1\%$$

$$€(\text{Walmart} - \text{VW}) = 7.0 - 6.0 = 1\%$$

$$\text{And thus the QSD} = -1\% - (1\%) = -2\%$$

Whenever the QSD is not equal to zero, there are potential gains from the trade. Currency swaps reduce borrowing costs when each party borrows in the market in which it has a comparative advantage, and then swaps into its preferred currency. In this case, a total potential savings of 2% is at stake, which can be shared between the counterparties and the swap bank. There is no reason to presume that the gains will be shared equally. In this example, Walmart received 0.9% of the gains, VW received 0.85%, and the remaining 0.25% (= 2.0 − 0.9 − 0.85) went to the swap bank.

12.6.7 More Complex Swaps

Several more complex kinds of swaps exist. They are often referred to as *exotic swaps*. A few examples:

- *Swaption:* A contract between two counterparties in which one has the right, but not the obligation, to enter into a specific swap in the future (the terms of the swap are set in advance, at the time the contract is signed).
- *Basis swaps:* Parties exchange the difference between two floating rates.
- *Deferred swaps:* The exchange of interest payments begins at some defined point in the future.
- *Amortizing swaps:* The notional amount decreases over time according to a formula (that is related to time, interest rates, amortization of other securities, etc.).
- *Step-up swaps:* The notional amount increases over time according to a formula.
- *Quanto swap:* Depends on the joint movement of floating rates (EURIBOR, LIBOR, etc.) and foreign exchange markets.
- *Power swap:* Swaps where the floating leg pays a power function of the LIBOR rate (LIBOR squared, LIBOR cubed, etc.).
- *Range accrual swaps:* The coupon on one of the legs of the swap is conditional on some event happening. For instance, this could be the number of days the EURIBOR is within a predefined range, set using an upper and a lower barrier. But it could also be linked to any other financial asset (stock indices, commodities, etc.).
- *Snowball swaps:* The payoff of each coupon is dependent on the payoff of the immediately preceding period.

It is important to emphasize that most of these exotic swaps are highly speculative. Some have potential hedging uses in the asset–liability management of financial institutions and pension funds, but for the most part, they represent highly leveraged bets on the direction of the market. Many companies and even government institutions (for example, the city of Milan and the Greek government) have used complex swaps as a purely speculative instrument to try to push some of their liabilities into the future. Many of these ill-advised speculative forays end in disaster.

SUMMARY

Risk management or hedging is the main reason for using futures and forwards. Companies can use these derivatives to protect themselves from uncertain changes in the price of different assets.

Futures and forwards are derivatives contracted today, fixing the terms of a trade that will occur at a specific time in the future. For instance, interest rate futures allow investors to fix today an interest rate that will be used in the future (for either a loan or a deposit). And foreign exchange derivatives allow companies to fix today a certain exchange rate that will be used for a certain transaction in the future.

The main differences between futures and forwards are the customization and liquidity implications. Futures contracts are traded on organized exchanges, under standard contracts in terms of amount, maturity, dates, and the like. Forwards can be tailor-made to suit the circumstance; they are bilateral agreements between two parties (and thus subject to counterparty risk).

In terms of liquidity, when using futures, investors must consider the required margins, as well as the mechanics of the marking-to-market. Indeed, marking-to-market may require investors to place additional money in the margin account, which could have liquidity implications. In the case of forwards, no intermediate payments occur, and all cash flows occur only at maturity.

In this chapter, we have looked at the pricing rationale for futures and forwards on different assets, including stocks, indices, interest rates, and exchange rates. Overall, the futures price does not reflect expectations, but rather the only derivative price that can prevent brokers from exploiting arbitrage opportunities

We also introduced swaps and their role. Non-financial corporations can use swaps in many risk management situations, which helps explain why they are among the most widely used derivatives.

Management of Corporate Risks with Options

An option is a derivative contract that gives its owner the right to buy or sell an underlying asset at a fixed price over a period of time (or at a specific date). Options contracts exist for a variety of underlying financial assets, including stocks, interest rates, bonds, stock indices, and currencies. But there are also options on non-financial assets such as commodities and even the weather.

There are two kinds of options: calls and puts. A *call option* gives the holder (buyer or *long call* [1]) the right to buy a certain asset, at pre-specified terms. There is always a counterparty, who is the seller of the option (*option writer* or *short call*). The seller of the option is obliged to sell the asset (at the specified terms) should the holder of the option wish to exercise it. Call options are increasingly popular in executive compensation programs. Indeed, since the early 1990s, many companies have introduced stock option programs, giving employees the right, but not the obligation, to buy shares at a certain price.

A *put option* gives the holder of the option (buyer or *long put*) the right to sell. The seller of the option (or *writer* or *short put*) is obliged to buy the asset (at the specified terms) should the holder of the option wish to exercise the option to sell.

In the case of both calls and puts, the buyer of the option pays a premium to the seller in exchange for these rights (to buy something — call; to sell something — put). This premium depends on a number of variables, including the market price of the underlying asset.

Companies can use options to protect themselves from uncertain changes in the price of various assets. This is often referred to as *hedging* and consists of reducing or even eliminating risk. This chapter addresses the following topics:

- The different types of options
- How and when options are traded
- The payoffs of options

---

[1] A long position means you have invested in or bought something; a short position is equivalent to selling.

- Possible strategies using options and why they are useful
- How options are valued

13.1   THE PAYOFFS OF OPTIONS

In this section, we analyze the payoffs of different types of options at expiration.[2] They are illustrated using examples of stock options, but are generalizable to any other asset.

13.1.1 Call Options

At the expiration date, the payoff of the option is either zero (if it is not exercised) or the difference between the underlying price and the exercise price. The payoff for the option buyer (also called the holder or long call) can be described as

$$\text{Long Call Payoff} = \text{Max}\,(0, S - X) \tag{13.1}$$

| S is the price of the underlying stock and X is the exercise price.

Thus, if the stock price at expiration is above the exercise price, this is good news for the buyer of the option because in that case its payoff is positive. However, if the stock price is below the exercise price, the buyer will have a payoff of zero.

The payoff for the seller of the option (short call) can be described as

$$\text{Short Call Payoff} = \text{Min}\,(0, X - S) \tag{13.2}$$

| S is the price of the underlying stock, and X is the exercise price.

Thus, if the stock price at expiration is below the exercise price, this is good news for the seller of the option because in that case its payoff would be zero. However, if the stock price is higher than the exercise price, the seller will suffer a negative payoff as the buyer will exercise the right to buy the stock.

> Consider a call option on the stock of Exxon. The exercise price of this option is $100. This call option entitles its holder (the *buyer* of the option, or *long call*) to buy a share of Exxon at the expiration date for $100.
>
> If at maturity the price of Exxon is $80, the payoff of the option would be $0, and the option would not be exercised. However, if at the expiration date the stock price is $120, the payoff would equal

---

[2] All these payoffs correspond to the cash flows that will occur at maturity (exercise date), and do not take into consideration the price paid for the options (also called premium).

$20 ($120 − $100). The holder of the option can exercise it by paying $100 and selling immediately at the market price of $120, thus obtaining a net +$20.[3] The following graph describes the payoffs for the buyer of a call option at expiration for different stock prices.

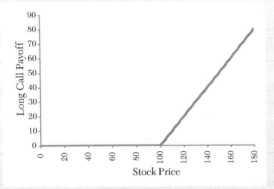

Because the call has an exercise price of $100, stock prices below that value lead to a zero option payoff at maturity. But if the price is above $100, the payoff of the long call is equal to the difference between the stock price and the exercise price.

Conversely, at expiration the payoffs for the *option writer* (*seller*, or *short call*) will be the opposite of those described above. Indeed, at expiration, the seller of the option has no rights and is obliged to sell the Exxon stock for $100 if the holder of the option decides to exercise it. The following graph describes the payoffs for the seller of a call option at expiration for different stock prices.

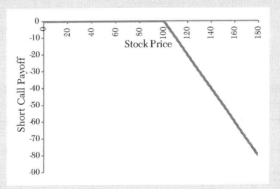

This is a mirror image of the payoffs for the call buyer. Any price above $100 will produce a negative payoff. For instance, if the price is $120, the short call will have a payoff of −$20. As the graph shows, the payoffs for the option seller (the call writer) can be negative and are not bounded. Obviously, the call writer, who is exposed to losses, agrees to incur this risk in exchange for the premium he or she receives at the time of selling the option.

---

[3] Note that the holder of the option does not need to keep the Exxon stock. The holder has the right to buy it at $100, but nothing prevents him or her from exercising the option and immediately selling the underlying stock at the market price.

13.1.1 Put Options

The right to sell an asset at a pre-specified price is a put option. For an investor who holds a put option (long put) at the expiration date, the payoffs are either zero (if it is not exercised) or the difference between the exercise price and the underlying stock price. The payoffs can be described as follows:

$$\text{Long Put Payoff} = \text{Max}\,(0, X - S) \qquad (13.3)$$

| S is the price of the underlying stock, and X is the exercise price.

The payoffs for the seller of the option (short put) can be described as

$$\text{Short Put Payoff} = \text{Min}\,(0, S - X) \qquad (13.4)$$

| S is the price of the underlying stock, and X is the exercise price.

Consider a put option on the stock of Exxon. The exercise price of this option is $100. This put option entitles its holder (the *buyer* of the put option, or *long put*) to sell a share of Exxon at the expiration date for $100.

If at maturity the price of Exxon is $150, the payoff of the option is $0. The holder of the option will never exercise the option, because it is not reasonable to sell for $100 something that is priced in the market at $150. In other words, the holder of the option will not exercise the option unless the stock is worth less than the exercise price.

However, if at the expiration date, the stock price is $70, the payoff equals $30 ($100 − $70). The holder of the option can exercise the option and buy the underlying stock for $70. Because the holder sells for $100 (fixed exercise price) and buys for $70, this generates a net +$30. The following graph describes the payoffs of this *long put* at expiration.

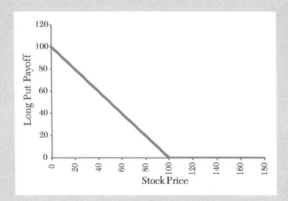

Conversely, at expiration, the payoffs for the *option writer* (also called the *seller* of the put option, or *short put*) will be the opposite of those described above. Indeed, at expiration the seller of the put option has no rights and is obliged to buy the stock in exchange for $100 should the holder of the option decide to exercise it. The following graph describes the payoffs for the seller of a put option at expiration.

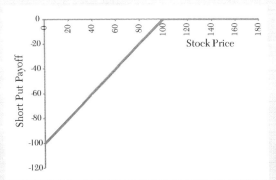

Thus, if the stock price at expiration is above the exercise price, this is good news for the seller of the option because the option would be worthless. However, if the stock price is below the exercise price, the seller will experience a negative payoff (at any price below $100 the payoffs are negative). For instance, if the price is $60, the short call will have a payoff of -$40. The seller's payoff at maturity is, however, bounded at –$100. Indeed, the worst-case scenario would be if he or she is forced to buy a stock that has a value of zero for $100, thereby generating a $100 loss.

13.1.3 How and When Options Are Traded

All options have a specified deadline (also called the *exercise date* or *maturity date*). But there are two possibilities regarding when the option can be exercised:

- A *European option* can only be exercised at a specific point in time.
- An *American option* can be exercised at any time until the maturity of the option.

These terms have nothing to do with where the options are traded, Europe or the US. Both options are traded on both sides of the Atlantic.

The majority of exchange-traded stock options, for example, those issued for companies such as Microsoft or General Electric, are American-style options. Index options can be either American- or European-style options. For example, the S&P 100 Index options are American-style options, whereas the Nasdaq 100 Index options are European-style options.

The fixed price at which the holder can buy (call option) or sell (put option) the underlying asset is called the *exercise price* or *strike price*.

At any time prior to expiration, it is common to talk about "moneyness" and whether a particular option is in-the-money or out-of-the-money. This terminology refers to cash flows that would potentially occur should the option be exercised at that moment, given the current price of the underlying asset.

For instance, a call option is

- *In-the-money* when the value of the underlying asset is higher than the exercise price — thus, exercising the option at that time and simultaneously selling the just-acquired underlying asset at the current market price would produce a positive cash flow.

- *Out-of-the-money* when the value of the underlying asset is lower than the exercise price.

- *At-the-money* when the value of the underlying asset is equal to the exercise price.

Conversely, a put option is

- *In-the-money* when the value of the underlying asset is lower than the exercise price — thus, exercising the option at that time and simultaneously buying the underlying asset at the current market price would produce a positive cash flow.

- *Out-of-the-money* when the value of the underlying asset is higher than the exercise price.

- *At-the-money* when the value of the underlying asset is equal to the exercise price.

13.2 HEDGING CORPORATE RISKS USING OPTIONS

Companies can thus use options to protect themselves — hedge — against uncertain changes in the prices of different assets. An important difference exists between using options and futures for risk management. When using futures (or forwards) contracts, two parties agree today on the conditions under which a certain trade will occur in the future. When the contract is signed, no payment is made. However, the trade *will* occur at a specific time in the future, whether or not the buyer of the future profits from it. In the case of an option, the holder of the option has the right, but not the obligation, to exercise it. This means that if market prices evolve in such a way that exercising the option is not profitable, the holder of the option just walks away, and there is no payment at maturity. But this flexibility comes at a price. When using options, a premium must be paid up front to the seller of the option, which is not the case when using futures.

For instance, call options on a commodity such as copper offer the right but not the obligation to buy or sell copper at a specified strike price, at a specified date. Copper is widely used in construction, infrastructure, and equipment manufacturing (cables, wiring, and electrical goods). An equipment manufacturer may be interested in using options on copper to hedge its price risk. Indeed, the copper market is vulnerable to many supply-side constraints, and the price of copper can be very volatile. By hedging this risk with a call option, the equipment manufacturer can place a cap on the price of this raw material. If copper prices are below the strike price of the option, the company benefits and can buy the copper directly on the spot market at reduced prices (letting the option expire unused). However, if copper prices increase, the company will exercise the option to buy at a pre-specified price. Thus the option effectively caps the raw material costs. Of course, in order to have this option, the manufacturer must pay a premium up front, which can be seen as the cost of insurance against raw material price increases.

Buying put options can be seen as guaranteeing an effective floor on the price at which an asset will be sold. Consider a company that sells oil and that decides to buy a put option on oil. Suppose the put option allows it to sell oil in one year for $100 a barrel. If the oil price increases above $100 per barrel during the course of the year, the company can simply sell on the spot market and thus generate higher profits from the higher selling price. But if the oil price drops, the company can exercise the put option to sell the oil at the fixed price of $100. Thus, by using a put option the company is hedging itself against drops in the oil price. The put option establishes a floor (the payoff will never be below $100), but allows the company to keep the upside in case the oil price rises above $100.

Similarly, options on currencies, interest rates, and other commodities can be useful hedging instruments for companies exposed to these risks.[4]

KEY LEARNING POINT ✓

Options on interest rates, foreign exchange rates, stocks and bonds, commodities, and weather allow companies to hedge risks, while still benefiting from the upside.

---

[4] Several agricultural, metals, energy, foreign exchange, interest rate, and equity contracts exist and are traded on different exchanges, e.g., Chicago Board of Trade, Intercontinental Exchange (ICE), and NYSE Euronext Liffe.

Alfa Romeo, an Italian car manufacturer, regularly buys raw materials from Japan. It pays its suppliers in Japanese yen. Its cars are sold mostly in euros and are competitively priced in the market. The company knows that it has a limited capacity to pass exchange rate movements on to its customers. That is, if the price of raw materials stays constant in yen, but the yen appreciates, the real euro cost of the raw materials goes up. In this case, the company's margins will go down. The company could buy a foreign exchange option (FX option) on the yen, for which it must pay a certain premium. This FX option will give it the right, but not the obligation, to buy yen on a specified date in the future at a specified exchange rate. If the yen appreciates, Alfa Romeo can exercise the option and buy yen at the fixed price. If the yen devalues, the company lets the option expire and simply buys the yen cheaper on the spot market. Using FX options effectively allows the company to put a cap on the yen cost, but also to benefit from favorable exchange movements.

Patek Philippe, a Swiss watchmaker, exports to the US. It knows it will receive $10 million in a certain export contract. But because its costs are in Swiss francs (CHF), it will be subject to a foreign exchange risk. Patek Philippe can use FX options to hedge this risk by buying put options on dollars (for instance, allowing it to convert $1 for CHF 1.15). In this way, the company effectively puts a floor on the amount of Swiss francs it will receive (CHF 11.5 million, that is, the original $10 million, converted at the exercise price of $1 for CHF 1.15). But if the dollar appreciates (that is, each dollar becomes worth more Swiss francs), Patek Philippe lets the option to sell at a fixed amount expire, and sells the dollars in the spot market for more Swiss francs. For instance, if the dollar appreciates to $1 = CHF 1.5, then Patek Philippe converts its $10 million into CHF 15 million, and lets the option to sell dollars (at 1.15 CHF) expire unused.

Weather derivatives have traded since 1999. These products can be used to hedge price and volume risks that a company may face. For example, a gas distributor sells less gas in a hot winter, thereby reducing its profits. Most weather derivatives are traded in the over-the-counter (OTC) market, although some contracts are also listed on the Chicago Mercantile Exchange (CME). Two of the most common ones are Heating Degree Days (HDD) and Cooling Degree Days (CDD). An HDD index is calculated using daily temperatures above 18°C (65°F in the US). This represents the point at which heating in a building is typically switched on, and the HDD index thus proxies for the demand for heating. The CDD is calculated based on the daily temperatures below 18°C, which reflects the demand for power to drive air-conditioning. Companies in different sectors (energy, hotel and restaurant chains, entertainment parks, water utilities, retail, construction, and clothing manufacturers) use options on these products to suit their particular exposures to these risks.

KEY LEARNING POINT

Options allow companies to hedge risks by effectively setting boundaries (caps or floors) at which a particular asset will be traded in the future.

13.3   POSSIBLE STRATEGIES USING OPTIONS AND WHY THEY ARE USEFUL

Numerous strategies can be implemented using combinations of calls and puts together with underlying assets. In this section, we analyze some of the key strategies that options enable as well as examples of why they are useful.

13.3.1 Covered Call

This consists of a stock and a short call (selling a call option). The writer receives a premium upon selling a call and is therefore obliged to sell the stock at the pre-specified price (if the option is exercised). In this case, the call is said to be covered because the risk of having to potentially deliver the stock is covered by the stock held in the portfolio.

At expiration the covered call has the following payoffs

	S < X	S >= X
Stock	S	S
Short call	0	−(S − X)
Covered call	S	X

S is the price of the underlying stock, and X is the exercise price.

Assuming that an investor holds a stock of Exxon and a short position on a call option with an exercise price of $100, the following graph describes the payoffs of this covered call at expiration.

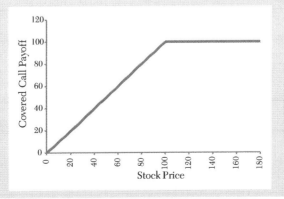

That is, if at maturity the price of Exxon is above $100, the value of the covered call will still be $100. If at maturity the stock price is below $100, the covered call payoff will equal the value of the underlying stock. Effectively, a covered call strategy caps the upside of the stock, so even if the stock price goes above the exercise price, the covered call owner will not benefit from additional gains. In exchange, the investor gains a premium ex-ante from selling this option.

A covered call is a useful strategy for an investor who has a price target of $100 for a stock in his or her portfolio. This means that he or she will sell the stock in the market if the price reaches $100. In this situation, the investor can profit from the options market, and in particular from a covered call strategy. If the investor sells a call option with a strike of $100 and simultaneously has a portfolio containing the underlying stock, he or she is effectively committing to selling the stock for $100, but also receives a premium at the time of selling the call. The covered call thus allows this investor to preserve his or her initial objective of selling at $100, while profiting from a guaranteed premium received at the time of writing the call.

13.3.2 Protective Put

Buying a put option protects the buyer against price drops. Holding an asset and a put is called a protective put. At expiration, the payoffs of the protective put are as follows:

	$S < X$	$S >= X$
Stock	S	S
Long put	$X - S$	0
Protective put	X	S

In effect, a protective put strategy limits the downside without capping the upside. If the stock price goes up, the investor profits from it. But if it goes down, the investor is protected up to a certain limit (the exercise price of the put). In exchange for this protection, the buyer must pay a premium for the put option.

An investor holds stocks of Exxon that are currently priced at $100. In two years, the investor will need most of the money invested in that stock for a house down payment. Instead of selling the stocks today and putting the money in a bank account, the investor can buy a protective put. By buying a two-year put option with a strike price of $100, for instance, the investor will be protected from price drops below this level. The following graph describes the payoffs of the protective put at expiration:

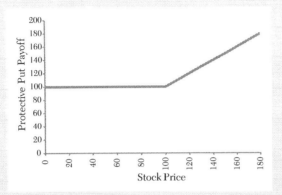

The investor thus preserves the upside on Exxon stock for these two years and effectively guarantees at least $100 at expiration. If after two years the stock price is above $100, he or she can sell the stock in the market. However, if the stock price has fallen below $100, he or she exercises the option and receives the guaranteed $100 (exercise price). Of course, in exchange for this protection, the investor must pay a premium to acquire the put option.

13.3.3 Straddle

A straddle is established by buying a put and a call option on a stock with the same exercise price. This is a useful strategy for an investor who believes a stock will move significantly but is uncertain about the direction of movement. At expiration, the payoffs of the straddle are as follows

	$S < X$	$S >= X$
Long call	0	$S - X$
Long put	$X - S$	0
Straddle	$X - S$	$S - X$

Assuming the investor holds long positions in call and put options, both with an exercise price of $100, the following graph describes the payoffs of this straddle at expiration.

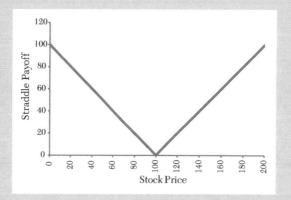

That is, if at maturity the price of Exxon is above $100, the investor benefits from exercising the call option. Alternatively, if the Exxon price is below $100, the investor benefits from the put option. Effectively, a straddle has no downside, and its upside depends on the volatility of the stock. Of course, in exchange the investor must pay the option premiums to purchase the call and put.

13.3.4 Collar

A collar essentially brackets a portfolio's value between two bounds. It is defined as a long stock plus a long put and a short call. The put option provides downside protection, or a floor. The short call (with a higher exercise price than the put) provides the upper limit, or a cap. A collar is thus an asset that has a capped upside and a capped downside.

This is a strategy that allows a certain protection against changes in the value of a certain asset, while minimizing the costs of that hedging strategy. The main idea of a collar strategy is to give the investor downside protection at a low cost today. To raise the money for the put, the investor sells a call (short call) with a higher exercise price. Often, the short call is selected in such a way that its premium covers the premium paid for the put. Thus, the investor does not spend any money on the options and, in exchange for the floor on negative returns, accepts a cap on the gains.

Consider an investor who has a stock with a current share price of $100. The investor could construct a collar by buying a put with a strike price of $80 and selling a call with a strike price of $120. The following graph describes the payoffs of the collar at expiration.

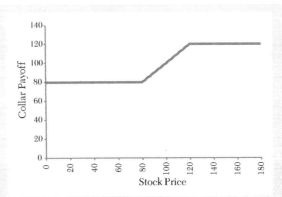

The cap (short call) will limit the gain on the portfolio to $20; it will also limit the loss to $20 (through the put with an $80 exercise price).

Collars are frequently used on interest rates. On the one hand, a company that uses a collar strategy effectively protects itself against a large interest rate increase (and thus higher financing costs). On the other hand, the company accepts that if the interest rate decreases significantly, the benefits would be capped.

13.3.5 Butterfly Spread

A butterfly spread is a strategy based on the expectation of low volatility of the underlying asset. It is established by buying two call options with different strike prices, and selling two calls with another strike price.

An investor could construct a butterfly spread by buying a call with a strike price of $80, buying another call with a strike price of $120, and selling two calls with a strike price of $100. The following graph describes the payoffs of the butterfly spread at expiration.

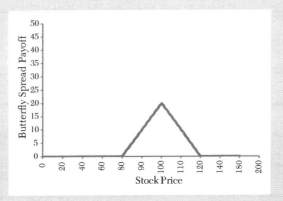

That is, if at maturity the price of the stock is between $80 and $120, the investor will benefit from the butterfly spread. Alternatively, if the price is below $80 or above $120, the investor will get no payoff at maturity. This is a useful strategy for an investor who believes a stock will not move significantly. Provided that at maturity the stock price is between $80 and $120, the payoff will be positive.

13.4   HOW OPTIONS ARE VALUED

As seen above, the payoffs for holders of options (call or put) are always positive at maturity (or zero if the option is not exercised). Obviously, the writer of these options (the seller), who is exposed to losses, agrees to incur this risk in exchange for a premium at the time of initially selling the option. In this section, we analyze how options are priced.

First, we need to introduce the concept of arbitrage. Arbitrage occurs when you can make money: (1) today, (2) without risk, and (3) without using capital. For instance, if the same asset is traded in two different markets at different prices, there is an arbitrage opportunity.

Arbitrage example

Consider the stock of British Telecom, which is simultaneously traded in London and New York. If it traded simultaneously in New York for $50 and in London for $55, you can buy the share in the cheap market (New York) for $50 and sell it immediately in the expensive market (London) for $55. Because you have no net position in the stock, it is irrelevant whether its price moves up or down.

If the transactions are executed simultaneously, you have a riskless profit, which means there was an arbitrage opportunity You make an easy $5 profit without having to be rich to do so and without needing funds of your own because you use the proceeds from selling the stock in London to pay for the purchase in New York.

One of the key principles of modern finance, and in particular option pricing, is that arbitrage opportunities do not exist. Or if they do, they quickly disappear. For instance, in the above example, you would have massive amounts of buy orders in New York and sell orders in London. This would continue until the prices in the two markets converged, and arbitrage were no longer possible.

Derivatives are usually valued using this no-arbitrage principle, which states that equilibrium prices are reached when no arbitrage opportunities are available. Using this principle, Black, Merton, and Scholes show how an option (for instance, on a stock) can be replicated exactly by holding a certain number of stocks and risk-free assets.[5] That is, the payoffs of a

---

[5] Black and Scholes (1973); Merton (1973).

call option are similar to those of a portfolio of stocks and risk-free assets. Thus, the price of the option must be equal to the value of that portfolio.

13.4.1 Call Option Value

The most commonly used formula for option pricing is the Black–Scholes formula. It is also used to evaluate the value of stock options provided to employees under many companies' long-term incentive plans. The formula, which calculates the value of call options,[6] was one of the main breakthroughs in finance theory:

$$C = S \times N(d_1) - \frac{X}{e^{rt}} \times N(d_2) \qquad (13.5)$$

| $d_1 = \dfrac{\ln\left(\dfrac{S}{X}\right) + \left(r + \dfrac{1}{2}\sigma^2\right) \times t}{s\sqrt{t}}$ and $d_2 = d_1 - \sigma\sqrt{t}$

| C is the call option price, S is the spot price[7] of the underlying stock, X is the exercise (or strike) price, r is the risk-free rate,[8] t is the time to expiration, and σ is the implied volatility.[9] $N(.)$ is the value of a normal distribution.[10]

13.4.2 Black–Scholes in Practice

The following steps should be taken to compute an option value using the Black–Scholes formula:

1. Get data on:

    S – Current stock price

    X – Exercise price

    σ – Volatility of the stock (annualized)

    t – Time to maturity (% of year)

    r – Continuously compounded risk-free rate

---

[6] The Black–Scholes formula gives a theoretical estimate of the price of European-style options. For American-style options, in most cases it is acceptable to value them with the Black–Scholes formula. Indeed, American options are rarely exercised before the expiration date, so the European pricing is a good approximation. Alternatively, the Roll–Geske–Whaley option pricing model can be used for American options on dividend-paying stocks — see Roll (1977), Geske (1979, 1981), and Whaley (1981).

[7] The current price at which a security is traded in the market.

[8] This should be the annualized continuously compounded rate on a risk-free asset with the same maturity as the option.

[9] This is the standard deviation of the stock returns on the underlying stock (expressed in annual terms).

[10] It is the cumulative distribution function of the standard normal distribution.

2. Calculate N(d1), N(d2), where N(d1) and N(d2) represent normal probabilities based on the values of d1 and d2.[11]

3. Calculate the Black–Scholes price.

We want to value a two-year call option on Exxon. Exxon's current stock price is $100. The exercise price of this option is $120. The risk-free rate is 4%,[12] and the company pays no dividends. The volatility of the stock price is 20%. Replacing these inputs in formula (13.5), we obtain

$$d_1 = \frac{\ln\left(\frac{100}{120}\right) + \left(0.04 + \frac{1}{2}0.2^2\right) \times 2}{0.2\sqrt{2}} = -0.220$$

$$d_2 = d_1 - \sigma\sqrt{t} = -0.220 - 0.20\sqrt{2} = -0.503$$

Using the Excel NORMSDIST formula, we obtain $N(d_1) = 0.413$, $N(d_2) = 0.309$.

Replacing the above inputs in the Black–Scholes formula:

$$C = S \times N(d_1) - \frac{X}{e^{rt}} \times N(d_2) = 100 \times 0.413 - \frac{120}{e^{0.04 \times 2}} \times 0.309 = 7.12$$

So the value of this two-year call option is $7.12.

13.4.3 Option Value Determinants

There are thus five factors that affect the value of a call option:

1) *Stock price*

The value of the call increases with the stock price. Returning to the previous example (a two-year call option on Exxon, with an exercise price of $120), we can build the following table, which shows how sensitive the call value is to changes in the underlying stock price.

Underlying stock price	$80	$90	$95	$100	$105	$110	$120
Call option value	$1.59	$4.00	$5.24	$7.12	$9.34	$12.34	$17.98

[11] A number of ways exist to obtain N(d1) and N(d2). In Excel, the function "=NORMSDIST(…)" provides the values of the normal probabilities we need.

[12] The Black–Scholes formula requires the use of a continuously compounded rate. Using annually or semi-annually compounded rates produces small variations in the final option price.

Higher current stock prices increase the likelihood that the call option will be exercised (at its strike of $120). This makes the value of the call option higher.

2) *Exercise price*

The value of the call goes down for higher values of the exercise price.

Exercise price	$110	$120	$130	$140	$150
Call option value	$10.86	$7.12	$5.08	$3.09	$1.98

Intuitively, higher strike prices lower the probability that the option will be profitably exercised by the maturity date. Thus, today the value of the option is lower. For instance, using today's stock price of $100, the value of a two-year call on Exxon with a strike of $150 is $1.98.

3) *Interest rate*

A higher interest rate decreases the present value of the exercise price, thus increasing the call option's current value.

4) *Time to expiration*

A longer time to expiration increases option value. The more distant the expiration date is, the more unpredictable future events are, and thus the more variable the stock price will be.

5) *Implied volatility of the stock price until expiration*

Higher volatility leads to a higher option value. Because the option payoffs have a lower bound at 0, higher volatility increases the potential payoff of the option in a rising-stock scenario. In the case of good stock performance, the option holder prefers the volatility to be as high as possible, thus increasing the option's expected payoff.

13.4.4 What If the Stock Pays Dividends?

Dividends affect option valuation negatively. Indeed, higher dividend payments (unless there is new information on the company) will reduce the stock price on the day of the dividend payment. This is bad news for the call option holder.

The most standard approach for dealing with dividends in the Black–Scholes formula consists of adjusting the stock price downward by the value of the dividends to be paid until expiration (in present-value terms).

In the above example, suppose the stock will pay a dividend of $2 in one year's time and $3 in two years (right before the expiration of the option).[13] The risk-free interest rate equals 4%.

In order to use the Black–Scholes formula (13.5), we must calculate the adjusted stock price (S'), which is obtained by computing

$$S' = S - PV(Dividends) = 100 - \frac{2}{1.04} - \frac{3}{1.04^2} = 100 - 1.92 - 2.77 = 95.30$$

Replacing this dividend-adjusted stock price in the Black–Scholes formula (13.5) leads to a call value of $5.34.

KEY LEARNING POINT ✓

When valuing an option on a stock that pays dividends, a dividend-adjusted stock price must be used in the Black–Scholes formula.

13.4.5 Put Option Value

Formula (13.5) *is the call option pricing formula.* In order to obtain the equivalent put option pricing formula, we must introduce the *put-call parity*. This formula is based on the concept of arbitrage. Consider the following two portfolios:

1.   A call with a strike price of X plus a riskless bond with face value X (the option's exercise price).

2.   A stock plus a put with a strike price of X.

It can be shown that the two portfolios generate exactly the same payoffs.

Thus, if in the future they generate the same payoffs, today the call plus bond portfolio must cost the same as the stock and put portfolio[14]:

$$P + S = C + PV(X) \tag{13.6}$$

| P is the put value, C is the call value, S is the underlying stock price, and PV(X) is the present value of the exercise price.

---

[13] If the dividends are paid after the expiration of the option, they are no longer relevant.

[14] If this parity is ever violated, an arbitrage opportunity arises. To exploit it, an investor must buy the cheap portfolio (either 1 or 2 above) and sell the expensive one. This will generate an immediate gain, without using any capital (the sale of the expensive portfolio pays for the acquisition of the cheap one) or causing any risk (the payoffs are the same at maturity). These arbitrage opportunities are not usual, and if they do happen, they are quickly dissipated in the market, and the put–call parity is restored.

Given the *put-call parity* in (13.6), the value of a put option is

$$P = C + PV(X) - S$$

We can replace C by the Black–Scholes call option value in the above put–call parity formula (13.6) to obtain the put option value:

$$P = \frac{X}{e^{rt}} \times \left[1 - N(d_2)\right] - S \times \left[1 - N(d_1)\right]$$ (13.7)

| (as before) $d_1 = \dfrac{\ln\left(\dfrac{S}{X}\right) + \left(r + \dfrac{1}{2}\sigma^2\right) \times t}{s\sqrt{t}}$ and $d_2 = d_1 - \sigma\sqrt{t}$

We want to value a two-year put option on Exxon. Exxon's current stock price is \$100. The exercise price of this option is \$90. The risk-free rate is 4%, and the company pays no dividends. The volatility of the stock price is 20%.

$$d_1 = \frac{\ln\left(\dfrac{100}{90}\right) + \left(0.04 + \dfrac{1}{2}0.2^2\right) \times 2}{0.2\sqrt{2}} = 0.797$$

$$d_2 = d_1 - \sigma\sqrt{t} = 0.797 - 0.20\sqrt{2} = 0.514$$

$$P = \frac{90}{e^{4\% \times 2}} \times \left[1 - 0.695\right] - 100 \times \left[1 - 0.788\right] = 4.16$$

Under these conditions, the value of the put option is \$4.16.

The value of the put decreases as the current stock price increases. The following table shows how sensitive the put value is to changes in the underlying stock price (keeping the exercise price constant at \$90).

Underlying stock price	\$80	\$90	\$95	\$100	\$105	\$110	\$120
Put value	\$11.01	\$6.56	\$5.37	\$4.16	\$2.93	\$2.20	\$1.22

Higher current stock prices decrease the likelihood that the put option will be exercised (at its strike of \$90), thus decreasing the value of this selling option.

Conversely, the value of the put goes up for higher values of the exercise price.

Exercise price	\$80	\$85	\$90	\$95	\$100	\$105	\$110	\$120
Put value	\$1.70	\$2.63	\$4.16	\$5.75	\$7.29	\$9.49	\$12.41	\$17.89

Indeed, a put option that allows its holder to sell (if he exercises the option in two years) for a price of \$105 has a greater value than one that only allows the sale at \$90.

13.4.6 Delta Hedging

The relationship between option value and some of its determinants is governed by a set of risk measures commonly called the *Greeks* because they use Greek letters.

The most common Greek is delta. It is the relationship between the option value and the underlying stock price[15]:

$$\text{Delta} = \text{Change in Option Price} / \text{Change in Stock Price} \qquad (13.8)$$

In the Black–Scholes formula (13.5), delta equals $N(d_1)$ for calls and $N(d_1) - 1$ for puts (formula 13.7).

For instance, in the above example of a two-year call on Exxon, $N(d_1)$ equals 0.413. This means that for each $1 change in the price of Exxon, we should expect

- A change in the call option price = $0.413 \times \$1 = \$0.413$
- A change in the put option price = $(0.413 - 1) \times \$1 = -\$0.587$

Delta is an important metric for constructing hedges or replicating options. In this case, the price of a call option increases by 41.30% of the original stock increase, and the put option price decreases by 58.7% of the stock price increase. So if we sold 100 call options with the above delta and then added a long position on 41.3 stocks, we would have a hedged position that would maintain its value regardless of the value of the underlying asset. This is called *delta hedging*, or *dynamic hedging*.[16]

13.4.7 How to Estimate Volatility

Higher volatility is associated with higher option values (calls or puts). Because the option holder only exercises an option when it is profitable, he or she cannot lose any money at maturity (apart from the premium originally paid). Higher volatility will translate into more uncertain future stock prices, and thus higher expected payoffs. Thus, the option holder always benefits from increased volatility.

---

[15] Other Greeks include *vega*: a measure of the sensitivity of the option price to changes in the volatility of the underlying stocks; *theta*: a measure of the sensitivity of the option value to time to expiration; *rho*: a measure of the sensitivity of the option value to changes in the risk-free rate; and *gamma*: a measure of the sensitivity of *delta* to changes in the underlying price.

[16] Alternatively, we also know that we can replicate the payoffs of the call options by holding the delta number of shares and an appropriate position in the risk-free asset. This can also be used to build options on different assets for which, due to the terms — maturity, size, exercise price — no liquid trading exists on the derivatives exchange.

KEY LEARNING POINT ✓

Volatility is always associated with higher option values (for both calls and puts).

It is important to highlight that all the inputs for the option value can be readily observed, except for the volatility. What matters is the volatility over the life of the option (forward-looking volatility), not past volatility. So how is future volatility estimated?

One option is to use historical volatility as a benchmark, for instance, by estimating the volatility in stock returns based on a certain number of past periods. We can use, for instance, weekly data on stock prices, and then estimate the volatility of weekly returns based on the last two years. In Excel, this can be obtained using the STDEV(.) formula.

It is important to express the volatility (or standard deviation) in annual terms. If the data used to compute volatility is weekly stock returns, the resulting metric will be expressed in weekly terms so we multiply that by $\sqrt{52}$. If we were using daily data, we would multiply the resulting daily volatility by $\sqrt{255}$ to reflect the average number of trading days in a year.

We also need to decide how far back in time to go. The farther back we go, the more observations we will have, but the less current the data will be. But there is no absolute truth here. Remember that σ in the Black–Scholes formula is the implied volatility of the option in the future. As in all cases, past data can be good or bad descriptors of the future.

In the markets, options are commonly traded based on implied volatility. That is, traders quote one another's implied volatilities. For instance, you post a buy order on a particular option accepting to pay a price consistent with an implied volatility of 25% (that is, the price that is obtained by using $\sigma = 25\%$ in the Black–Scholes formula).

Consider a two-year call option where the current stock price is $100, the exercise price is $100, the risk-free rate is 4%, and there are no dividends. Different option values are obtained using different volatility estimates.

	Volatility				
	10%	15%	20%	25%	30%
Call value	$10.39	$12.46	$14.98	$17.55	$20.12
Put value	$2.70	$4.77	$7.29	$9.86	$12.43

Higher volatility increases the likelihood that an option will be profitably exercised upon maturity.[17]

Given the above inputs, if the call option is priced in the market at $17.55, we can infer that the implied volatility in that price is 25%. Similarly, if someone is willing to trade this call option at an implied volatility of 25%, the result is a premium of $17.55.

The implied volatility has other uses in addition to option pricing. The implied volatility of equity markets is sometimes used as an indicator of how risky the current environment is (and how uncertain the future is). For instance, the VIX index[18] is commonly referred to as the "fear index." It is based on the traded prices of options on the S&P 500 index and represents the market expectation of stock volatility over the next 30 days (see **Figure 13.1**).

FIGURE 13.1: Implied volatility given by the VIX index.

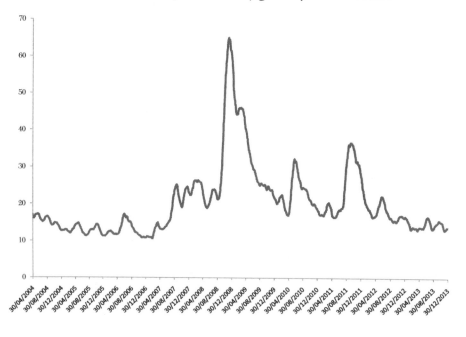

Source: http://www.cboe.com/micro/vix/historical.aspx.

---

[17] If there is no volatility, there is no uncertainty. For instance, in this example, both call and put options are issued with an exercise equal to the current stock price ($100). If there is no uncertainty and the stock price stays flat for two years, none of the options will have any value at maturity, and thus the value today is also zero.

[18] The VIX index is defined as 30-day implied volatility on the S&P 500. Data on the VIX can be obtained at http://www.cboe.com/micro/vix/historical.aspx.

The VIX long-term average is approximately 20%. However, it can clearly be seen that it rose significantly in the aftermath of the 2008/2009 financial crisis, thus reflecting investors' uncertainty about the future.

KEY LEARNING POINT ✓

Implied volatility can be seen as the market perception of uncertainty in the future.

SUMMARY

In this chapter we have introduced options and the way they work. In addition, we have looked at several different hedging strategies and a variety of structured strategies that are possible using options.

An option is a financial asset that entitles the holder to buy or sell an underlying asset at some pre-specified conditions (when and how much). There are two classes of options. Call options give the right to buy. Put options give the right to sell.

Having an option has value (for its owner). Thus, the buyer of any option must pay a price (also called the premium) to acquire the above-mentioned rights (to buy or sell). The Black–Scholes method is the standard valuation technique in the market. It requires five inputs in order to compute the value of any option: the current stock price, exercise price, volatility, option maturity, and the risk-free rate. It is used not only by financial market professionals, treasurers, and CFOs but also by compensation consultants and boards when evaluating executive compensation schemes that use stock options.

Options are available for many different assets, including interest rates, foreign exchange rates, stocks and bonds, commodities, and even the weather. Overall, these instruments allow companies to hedge risks while still benefiting from the upside. With appropriate use, options allow companies to put boundaries (caps or floors) on the value of a particular asset to be traded in the future.

REFERENCES

Black, F., and M. Scholes, 1973, *The Pricing of Options and Corporate Liabilities, Journal of Political Economy*, Vol. 81: 637–654.

Geske, R., 1979, A Note on an Analytical Valuation Formula for Unprotected American Call Options on Stocks with Known Dividends, *Journal of Financial Economics*, Vol. 7: 375–380.

Geske, R., 1981, On the Valuation of American Call Options on Stocks with Known Dividends: A Comment, *Journal of Financial Economics*, Vol. 9: 213–215.

Merton, R.C., 1973, *Theory of Rational Option Pricing, The Bell Journal of Economics and Management Science*, Vol. 4: 141–183.

Roll, R., 1977, An Analytic Valuation Formula for Unprotected American Call Options on Stocks with Known Dividends, *Journal of Financial Economics*, Vol. 5: 251–258.

Whaley, R.E., 1981, On the Valuation of American Call Options on Stocks with Known Dividends, *Journal of Financial Economics*, Vol. 9: 207–211.

Index

Company index

55063395R00194

Made in the USA
Lexington, KY
10 September 2016